the future of literacy studies

Palgrave Advances in Linguistics

Consulting Editor:
Christopher N. Candlin,
Macquarie University, Australia

Titles include:

Mike Baynham and Mastin Prinsloo (*editors*)
THE FUTURE OF LITERACY STUDIES

Noel Burton-Roberts (*editor*)
PRAGMATICS

Susan Foster-Cohen (*editor*)
LANGUAGE ACQUISITION

Monica Heller (*editor*)
BILINGUALISM: A SOCIAL APPROACH

Martha E. Pennington (*editor*)
PHONOLOGY IN CONTEXT

Ann Weatherall, Bernadette M. Watson and Cindy Gallois (*editors*)
LANGUAGE, DISCOURSE AND SOCIAL PSYCHOLOGY

Forthcoming:

Charles Antaki (*editor*)
APPLIED CONVERSATIONAL ANALYSIS:
CHANGING INSTITUTIONAL PRACTICES

Barry O'Sullivan (*editor*)
LANGUAGE TESTING: THEORIES AND PRACTICES

the future of literacy studies

edited by
mike baynham and
mastin prinsloo

palgrave
macmillan

First published 2009 by
PALGRAVE MACMILLAN

Palgrave Macmillan in the UK is an imprint of Macmillan Publishers Limited,
registered in England, company number 785998, of Houndmills, Basingstoke,
Hampshire RG21 6XS.

Palgrave Macmillan in the US is a division of St Martin's Press LLC,
175 Fifth Avenue, New York, NY 10010.

Palgrave Macmillan is the global academic imprint of the above companies
and has companies and representatives throughout the world.

Palgrave® and Macmillan® are registered trademarks in the United States,
the United Kingdom, Europe and other countries.

ISBN: 978–0–230–55370–5   hardback
ISBN: 978–0–230–55371–2   paperback

This book is printed on paper suitable for recycling and made from fully
managed and sustained forest sources. Logging, pulping and manufacturing
processes are expected to conform to the environmental regulations of the
country of origin.

A catalogue record for this book is available
from the British Library.

A catalog record for this book is available
from the Library of Congress.

To Ron Scollon and Pippa Stein

contents

advances in linguistics series
consultant editor's preface

This new *Advances in Linguistics Series* is part of an overall publishing programme by Palgrave Macmillan aimed at producing collections of original, commissioned articles under the invited editorship of distinguished scholars.

The books in the Series are not intended as an overall guide to the topic or to provide an exhaustive coverage of its various sub-fields. Rather, they are carefully planned to offer the informed readership a conspectus of perspectives on key themes, authored by major scholars whose work is at the boundaries of current research. What we plan the Series will do, then, is to focus on salience and influence, move fields forward, and help to chart future research development.

The Series is designed for postgraduate and research students, including advanced level undergraduates seeking to pursue research work in Linguistics, or careers engaged with language and communication study more generally, as well as for more experienced researchers and tutors seeking an awareness of what is current and in prospect in adjacent research fields to their own. We hope that some of the intellectual excitement posed by the challenges of Linguistics as a pluralistic discipline will shine through the books!

Editors of books in the Series have been particularly asked to put their own distinctive stamp on their collection, to give it a personal dimension, and to map the territory, as it were, seen through the eyes of their own research experience.

The Future of Literacy Studies suggests not just a time-related projection but one which has something of a manifesto ring about it, engaged, social, political even, certainly ambitious, and a title that sets out an agenda. This is borne out in this rich and varied contribution to the *Advances in Linguistics* Series. More than just an agenda, though, it offers a landscape and a vision worthy of the expansive cartography of its editors Mike Baynham and Mastin Prinsloo. Not just a map, either, more a chart for new directions of travel, where each chapter adds to our appreciation of the widening presence of Literacies as evidence for understanding the social order and its members. Understanding, or rather, the making of meanings, is in many ways the *leitmotiv* of this carefully constructed collection of original contributions from a distinguished panel of authors. Meaning seen as emerging, or perhaps better quarried, from events and social practices, the evidence for which are literacy behaviours personal as well as institutionally and organizationally mediated. Literacies, then, as signals of purposefulness, what is done with texts of all kinds, but also as markers of networks of communication, local, national and transnational, affording access to meanings across diverse contexts of value and use. Literacy, in the metaphor cited in one of the chapters in this remarkable collection, is a *contact zone*, in Mary Louise Pratt's words, a *'social space where disparate cultures meet, clash and grapple with each other'*, and which, as such, issues a challenge to chart the trajectories of literacy across institutions and local worlds. As the chapters evidence, these worlds are richly and diversely textualized, increasingly digitalized, and dispersed, requiring great efforts of ingenuity to explore and inhabit. Yet, as the Editors outline in their masterly Introduction, this dispersal and this complexity will be the essence of the future of Literacy Studies, a future which, as another author puts it in this remarkable and imaginative book, is social as well as *textual*. The social has its boundaries, however; there is another personal, aesthetic, and imaginative dimension to be emphasized, one which addresses the *stories* in Literacies, linking texts to education, to individuals' social and cognitive development. Chapters in this book highlight this dimension, making the case for an aesthetic turn in Literacy studies. So, as the Editors make plain, Literacies are, in the telling conception of the late and much admired Ron Scollon, at the heart of a *nexus* of practice, where many strands converge, suggesting that although the future of Literacy Studies may indeed be textual, its challenges and opportunities lie in appreciating and valuing its *textures*.

Christopher N. Candlin
Macquarie University, Sydney

acknowledgements

This volume was planned during the 2005 International Applied Linguistics association AILA Congress at Madison, Wisconsin and discussed on the terrace of Frank Lloyd Wright's visionary conference centre on the shore of Lake Monona—as good a place as any to conceive a book on the future of Literacy Studies. The intellectual work on which we draw upon owes much to the opportunities afforded by the AILA Scientific Commission (now Research Network) on Literacy, which brought together literacy researchers from around the world in a series of meetings over a sustained period from the late 1990s onwards, laying the collaborative groundwork for this collection. We would like to acknowledge the foresight of our series editor Chris Candlin for his clear and constructive vision of what books in the series should look like, also the team at Palgrave, notably Jill Lake then Priyanka Pathak and Melanie Blair, who supported the project at all stages. Finally we would like to remember two scholars whose work despite their untimely deaths continues to influence the future of Literacy Studies: Ron Scollon, whose ideas inspired us at many points in the collection and Pippa Stein who was to be a contributor. To them we dedicate this volume.

contributors

David Barton is Professor of Language and Literacy at Lancaster University and Director of the Lancaster Literacy Research Centre. He has been concerned with rethinking the nature of literacy (*Literacy*, Blackwell, second edition. 2007), carrying out detailed studies of everyday literacies (*Local Literacies*, Routledge, 1998; *Situated Literacies*, Routledge, 2000; *Letter Writing as a Social Practice*, John Benjamins 2000) and the relations of literacy and learning (*Beyond Communities of Practice*, Cambridge University Press, 2005; *Literacy, Lives and Learning*, Routledge, 2007; *Improving Learning in College*, Routledge 2009). Current interests include the changing nature of literacy in contemporary society; literacy and social justice; research methodologies; reading and writing Flickr; the history and future of dictionaries.

Mike Baynham is Professor of TESOL at the University of Leeds and Director of the Centre for Language Education Research. A sociolinguist by training and applied linguist by affiliation, he has long-standing research interests in literacy, narrative and language, and migration. Co-convenor with Mastin Prinsloo of the AILA Scientific Commission (now Research Network) on Literacy from 1996–2001, he is currently co-convenor with Stef Slembrouck of the AILA ReN on Language and Migration. Recent publications include a translation into Greek of his 1995 book *Literacy Practices* (with Metaixmion 2002), *Literacy Practices Global and Local* (with Benjamins 2008), edited with Mastin Prinsloo and *Dislocations/Relocations: Narratives of Displacement* (published by St Jerome 2005) with Anna de Fina.

Deborah Brandt is Professor of English at the University of Wisconsin-Madison, where she teaches undergraduate writing and graduate courses in Literacy Studies and contemporary writing theory. Her work focuses on relationships between literacy and economic change as they bear on the lives of everyday people. She is author most recently of *Literacy in American Lives* (Cambridge University Press, 2001) and *Literacy and Learning: Reflections on Writing, Reading and Society* (Jossey-Bass 2009).

Lesley Farrell is Professor at the University of Technology, Sydney, Australia. She has an international reputation in the field of language and global work and has published widely. Her research and publications have focused on language and social change in globally distributed workplaces, paying particular attention to the development of new forms of ICT-enabled workplace literacy, the effects of globalization on local work practices and local knowledge-building, and the role of local work-related education in the production of the global knowledge economy. Recent publications include *Educating the Global Workforce: Knowledge, Knowledge Work and Knowledge Workers* (eds) Lesley Farrell, Tara Fenwick (Routledge 2007).

Glynda A. Hull is Professor of English Education at New York University, and Director of the Ruth Horowitz Center for Teacher Development. Her research examines digital technologies and new literacies; adult literacy and changing contexts and requirements for work; writing and students at risk; and community/school/university partnerships. Her books include *Changing Work, Changing Workers: Critical Perspectives on Language, Literacy, and Skill* (SUNY Press); *The New Work Order: Education and Literacy in the New Capitalism* (Allen & Unwin; with James Gee and Colin Lankshear); and *School's Out! Bridging Out-of-School Literacies with Classroom Practice* (Teachers College; with Katherine Schultz).

Roz Ivanič is Professor Emerita of Linguistics in Education at Lancaster University. Her landmark monograph on academic literacies *Writing and Identity: The Discoursal Construction of Identity in Academic Writing* was published by Benjamins (1998). From 2004 to 2008 she directed the research project 'Literacies for Learning in Further Education' funded by the Economic and Social Research Council Teaching and Learning Research Programme and is the lead author for *Improving Learning at College: Rethinking Literacies across the Curriculum* (Routledge 2009).

Catherine Kell is a Senior Lecturer in the School of Language and Social Sciences, Auckland University of Technology and in the School of Education at the University of Waikato, New Zealand. She teaches in the area of Literacy Studies and adult learning. Previously she worked at the University of Cape Town and much of her ethnographic research has been done in South Africa. Her main interests are adult literacy theories, policies and pedagogies, and she studies these in community, workplace and development contexts.

Mark Evan Nelson is Assistant Professor of English Language and Literature at the National Institute of Education in Singapore. Mark's research is chiefly concerned with understanding the semiotic, sociocultural and pedagogical implications of multimodal textual communication, with a particular focus on visual/pictorial and linguistic channels. Notable publications on the subject include *Locating the Semiotic Power of Multimodality* (with Glynda Hull in *Written Communication*) and *Mode, Meaning and Synaesthesia in Multimedia L2 Writing* (in *Language Learning & Technology*).

Mastin Prinsloo is Associate Professor in the School of Education at the University of Cape Town, working in Applied Language and Literacy Studies. He was co-convenor from 1996–2001 with Mike Baynham of the AILA Scientific Commission (now Research Network) on Literacy. He was Director of the Social Uses of Literacy (SOuL) research project and his publications include *The Social Uses of Literacy* (co-edited with Mignonne Breier) and *Literacies, Global and Local* (co-edited with Mike Baynham).

Ilana Snyder is Professor in the Faculty of Education, Monash University. Author of a number of influential books on literacy in the digital age, her most recent book, *The Literacy Wars*, published in 2008, analyses contemporary media debates around literacy education. Much of her research has focused on the changes to literacy, pedagogical and cultural practices associated with the use of digital technologies and the implications for the teaching of English.

Brian Street is Professor of Language in Education at King's College, London University and Visiting Professor of Education in the Graduate School of Education, University of Pennsylvania. He has a long-standing commitment to linking ethnographic-style research on the cultural dimension of language and literacy with contemporary practice in education and in development and has recently extended this to research on social dimensions of numeracy practices. He was the 2008 winner of the National Reading Conference's Distinguished Scholar Lifetime Achievement Award which was initiated to recognize scholars for 'a lifetime contribution that has had significant impact on the field of literacy theory, research, and practice'. He is currently involved in international development projects applying ethnographic perspectives to literacy learning and teaching.

Doris S. Warriner is Assistant Professor of Language and Literacy and Applied Linguistics at Arizona State University. Her teaching and research on immigration, second language learning and literacy draws from the insights of critical applied linguistics, educational anthropology and linguistic anthropology. Her work with immigrant families, their communities and the institutions that they encounter focuses on questions of access, engaged participation and identity. Her work has appeared in *Anthropology and Education Quarterly; Journal of Language, Identity and Education; Linguistics and Education;* and *Women Studies Quarterly*.

Mark Warschauer is Professor of Education and Informatics at the University of California, Irvine and director of the university's Digital Learning Lab. His research focuses on the relationship of digital media use to language and literacy practices of culturally and linguistically diverse learners. His most recent book is *Laptops and Literacy: Learning in the Wireless Classroom* (Teachers College Press). Warschauer also directs the PhD in Education programme at UCI, which includes a specialization in Language, Literacy and Technology. He can be reached through his website at http://www.gse.uci.edu/markw.

introduction: the future of literacy studies

Mike Baynham and
Mastin Prinsloo

a practice is a mediated action with a history.

Scollon 2001: 66

the 'new' literacy studies

It is now some twenty-five years since Literacy Studies took a new direction, turning away from questions of pedagogy and the psycholinguistic processes of the individual reader–writer and looking outside the classroom to study literacy in its social context. Foundational works in this approach were Shirley Brice Heath's *Ways with Words* (Heath 1983) and Brian Street's *Literacy in Theory and Practice* (Street 1984). Both studies memorably shifted the focus of literacy research onto domains and contexts beyond the classroom. Along with Scribner and Cole's landmark *Psychology of Literacy* (Scribner & Cole 1981) which again emphasized the local and contextual practices by which literacy operates in social groups these are what Baynham (2004) calls the *first-generation* Literacy Studies. *Second generation* works such as Barton and Hamilton (1998), Besnier (1993), Kulick and Stroud (1993), Prinsloo and Breier (1996) developed these approaches in a series of significant empirical studies. In this book we ask what the future of Literacy Studies is, inviting a number of scholars actively involved in shaping the field of Literacy Studies both to take stock of the current state of activity and to point to future directions for literacy research. In doing so, this book provides an introduction to current *third-generation* empirical work which is pushing the boundaries of literacy research in a number of

1

key directions: the focus has shifted from the local to the translocal, from print based literacies to electronic and multimedia literacies and from the verbal to the multimodal. Dynamic changes in the object of inquiry, brought about by both social and technological change, have challenged literacy researchers to revisit foundational principles and constructs to deal with new contexts and new data.

The chapters in this collection all take the conceptual turn that sees literacy, as Street (this volume, p. 21) puts it, 'not as an issue of measurement or of skills but as social practices that vary from one context to another'. They draw upon, and, indeed have mostly been influential shapers of this direction of research, often called the New Literacy Studies (NLS). Literacy is seen in this approach as variable with regard to its forms, functions, uses and values across social settings, and thus varying in its social meanings and effects. This work has drawn in researchers from a range of disciplines. They have studied literacy in everyday social life, on the understanding that literacy goings-on are always and already embedded in particular forms of activity; that one cannot define literacy or its uses in a vacuum; that reading and writing are studied in the context of social (cultural, historical, political and economic) practices of which they are a part and which operate in particular social spaces. This work opposes the position which views literacy as merely a matter of generic skills, as a unitary process, one where 'readers' and 'writers' are generalized subjects without any social location and who are more or less efficient processors of text.

In this introductory chapter we examine what the study of literacy as social practice has entailed and explore, in particular, the issue of what is meant by 'practice', in the study of literacy and how this idea has both been productive and challenging. The issues that confront literacy researchers in everyday settings and in educational, work and other institutional contexts have changed, dramatically in some ways, in the past twenty-five years and we can ask how some of the key understandings of the social literacies approach have changed. We ask how practices have been theorized in Literacy Studies and examine how literacy practices and literacy events have been enabling terms and concepts in this work and how they have been applied and revised.

what is meant by practice in literacy studies?

One of the key early texts in the social practices approach to literacy, that of Scribner and Cole (1981: 236), drawing closely on the work of Vygotsky, defined practice as 'a recurrent, goal-directed sequence of activities using a particular technology and particular systems of knowledge'. They contrasted this concept with that of 'skills', 'the coordinated sets of actions involved in applying this knowledge in particular settings' and saw skills as comprising sensory-motor, linguistic and cognitive skills. So, the practice of law, on the one hand, and basket weaving, on the other, both required all three of those components of skills, but in different ways. This notion of 'practice' guided the way that Scribner and Cole sought to understand literacy, as always constituted within socially organized practices which make use of a symbolic system or systems as well as a technology for producing and disseminating it. The nature of these practices, including of course, their technological aspects, would determine the balance of skills and the consequences associated with literacy. Scribner and Cole thus noted that letter writing amongst the Vai in Liberia (perhaps using the Vai script and language) must be considered as a literacy practice different from, for example, the keeping of a personal diary, or a ledger, since each of these required different measures and weightings of technology, knowledge and skills as they were part of different social activities, or practices.

A somewhat different and highly influential view of how literacy and language were embedded in socio-cultural practice was presented in Shirley Heath's seminal ethnographic research (e.g. 1982, 1983) which contrasted the home and school language and literacy practices of two working class communities, black and white, with middle class people in the same town in the Piedmont Carolinas, USA, at a time when legal desegregation was newly in place and racially integrated schooling was a relatively new phenomenon. Heath focused empirically on 'literacy events', which she described as 'the occasions in which written language is integral to the nature of participants' interactions and their interpretive processes and strategies' (Heath, 1982: 50).

She followed Dell Hymes in insisting that what counted in effective communication was not a generalized competence (e.g. being able to 'speak English' or 'code and decode letters') but a situated, communicative competence embedded in acquired, 'deep' cultural knowledge and learnt models of using situated language in specific ways. She concluded that patterns of language and literacy use varied across local communities (and across social classes) and were consistent with other cultural practices, such as 'space and time orderings, problem-solving techniques, group loyalties, and preferred patterns of recreation' (Heath 1983: 344). She argued persuasively that children's successes and failures could not be adequately explained with reference to single-factor explanations, such as relative amounts of parent–child interaction or formal language, structural differences across home and school. They needed, rather, to be understood with reference to wider and deeper cultural practices, the situated 'ways of knowing' that children took to school, that then encountered the schools' ways.

Street's (1984) study of literacy in an Iranian village developed a complementary perspective. In a setting where government educators and planners identified villagers as predominantly 'illiterate', Street studied the complexities of the literacy practices in the village which varied from religious to market to school-based practices. As he describes it in this volume, he called for a more developed conceptualization of the theoretical and methodological issues involved in understanding and representing local literacy practices. Street criticized what he referred to as the autonomous model of literacy, which suggests that literacy functions outside of political contexts. Street's ideological model (1983, 1995) of literacy sees 'literacy' as a shorthand term for literacy practices which are rooted in social, cultural and political contexts and which can be studied ethnographically.

David Barton, together with Mary Hamilton, Roz Ivanic and colleagues in Lancaster developed a body of work that focuses on practices in Literacy Studies primarily as 'everyday practices', which starts out from what people do in their lives. Their work complemented similar work done elsewhere (Baynham 1995, as one example, stressed the combination of talk and texts and the roles of literacy mediators in multilingual settings). Noting that various texts, including notes, newspapers, books, schedules, documents, diagrams, images and standardized forms, permeate daily activities, Barton, Hamilton and colleagues argued that large parts of social interactions are literacy practices, influenced by literacy texts and practices. The way into understanding these practices, as they saw it, was through the study of particular events, as part of situated practices.

Researchers working with the resources of this 'social literacies' approach, such as those described above, have since become increasingly aware that the focus on literacy practices as located in immediate social, cultural and political contexts has to be tempered with a sense of how remote sites, and remote literate practices shape and constrain local literacy practices. As Brandt and Clinton (2002: 338) argued, if 'reading and writing are means by which people reach – and are reached by – other contexts, then more is going on locally than just local practice'.

The theme of how literacy practices are, in many contemporary cases, so often translocal and transnational practice, is taken up and examined in several of the chapters in this volume and is one reason for looking again at the concepts of practice and literacy events in Literacy Studies. Another reason is the growing concern with the multiple communicative modalities that underwrite literacy practices in contemporary times, besides print, including images, sound and movement, particularly with regard to screen-based multimedia literacies (Kress 2003; also see Kress & van Leeuwen 1996, 2001). There is a conversation going on amongst researchers working on multimodal studies, who stress that communication is nearly always multi-sensory and therefore multimodal, and between researchers who have focused on literacy as situated social practice. Increasingly, researchers are drawing on resources from both these approaches (e.g. Pahl & Rowsell 2005). A question that has been examined is whether the affordances of particular media (e.g. that language and sound are associated with sequence and time and images lend themselves to displays of relationships, proportionality and simultaneity) have an autonomy independent of social relationships, and whether they maintain their semiotic affordances and communicative functions when they appear in different settings, as part of different social practices. It is as likely that they are themselves socially shaped and situationally variable resources, whose affordances are shaped by social practices. In the light of these concerns we go on to look closer at practice accounts of literacy, its roots and various directions in Literacy Studies.

The sense in which practice is used as a productive theoretical category in Literacy Studies can be traced via the work of Bourdieu to the early Marx of the theses on Feuerbach:

> The principal defect of all materialism up to now – including that of Feuerbach – is that the external object, reality, the sensible world is grasped only in the form of *an object* or *an intuition*; but not as concrete human activity, as practice. ... (Marx *Theses on Feuerbach* epigraph to Bourdieu's Outline of a Theory of Practice (1977))

This kind of practice is a combination of action and reflection. The concept of practice is thus used in different senses in social practice theory, first from practice to refer to a more or less coherent or coordinated entity or activity (such as schooling, cuisine or fashion) and, second, to a performance or the carrying out of an action. Reckwitz (2002: 249–50) defines the concept as follows:

> A 'practice' ... is a routinized type of behaviour which consists of several elements, interconnected to one another: forms of bodily activities, forms of mental activities, 'things' and their use, a background knowledge in the form of understanding, know-how, states of emotion and motivational knowledge. A practice ... forms so to speak a 'block' whose existence necessarily depends on the existence and specific interconnectedness of these elements.

For Scollon, apparently following in this tradition, a practice is a mediated action with a history (cf. Scollon [2001: 66–9]). One of the issues about practice as a construct however is one of scope, and indeed Scollon raises this explicitly. On the one hand, practice can be treated as perhaps the smallest identifiable unit of the social world, comparable to an action, albeit an action with a history. At the other end of the scale, for social theorists like Bourdieu (1977, 1991), Foucault (1977), Chouliaraki and Fairclough practices are something bigger, less definable in the interactional here-and-now. For Althusser practices hail or interpellate the subject (Althusser 1994: 128–32). We are no longer talking about single actions but of the sustained operations of institutions and ideologies over time. Perhaps the scale of such conceptualizations of practice creates a disconnect between the worlds of practice and the interactional here-and-now. This would be Scollon's position and his solution is to write practice small. In Literacy Studies, it's fair to say, the notion of practice operates less on the micro or macro end of the practice scale, more at some meso level though with some slippage between issues of scale. Here is how Tusting, Ivanic and Wilson put it:

> The term practices is central to the NLS approach to literacy. The term is used in two ways:
>
> • to refer to observable, collectable and/or documentable specific ethnographic detail of situated literacy events, involving real people, relationships, purposes, actions, places, times, circumstances, feelings, tools, resources The term 'practices' in this sense often *contrasts with, and hence complements* the term 'texts', since it refers to those other aspects of literacy which go beyond the text itself.
> • To refer to culturally recognizable patterns of behaviour, which can be generalised from the observation of specifics. The term practices in this sense often *includes* 'textual practices' the culturally recognisable patterns for constructing texts. (Tusting, Ivanic & Wilson 2000: 213)

Arising from this, another distinction worth making is between the notice of practice as a property of human activity and practice as a property of non-human entities, institutions, texts. In this further sense we can talk about institutional practices, disciplinary practices, discursive practices, textual practices with the further implication that human subjects are hailed, interpellated, subjected to these discourses and practices in the Althusserian sense. The sociologist Bob Connell (Connell 1987) further extends our understanding of such institutional, social or discursive practices in relation to gender, by talking about them not just in terms of constraints but also in terms of affordances or opportunities. So being interpellated, hailed or subjected to a particular discursive practice (say, for example, by particular kinds of academic writing, or by gendering practices) creates opportunities and affordances as well as constraints.

bourdieu, practice and literacy habitus

We go on to look more closely at notions of practice in the work of Bourdieu and Latour, as they have been explicitly drawn on in recent Literacy Studies, to address issues of the social and political location of practices and the links between the social and the material in such practices. We find, again, that this work has been used to suggest both more constrained and less constrained understandings of agency with regard to literacy in social interaction.

Bourdieu (1991) critically engaged with what he identified as *objectivist* epistemologies (both Marxist and structuralist/post-structuralist) which sought to construct the objective relations which structure practices. His alternative was that of an epistemology of *practice*, where a specific structure or order is given to social institutions or social fields by the ways in which people think, act and interact, and such human activity is simultaneously structured by institutional forces, such that it cannot be said that one precedes the other.

According to Bourdieu, the social and material conditions that pertain to an individual's experience, and in collective history, dispose individuals in certain ways, rather than others, which both enable and constrain them in particular ways. Individuals bring to those interactions their *habitus*, which is made up of those durable, transposable dispositions, or embodied history internalized as second nature and so forgotten as history (Bourdieu 1991: 12). *Habitus* reflects those possibilities and resources, and their limitations which people tacitly draw upon in their actions and interactions. *Habitus* also refers to a person's competence as a strategic player in a social field, and how such personal resources are continually being sanctioned by relative successes and failures in social interaction. A notion of social practice that draws upon the concept of *habitus* sees semiotic production not as the outcome of static norms or pre–given social and cognitive techniques, but rather as the effects of the dynamic positioning of individuals within a linguistic, semiotic and conceptual 'market' (Bourdieu 1991: ch 1). *Habitus* outlines a mechanism of regulated/regulating behaviour as well as for structured creativity on the part of individuals. *Habitus* is located and developed in social fields which are constituted by interactions among individuals holding relative positions of social power within such fields.

Bourdieu's concepts of habitus, cultural capital and social fields account for both the interactive and micro-dimensions of social practices combined with a theory of social structure. Habitus for Bourdieu is the principle of the generation and structuring of practices and representations and produces systems of durable, transposable dispositions. Bourdieu describes habitus as a set of historically rooted, socially organized dispositions. Persons who have been socialized into these dispositions are able to interpret and creatively engage in the flow of social practices. Habitus is the socially induced strategic 'sense of the game' which practitioners draw upon both to sustain a social field and their standing within it. They display a 'feel for the game' that is at hand. Habitus affords both regularity and improvisation in social life, yielding social practices that are 'spontaneously orchestrated' (Bourdieu 1991: 80).

Hasan (2002) drew on Bourdieu to explain the interactive dynamics that she found in the concept of *invisible semiotic mediation*. She identified semiotic mediation as referring to how the unself-conscious everyday discourse mediates mental dispositions, tendencies to respond to situations in certain ways and how it puts in place beliefs about the world one lives in, including both about phenomena that are supposedly in nature and those which are said to be in our culture. She claimed the primacy of this invisible semiotic mediation in a person's life, not simply because it regulates cognitive functions, but because it is also 'central to the shaping of "dispositions, identities and practices"' (Hasan 2002: 26). Hasan's view here presents a perspective on practice theory which stresses their determining effects on individual behaviour. An alternative perspective stresses that practices are constructed by what people do, 'they are "enacted" in specific events of communicative conduct, and their effectivity depends on the conditions of enactment' (Collins and Slembrouck 2004: 9). A more reflexive model (e.g. in Bloome and Egan-Robertson 1993) thus stresses the indeterminacy of outcomes. Such indeterminacy is a positive resource in so far as it means that things are never settled, there is always the possibility of contestation and reformulation. Interactive social activity is not simply the acting out of predetermined codes. There is a creative dimension to interaction, in that new meanings, consequences and adaptations are possible, not excluding those that are conflictual or misunderstood.

Pahl (2008) offers one good example of a Literacy Studies approach that draws upon the concept of habitus to describe the relationship between social practice, repeated practices in home settings and the habitus. She examines instances of children's multimodal text-making (including the making of a map of Turkey using prayer beads, on the part of Turkish-English children) and connects these creative practices with the habitus, the disposition of the household and wider social-structural forces. She sees habitus as a heuristic device for making sense of how the literacy practices of the children in her study are shaped by resources from different social spaces and how they provide the material for creative design on the children's part. Hull and Nelson's chapter takes up this theme of creative design in their account of digital story-telling among urban youth and adults in California.

Gee (2005, 2008) also sees social interaction as only partly scripted. He sees that social practices give individuals what he calls 'models' for acting. Models are 'partial storylines, metaphors, routines, scripts, principles, rules of thumb, or images that help one act and interact in relatively typical situations in a domain' (p. 142). He describes these models through the lens of Bourdieu's habitus but with a particular concern with the design potential of such inherited resources: 'Models are the way in which history, institutions, and affinity groups think and act in and through us. We pick them up – often unconsciously – and operate in their terms, thereby reproducing traditional action, interaction, and thinking in the domain' (p. 143). Such models are multiple because of the multiple domains of social life, just as our semiotic resources (or 'social languages') are multiple. Gee views practices as semiotic domains which each have a 'design grammar' – a set of principles or patterns in terms of which materials in the domain (e.g. oral or written language, images, equations, symbols, sounds, gestures, graphs, artifacts and so forth) are combined to communicate complex meanings.

Schatzki (1996, 2001) distinguishes between two forms of practices: 'Dispersed practices' are general and appear in many different contexts, examples being describing, explaining and imagining. 'Integrative practices' are 'the more complex practices found in and constitutive of particular domains of social life'. Examples of integrative practices that Schatzki gives include farming practices, cooking practices and business practices (Schatzki 1996: 98). Schatzki suggests that integrative practices will often include some of the dispersed practices, sometimes in a specialized form. In these terms we might say that while literacy appears to some as a dispersed practice, it in fact takes on a specialized form as part of an integrated practice in almost all instances. Gee appears to draw on a related idea when he suggests that some semiotic domains (or practices) can be precursors for other domains. This is so, he says, because one or more of the elements associated with the precursor domain ('ways of situating meaning, pieces of a social language, cultural models') facilitates learning in the other domain. He suggests that children who come to school 'looking gifted' have probably been immersed in a wide variety of precursory practices, that give them easy access to the specialized practices of schools in particular contexts.

latour, actor network theory and literacy studies

Latour's work in Actor Network Theory (and also that of Law (2004), as well as Bowker and Starr (2003, 1999), amongst others) has become influential in Literacy Studies (cf. Hamilton 2001; Lemke 1998; Barton and Hamilton 2005; Baynham 2006; Clarke 2008; Prinsloo 2008), raising in particular the question whether the theorizations of the sociocultural in practice theories give due weight to the significance which material artefacts bear in the social world. Actor Network Theory (ANT) presents the idea of objects as *artefacts*, as 'things' which are necessary components of social networks or practices. Social networks, or practices in their historical variability, consist not only of humans beings and their intersubjective relationships but also simultaneously of non-human 'actants'; things that are necessary and are so-to-speak 'equal' components of a social practice. Artefacts provide more than just objects of knowledge but are necessary, irreplaceable components of certain social practices; their social significance does not only consist in their being 'interpreted' in certain ways but also in their being 'handled' in certain ways and in being constitutive, effective elements of social practices. For ANT, artefacts have the status of hybrids. On the one hand, they are definitively not simply part of the physical world alone as within practices they are socially and culturally interpreted and handled. On the other hand, they are definitely more than 'cultural representations': they are used and have effects in their materiality.

Latour applies what he calls the principle of generalized symmetry (1993: 103) which insists that all entities, human or non-human, must be subjected to the same processes of social analysis. Actor network theory studies ethnographically the resources that are mobilized to establish an object of knowledge: the configuration of people, devices, texts, decisions, organizations and inter-organizational relations, in varying degrees of extensiveness and complexity. Such research follows the chain of events, actors and artefacts, including documents, institutional domains, activities of experts and access to these by 'non-experts' (Latour 1987; Hamilton 2001).

One feature of networks that follows is that they draw local actors into broader configurations not of their making, which play out away from the local scene. Agents, both human and non–human are enrolled onto the network, and Latour's work draws attention to the places where this work gets done, where humans and non–humans are constructed as equivalent to assure that these networks stick together (Bowker and Star 1999: 301). In networked practices, material things are routinely drawn upon and applied by different agents in different situations. The objects handled again and again endure, thus making social reproduction beyond temporal and spatial limits possible.

the literacy event and 'eventness' in literacy studies

We have earlier identified the crucial issue of how a connection is retained between the interactional here-and-now and the world of practice, however broadly or narrowly construed. Literacy Studies has typically referred to the event as a unit of analysis which keeps us close to the empirically observable lifeworld. However, once you begin to look more closely there are also problems from a number of angles with 'eventness', which we will outline briefly. The notion of the event implies some distinct structured set of activities, which can be readily distinguishable, having a schematic structure. In that sense the notion of event, in the way characterized, for example, by Hymes and linguistic ethnography more generally has much in common with the linguistic notion of genre.

However, one of the problems with this discrete, as it were prototypical notion of the literacy event, as something that can be easily detached from its context for analytical purposes is that much literacy activity is not like this. If I am driving down to London on the M1, my peripheral vision is continually engaging with text as I pass motorway signs, and am aware of the instrumentation on the dashboard. Does this make my driving to London a literacy event? Similarly there are questions of temporal/spatial discontinuity: if at the supper table one of my children is texting a friend, what kind of event is that? The notion of event is postulated as it were on the Aristotelian unities of time and space. How does it work when participants are not in the same time/ space coordinates? What happens, as Cathy Kell has shown us in her analysis of literacy activity surrounding buildings in South African townships, when literacy activity extends over time and space in different locations? Where can events be identified? The truth is that we live in a text saturated world and the textuality of the world is not necessarily grouped into neatly differentiable event structures. Literacy activity spills over particular space/time coordinates, the immutable mobiles of text circulate in chains of entextualization which are only beginning to be studied seriously.

This question of the event bears some similarity with recent arguments made by Bamberg and Georgakopoulou (2008) concerning small narratives in contrast to prototypical narratives. Literacy events are like prototypical narratives, yet much small-scale incidental literacy activity, characteristic of our text saturated world, would slip through the net of the 'eventness'. We think it is also possible to argue that the focus on the event in the here-and-now is characteristic of the focus on the local in Literacy Studies, with context understood as something fixed and settled.

beyond the local: from local to translocal literacies?

One of the characteristics of the development of the NLS has been, as we have seen an emphasis on the situated, the local. This tendency is perhaps articulated most clearly in Barton and Hamilton's landmark *Local Literacies* (Barton and Hamilton 1998). Yet all around, as is apparent as well in *Local Literacies*, is evidence that the local exists in a networked global world, that literacies have to be seen as transnational or at least translocal. Looking at literacies from a translocal rather than local perspective raises questions of the processes by which texts are produced and consumed across contexts and localities, how written texts are talked up.

how to retain the focus on activity in the analysis of practices

In the analysis of practice there is a danger of slippage towards representation (cf. Scollon 2001: 6) 'Discourse is best conceived as a matter of social actions, not a system of representation or thought or values.' We would argue that there is an analytic bias towards losing the performativity of the object of analysis and reducing it to a set of representations. This is something that Bourdieu alerts us to:

> The 'knowing subject' as the idealist tradition rightly calls him, inflicts on practice a much more fundamental and pernicious alteration which, being a constituent condition of the cognitive operation, is bound to pass unnoticed: in taking up a point of view on the action, withdrawing from it in order to observe it from above and from a distance, he constitutes practical activity as an *object of observation and analysis*, a *representation*. (Bourdieu 1977: 2)

What the event construct brings with it is a focus on the here-and-now of the encounter; in this case the textually mediated encounter.

re-theorizing the relation between spoken and written language from the point of view of spoken language

In Literacy Studies we have tended to regard talk as the occasion for literate activity, rarely something that is of interest in its own right. Conversely those research traditions which have focused centrally on spoken language, for example Conversation Analysis (CA), have hardly reacted to the text saturation of talk, the shifts and blends which are so commonplace, but somehow below the radar of both Literacy Studies and CA. We are reminded again here of Alexandra Georgakopoulou's and Michael Bamberg's notion of the small narrative (Bamberg & Georgakopoulou [2008] Georgakopoulou [2007]), which similarly slips below the radar of canonical narrative analysis. Literacy Studies has been good at locating the event in (local) context and the practices implied and structuring the event. Maybe the analytical focus needs to shift to the subtle saturations of literateness in daily life, the ways that texts are talked up over time and space.

multimodality and literacy practices

Kress and others have presented an understanding of literacy as being multimodal in terms of the semiotic means through which it is communicated, where texts are not just products of language written down but also get their meanings through other modes of semiosis, including visual, aural and other modalities, besides written language (Kress and van Leeuwen 1996; Kress 1997, 2001; Kress and Jewitt 2003).

As Kress (2001: 1, 2) describes it:

> Representation and communication always draw in a multiplicity of modes, all of which contribute to meaning. First, material media are socially shaped to become over time meaning making resources, to articulate the (social and individual/affective) meanings demanded by the requirements of different communities. Second, the meanings of the modes of language-as-speech or language-as-writing, as of all other modes, are always interwoven with the meanings made with all other modes co-present and 'co-operating' in the communicative context. Third, what is considered a 'mode' is always contingent: resources of meaning are not static or stable; they are fluid. Modes of representation and communication are constantly transformed by their users in response to the communicative needs of society; new modes are created, existing modes are transformed.

Kress (1997: 137) made the argument that children happily combine various semiotic systems, such as talk, drawing, gesture, dramatic play and writing. He described 'multimodality' as 'an absolute fact of children's semiotic practices'.

In the context of reading and writing practices in screen-based media, where the 'old literacies' are print-based, paper-based and language-based, reading and writing associated with the 'new literacies' are seen to integrate written, oral and audiovisual modalities of interactive human communication within screen-based and networked electronic systems. Graphic resources such as pictures and diagrams have increasingly moved to front-stage, imparting information directly, rather than providing backup for knowledge that is text-based (Kress and van Leeuwen 1996; Kress 1997, 2001). Along these lines, Lemke argued that meanings in multimedia are not fixed or additive, in the way word-meaning and picture-meanings relate. Rather, they are multiplicative, where word-meaning is modified by image-context, and image-meaning in turn is modified by textual context (Lemke 1997: 287). Readers of the 'new literacies' must organize their reading across a range of media, flexible constructs and typologies that break from traditional grammar orthodoxies (Kress 1997).

beyond events/practices: scale theory?

What are the strategies for bringing into alignment the face-to-face encounter with phenomena at different scales, retaining the activity/

event orientation while bringing into the analysis the larger scale phenomena that have interested the theorists of practice? It is interesting
to compare the concerns articulated by Street (1993) at a comparatively
early stage in the NLS project with the problematic currently addressed
through scale theory by Blommaert, Collins and Slembrouck (2005) and
others. Street argues against the restricted notion of context then current in linguistics generally and pragmatics in particular (cf. Street 1993:
13–15 'Context in Linguistics and Anthropology'). In terms of the concerns of scale theory the question is how does an analysis account for the
effects of large scale, for example institutional, national, transnational
features, and how does it account for the Goffmanian dynamics of face-
to-face interaction? What we see then is a bringing back of the large-scale
social categories adumbrated by Street into face–to-face interaction.

contributions to the volume

The chapters of this book bring together current perspectives on
Literacy Studies from leading researchers. We start with a foundational overview of the development of the field by Street, illustrated
through his current work on Academic Literacies, Development studies, Multimodality. The chapter reviews some of the key features in
what has been called the 'New Literacy Studies'. Complementing
Street's chapter is another foundational overview chapter by Barton,
reviewing in addition to the focus on events and practices, key constructs such as mediators, mentors, brokers, networks and sponsors.
Barton contextualizes literacy in an increasingly, textually mediated
social world. The themes he identifies are picked up and developed in
other chapters, Ivanic on literacy practices in further education, Farrell
on the workplace and the knowledge economy, Hull and Nelson on the
aesthetics of literacy.

Brandt's chapter is built around historical arguments concerning
the emergence of literacy practices in nineteenth–twenty-first-century
America. She argues that there is currently a shift from the dominance
of reading to that of writing, documenting very different ideological
constructions of reading and writing practices. The point she makes
about the degree of regulation and surveillance involved in the production of writing is echoed and supported in Farrell's chapter on workplace writing practices. Brandt makes an interesting use of oral history
methods to document literacy practices.

Kell provides a critical review of some of the key constructs such as
practices and events, interrogating the local in Literacy Studies, via an

analysis of transcontextual literacy practices, modelling flows, cross-ing, text trajectories (particularly literacy activity associated with house building projects in the Khayalethu township, South Africa). To imple-ment the transcontextual analysis she advocates a methodology of long-term participant observation in multiple domains to track text tra-jectories. Her chapter has a thematic focus on materiality and agency; context and the local/global; and multimodality and multiliteracies, extending the notion of life history to the history of literacy objects and artefacts.

Ivanic's chapter has a focus on the study of literacy practices in edu-cational settings: 'uses of reading and writing to mediate learning'. She critiques the scope of the term 'practice' and develops a position similar to that of Scollon. According to Ivanic 'The Literacy Studies research paradigm can make invisible, discounted practices visible not only in the full panoply of people's lives, but also on courses of study in all disciplines and subject areas across all sectors of education.' In the research presented she documents a theoretical shift which is also adumbrated in Kell's chapter from 'situated' to what she terms 'border literacies', echoing Kell's transcontextual analysis. This involves the-orizing contact and crossing between vernacular literacies as studied in the classic studies of local literacies and literacy practices in educa-tional domains (here, Further Education), thus enabling an interest-ing reconceptualization of broad-brush cognitive constructs such as 'transfer'.

Warschauer and Snyder address the impact of electronic media of different sorts on literacy practices, albeit from slightly different per-spectives. According to Warschauer there is wide societal recognition of the importance of new technologies in daily life and learning. In con-trast Snyder points to considerable dissent in public discourse about the impact of new technologies. Warschauer focuses on identifying diverse semiotic modes and cross-language interaction, new forms of digital interaction. He proposes an ideological model of electronic literacy (indexing Street's productive formulation) and develops a discussion of digital literacies in relation to learning.

According to Snyder, literacy classrooms in schools remain over-whelmingly print-oriented in their approach to the teaching and learn-ing of reading and writing. Her media-based research identifies digital literacies as a site of controversy and struggle. She uses an analysis of media texts to understand broad-brush societal constructions of lit-eracy, identifying both trends towards and resistances to developing digital literacies. The chapter reviews research-based claims about how the use of digital technologies affects literacy learning and practices. She concludes that the literacy classroom of the future must involve the effective integration of print literacy and digital literacy and that teachers' attitudes to technological change are a key factor as are public discourses about literacy and new technology as exemplified in the media.

Warriner's chapter brings a preoccupation with global, transnational flows and literacy practices. The chapter suggests that transnationalism and literacy provide mutually enriching perspectives on both phenomena. Echoing Kell's focus on transcontextual methodologies, Warriner suggests that researching transnational literacy practices requires a radical rethinking of research methods to work across transnational sites.

Farrell's chapter examines literacy practices and the knowledge economy. As with a number of other contributions, there is a sustained examination of the impact of global/local practices, here in the globalized workplace. She emphasizes the power of remote sites to shape and constrain local literacy practices. The discussion of literacy and workforce regulation strongly echo points made by Brandt. Her emphasis on literacy and multimodality and the diversification of electronic literacy activity resonate with Warschauer's chapter. Farrell identifies differences in the way literacy education is conceptualized in a technologised workspace concluding that 'Local workplaces are the sites where the global movement of people, capital and ideas play out in urgent ways, generating new literate practices from the local and remote resources available to them, and the new identities, relationships and institutions that attend these new practices' (Farrell, this volume, p. 193).

According to Hull and Nelson 'being able and willing to communicate and understand within and across differences in language, ideology, culture, and geography reside at the heart of what it means to be literate now'. They place emphasis on multimodality, on 'literacies that are multimodal, aesthetically alert, and morally attuned' (Hull and Nelson, this volume, p. 199). They orient their approach to the work of the New London Group (1996), a consistent influence in a number of the contributions, particularly here the New London Group focus on design, that is the designing of multimodal meanings, where the 'online self' is most often both narrated and displayed by a combination of text and image. They conclude by invoking through examples 'the appropriation of multimodal textual forms to participate, undaunted, in local and global conversations that are respectfully alert to difference' (Hull and Nelson, this volume, p. 218).

conclusion

Over the past two decades, changes in the semiotic landscape, its dominant modalities and in the volume and rapidity of socio-economic interactions at global level have challenged what some have seen as the localism of Literacy Studies, resulting, as we will see in this volume, in re-evaluations, both theoretical and methodological, of the key contextual orientations laid down in foundational work in the field. Theoretically, the shift is from literacy situated in given places and times towards a conceptualization of dynamic transcontextual flows, from print to multimodal and digital literacies. Nor have key constructs such as practice gone unscrutinized: contributions to the volume emphasize the need for a rigorous approach to deploying such constructs. Alongside these theoretical re-orientations we see a developing awareness of the new methodologies required for transcontextual literacy research. We think that the readers of this volume will find evidence of continuity with the research parameters laid down in the foundational studies as well as change. The rich diversity of literacy practices identified by this research approach continues to challenge the narrow, decontextualized skills-based orientation that dominates many national literacy curricula.

references

Althusser, L. (1994) Ideology and ideological state apparatuses: notes towards an investigation. In S. Žižek (ed.) *Mapping Ideology*. London: Verso.

Bamberg, M. and A. Georgakopoulou (2008) Small Stories as a New Perspective in Narrative and Identity Analysis. *Text & Talk*, 28(3), 377–96.

Barton, D. and M. Hamilton (1998) *Local Literacies*. London: Routledge.

Barton, D. and M. Hamilton (2005) Literacy, reification and the dynamics of social interaction. In D. Barton and K. Tusting (eds) *Beyond Communities of Practice: Language, Power and Social Context*. Cambridge: Cambridge University Press.

Baynham, M. (1995) *Literacy Practices*. London: Longman.

Baynham, M (2004) Ethnographies of Literacy: Introduction. *Language and Education*, 18(4), 285–90.

Baynham, M. (2006) Agency and Contingency in the Language Learning of Refugees and Asylum Seekers. *Linguistics and Education*, 17, 24–39.

Besnier, N. (1993) Literacy and feelings: the encoding of affect in Nukulaelae letters. In B. Street (ed.) *Cross-Cultural Approaches to Literacy*. Cambridge: Cambridge University Press.

Blommaert, J., J. Collins and S. Slembrouck (2005) Spaces of Multilingualism. *Language and Communication*, 25(2): 197–216.

Bloome, D. and A. Egan-Robertson (1993) The Social Construction of Intertextuality in Classroom Reading and Writing Lessons. *Reading Research Quarterly*, 4(28), 304–33.

Bourdieu, P. (1977) *Outline of a Theory of Practice.* Cambridge: Cambridge University Press.

Bourdieu, P. (1991) *Language and Symbolic Power.* Cambridge, Mass: Harvard University Press.

Bowker, G. C. and S. L. Star (1999) *Sorting Things out: Classification and Its Consequences.* Cambridge, Mass.: MIT Press.

Bowker, G. C. and S. L. Star (2003) 'How things (actor-net)work: Classification, magic and the ubiquity of standards'. Pre-print copy of a paper published in a special issue of *Philosophia.* Downloaded from http://weber.ucsd.edu/~gbowker/actnet.html in March 2003.

Brandt, D. and K. Clinton (2002) Limits of the Local: Expanding Perspectives on Literacy as a Social Practice. *Journal of Literacy Research*, 34(3), 337–56.

Chouliaraki, L. and F. Norman (1999) *Discourse in Late Modernity. Rethinking Critical Discourse Analysis.* Edinburgh: Edinburgh University Press.

Clarke, J. (2008) Assembling 'skills for life': Actor network theory and the new Literacy Studies. In M. Prinsloo and M. Baynham (eds), *Literacies, Local and Global.* Amsterdam: John Benjamins, 151–72.

Collins, J. and S. Slembrouck (2004) Reading shop windows in globalized neighbourhoods. LPI Working Papers No. 2. http://bank.rug.ac.be/lpi/Accessed 13/7/2009.

Connell, R. W. (1987) *Gender and Power: Society, the Person and Sexual Politics.* Oxford: Polity.

Foucault, M. (1977) *Language, Counter-Memory, Practice.* Ithaca: Cornell University Press.

Gee, J. (2005) *An Introduction to Discourse Analysis: Theory and Method*, second edition. London: Routledge.

Gee, J. (2008) Learning in semiotic domains: a social and situated account. In M. Prinsloo and M. Baynham (eds) *Literacies, Local and Global.* Amsterdam: John Benjamins, 137–50.

Georgakopoulou, A. (2007) *Small Stories, Interaction and Identities. Studies in Narrative 8.* Amsterdam/Philadelphia: John Benjamins.

Hamilton, M. (2001) Privileged Literacies: Policy, Institutional Processes and the Life of the IALS. *Language and Education,* 15(2&3), 178–96.

Hasan, R. (2002) 'Semiotic Mediation, Language and Society: Three Exotropic Theories – Vygotsky, Halliday and Bernstein'. Paper presented at the Bernstein Symposium, Cape Town, July.

Heath, S. B. (1982) What No Bedtime Story Means: Narrative Skills at Home and School. *Language in Society,* 11(1), 49–76.

Heath, S. (1983) *Ways with Words: Language, Life and Work in Communities and Classrooms.* Cambridge: Cambridge University Press.

Kress, G. (1997) *Before Writing.* London: Routledge.

Kress, G. (2001) Keynote presentation, 'Writing, knowing, learning in the era of Multimodality'. International Literacy Conference, Literacy and language in global and local settings: New directions for research and teaching, 13–17. November 2001, Cape Town. Downloaded from http://www.ched.uct.ac.za/literacy/GuntherKress.html.

Kress, G. (2003) Perspectives on meaning-making: the differential principles and means of adults and children. In N. Hall, J. Larson and J. Marsh (eds) *Handbook of Early Childhood Literacy*. London: Sage, 154–66.

Kress, G. and C. Jewitt (2003) *Multimodal Literacy*. New York: P. Lang.

Kress, G. and T. van Leeuwen (1996) *Reading Images: The Grammar of Visual Design*. London: Routledge.

Kress, G. and T. van Leeuwen (2001) *Multimodal Discourse: The Modes and Media of Contemporary Communication*. London: Arnold.

Kulick, D. and C. Stroud (1993) Conceptions and uses of literacy in a Papua-New Guinea village. In B. Street (ed.) *Cross-Cultural Approaches to Literacy*. Cambridge: Cambridge University Press, 33–61.

Latour, B. (1987) *Science in Action: How to Follow Scientists and Engineers through Society*. Cambridge, Mass.: Harvard University Press.

Latour, B. (1993) *We Have Never Been Modern*. Cambridge, Mass.: Harvard University Press.

Law, J. (2004) And if the Global Were Small and Non-Coherent? Method, Complexity and the Baroque. *Society and Space* 22, 13–26.

Lemke, J. (1998) Metamedia literacy: transforming meanings and media. In D. Reinking, M. McKenna, L. Labbo and R. Kieffer (eds) *Handbook of Literacy and Technology: Transformations in a Post-Typographic World*. Hillsdale, NJ: Lawrence Erlbaum, 283–302.

New London Group (1996) A Pedagogy of Multiliteracies: Designing Social Futures. *Harvard Educational Review*, 66(1), 60–92.

Pahl, K. (2008) Habitus in children's multimodal text-making: a discussion. In M. Prinsloo and M. Baynham (eds) *Literacies, Local and Global*. Amsterdam: John Benjamins, 51–72.

Pahl, K. and J. Rowsell (2005) *Travel Notes from the New Literacy Studies: Instances of Practice*. Clevedon: Multilingual Matters.

Prinsloo, M. and M. Breier (1996) *The Social Uses of Literacy: Theory and Practice in Contemporary South Africa*. Amsterdam: John Benjamins.

Prinsloo, M. (2008) Literacy and Land at the Bay of Natal: Documents and Practices across Spaces and Social Economies. *English in Africa*, 35(1), 95–114.

Reckwitz, A. (2002) Toward a Theory of Social Practices: A Development in Culturalist Theorizing. *European Journal of Social Theory*, 5(2), 245–65.

Schatzki, T. (1996) *Social Practices: A Wittgensteinian Approach to Human Activity and the Social*. New York: Cambridge University Press.

Schatzki, T., K. Knorr-Cetina and E. von Savigny (2001) *The Practice Turn in Contemporary Theory*. London: Routledge.

Scollon, R. (2001) *Mediated Discourse: the Nexus of Practice*. London: Routledge.

Scribner, S. and M. Cole (1981) *The Psychology of Literacy*. Cambridge, Mass.: Harvard University Press.

Street, B. (1984) *Literacy in Theory and Practice*. Cambridge: Cambridge University Press.

Street, B. (ed.) (1993) *Cross-Cultural Approaches to Literacy*. Cambridge: Cambridge University Press.

Tusting, K., R. Ivanic and A. Wilson (2000) New Literacy Studies at the interchange. In D. Barton, M. Hamilton and R. Ivanic (eds) *Situated Literacies*. London: Routledge.

1
the future of 'social literacies'

brian street

This chapter addresses three areas of work in the field of social literacies where I can identify exciting developments: Academic Literacies in the University; Development Policy and Training Trainers in Literacy Programmes; the relationship of Multimodality to New Literacy Studies. The developments I am referring to can be identified in both theory – notably the bringing together of different fields such as social literacies and multimodal approaches – and of policy and pedagogy – such as the application of these ideas in the context of teacher training and course development, both in universities and in adult literacy programmes. They are all grounded in what I term as 'social literacies' approach that assumes reading and writing to be social practices that vary with context and use. Whereas dominant perspectives on literacy still tend to treat it as 'autonomous' of social context (cf. Street 1984) to be learned as a set of technical skills that are somehow universal (cf. UK National Literacy Strategy, US No Child Left Behind, parts of Unesco Global Monitoring Report on Literacy) a social practice perspective starts from the uses and meanings that participants bring to literacy practices in varied contexts. The implications of this for academic literacy in universities, for adult literacy programmes and for understandings of multimodality are followed through in the sections below.

social literacies

What do I mean by 'social literacies' and how it might offer 'directions' for 'cutting edge' work? I am using this term to refer to a body of work that for the past 20 years has approached the study of literacy not as an issue of measurement or of skills but as social practices that vary from one context to another. From my point of view, this social perspective stems from experiences living in Iranian villages during the 1980s and since reinforced by experience with literacy programmes in, amongst other places, Nepal, South Africa, India and the United States. I went to Iran during the 1970s to undertake anthropological field research (Street 1984). I had not gone specifically to study 'literacy' but found myself living in a mountain village where a great deal of literacy activity was going on. I was drawn to the conceptual and rhetorical issues involved in representing this variety and complexity of literacy activity at a time when my encounter with people outside the village suggested the dominant representation was of illiterate, backward villagers. Looking more closely at village life in the light of these characterizations, I noticed that not only was there actually a lot of literacy going on but also there were quite different practices associated with literacy: Those in a traditional Quoranic school, in the new State schools and amongst traders using literacy in their buying and selling of fruit to urban markets. If these complex variations in literacy, happening in one small locale, were characterized by outside agencies (e.g. state education, UNESCO, literacy campaigns) as illiterate, might this be the case in other situations, too?

I have kept this image in mind as I have observed and investigated literacy in other parts of the world such as urban Philadelphia, South Africa, India, and the United Kingdom. In all of these cases, I hear dominant voices characterizing local people as illiterate (currently media in the UK are full of such accounts, cf. Street 1997); while on the ground, ethnographic and literacy-sensitive observation indicates a rich variety of practices (Barton & Hamilton 1998; Heath 1983). When literacy campaigns are set up to bring literacy to the illiterate – 'light into darkness', as it is frequently characterized – I find myself asking first what are the local literacy practices and how do they relate to the literacy practices of the campaigners? In many cases the latter fail to take; few people attend classes and those who do drop out (cf., Abadzi 2003) precisely because they are being required to learn the literacy practices of an outside and often alien group. Even though in the long-run many local people do want to change their literacy practices and take on some of those associated with Western or urban society, a crude imposition of the latter that marginalizes and denies local experience is likely to alienate even those who were initially motivated.

Research, then, has a task to do in making visible the complexity of local, everyday, community literacy practices and challenging dominant stereotypes and myopia. This task indeed has become a major drive in my research, teaching, and writing, both in the research community and in the public arena. Following through its implications for pro-gramme design, including pre-programme research on local literacy practices and for curriculum, pedagogy, and assessment/evaluation, is a major task that requires first a more developed conceptualization of the theoretical and methodological issues involved in understanding and representing local literacy practices.

This approach has been particularly influenced by those who have advocated an ethnographic perspective, in contrast to the experimental and often individualistic character of dominant approaches to literacy in both research and policy. Much of the work in this ethnographic tradition (Barton & Hamilton 1999; Collins 1995; Gee 1999; Heath 1993; Heath and Street 2008; Street 1993) has focused on the everyday meanings and uses of literacy in specific cultural contexts and linked directly to how we understand the work of literacy programmes, which themselves then become subject to ethnographic enquiry (Robinson-Pant 2005; Rogers 2005).

In trying to characterize these new approaches to understanding and defining literacy, I have referred to a distinction between an 'autono-mous' model and an 'ideological' model of literacy (Street 1984). The autonomous model of literacy works from the assumption that liter-acy in itself, autonomously, will have effects on other social and cog-nitive practices. The autonomous model, I argue, disguises the cultural and ideological assumptions that underpin it and that can then be presented as though they are neutral and universal. Research in the social practice approach challenges this view and suggests that in prac-tice dominant approaches based on the autonomous model are simply imposing Western (or urban) conceptions of literacy onto other cul-tures (Street 2001). The alternative, ideological model of literacy offers a more culturally sensitive view of literacy practices as they vary from one context to another. This model starts from different premises than the autonomous model. It posits instead that literacy is a social practice, not simply a technical and neutral skill, and that it is always embedded in socially constructed epistemological principles. The ways in which people address reading and writing are themselves rooted in concep-tions of knowledge, identity, and being. Literacy, in this sense, is always contested, both its meanings and its practices, hence particular versions of it are always ideological; they are always rooted in a particular world-view often accompanied by a desire, conscious or unconscious, for that view of literacy to dominate and to marginalize others (Gee 1990). The argument about social literacies (Street 1995) suggests that engaging with literacy is always a social act, even from the outset. The ways in which teachers or facilitators and their students interact is already a social practice that affects the nature of the literacy learned and the ideas about literacy held by the participants, especially new learners and their positions in relations of power. It is not valid to suggest that literacy can be 'given' neutrally and then its social effects only experienced or added on afterwards.

For these reasons, as well as the failure of many traditional literacy programmes (Abadzi 1996; Street 1999), academics, researchers, and practitioners working in literacy in different parts of the world have come to the conclusion that the autonomous model of literacy, on which much of the practice and programmes have been based, was not an appropriate intellectual tool, either for understanding the diversity of reading and writing around the world or for designing the practical programmes this diversity required, which may fit better within an ideological model (Aikman 1999; Doronilla 1996; Heath 1983; Hornberger 1997, 2002; Kalman 1999; King 1994; Robinson-Pant 1997; Wagner 1993). The question this approach raises for policy makers and programme designers is, then, not simply that of the impact of literacy, to be measured in terms of a neutral developmental index, but rather of how local people take hold of the new communicative practices being introduced to them, as Kulick and Stroud's (1993) ethnographic description of missionaries bringing literacy to New Guinea villagers makes clear. Literacy, in this sense, is then already part of a power relationship and how people take hold of it is contingent on social and cultural practices and not just on pedagogic and cognitive factors. These relationships and contingencies raise questions that need to be addressed in any literacy programme: What is the power relation between the participants? What are the resources? Where are people going if they take on one form of literacy rather than another? How do recipients challenge the dominant conceptions of literacy?

This approach has implications for both research and practice. Researchers, instead of privileging the particular literacy practices familiar in their own culture, now suspend judgment as to what constitutes literacy among the people they are working with until they are able to understand what it means to the people themselves, and from which social contexts reading and writing derive their meaning. Many people labelled illiterate within the autonomous model of literacy may, from a more culturally sensitive viewpoint, be seen to make significant use of literacy practices for specific purposes and in specific contexts. For instance, studies have suggested that even non-literate persons find themselves engaged in literacy activities, so the boundary between literate and non-literate is less obvious than individual measures of literacy suggest (Doronilla 1996; Maddox 2005). Academics have, however, often failed to make explicit the implications of such theory for practical work. In the present conditions of world change, such ivory-tower distancing is no longer legitimate. Likewise, policy makers and practitioners have not always taken up such academic findings or have adopted one position (most often that identified with the autonomous model) and not taken account of the many others outlined here. These findings, then, raise important issues both for research into literacy in general and for policy in literacy education and training in particular.

academic literacies

My current research is in the area of student writing and faculty feedback in the university. This topic provides an opportunity to apply the theories and research on literacy as social practice to our own situation as writers at the university and also to consider what this tells us more broadly about discourse, identity, and power in the academy. The 'Composition' literature in the United States is already well developed, but recent work in the United Kingdom from an 'academic literacies' perspective has applied theories of power and discourse to what is often seen as simply a technical skills issue.

This approach developed from the New Literacy Studies perspective on literacy that treats it, as noted above, as a social practice rather than an autonomous skill. This tension is to be found in the academy as in other fields of life, in this case in the ways in which tutors and administrators attempt to support students in meeting the writing requirements of their courses. Mary Lea and I conducted research on such practices in a number of UK universities (Lea and Street 1998, 1999, 2006) and based on our analysis of the research data, we explicated three models of student writing. These we termed *study skills*, *socialization*, and *academic literacies*. The study skills model is based on the assumption that mastery of the correct rules of grammar and syntax, coupled with attention to punctuation and spelling, will ensure student competence in academic writing; it is, therefore, primarily concerned with the surface features of text. In contrast, the academic socialization model assumes students need to be acculturated into the discourses and genres of particular disciplines and that making the features and requirements of these explicit to students will result in their becoming successful writers. In some respects the third model, that of academic literacies, subsumes many of the features of the other two; we point out that the models are not presented as mutually exclusive and that each should be seen as encapsulating the other. Nevertheless, we argue that it is the academic literacies model which is best able to take account of the nature of student writing in relation to institutional practices, power relations, and identities, in short to consider the complexity of meaning making which the other two models fail to provide.

The explication of the three models we proposed has been drawn upon very widely in the literature on teaching and learning across a range of HE contexts (see, e.g. Thesen and van Pletzen 2006, on South Africa) and calls for a more in-depth understanding of student writing and its relationship to learning across the academy, thus offering an alternative to deficit models of learning and writing based on autonomous models of literacy.

This approach links well but is not exactly the same as the 'Writing in the Disciplines' (WiD) and 'Writing across the Curriclulum' (WAC) approach that has become popular in the United States (cf. Russell 1991; Bazerman 1988) and with work in the United Kingdom towards an 'embedded' approach (Mitchell 2006). A recent paper by US and UK theorists in these fields attempts to clarify the similarities and differences (Russell et al. 2007) and their conclusions and pointing forward is relevant to both the Widening Participation programme I will describe below and to the adult literacy programme discussed later:

> [T]here have been repeated calls for WAC to resist institutional practices and traditions that limit student writing and learning, calls which resonate with Lillis's (Lillis and Curry 2006) call for ACLITS to develop an academic literacies pedagogy which places the nature of dialogue at its centre and considers how to develop and validate alternative spaces for writing and meaning making in the academy. In WAC the ideological valences of writing pedagogies have been a source of controversy ... whereas it has been endemic to the ACLITS approach from the outset given its rooting in New Literacy Studies and the 'ideological model' of literacy. Research on teachers who take an explicitly political approach in the WACWiD classroom have found resentment and counter-resistance among students and most WAC programs take a much more indirect approach to institutional change. (Russell et al. 2007)

I provide here a brief account of a Widening Participation Programme at King's as an example of attempts to develop such theoretical issues in practice (Lea & Street 2006; Leung & Safford 2005; Scalone & Street 2006). In addition to drawing upon the two national traditions cited here – WACWiD in the United States and ACLITS in the United Kingdom–this programme also attempts to bring together aspects of the academic literacies approach with recent trends in EAL/ EAP (Leung 2005). The programme was designed to provide a non-credit bearing English language Development course for 'A' level (year 12 in the English school system) 17-year-old students from linguistic minority community backgrounds, attending schools in the locality of King's, who would like to further their studies at university. The programme currently accepts 50 students a year from local schools. The students attend a three-hour class on Saturdays during term times. Staff on the programme both teach and research the issues associated with academic literacies that the work raises. In particular, we use a teaching frame that draws attention to 'switching' of both genres and modes and this activity can be seen in the larger context of the academic literacies approach we have been considering (Scalone & Street 2006).

Using an academic literacies approach in this programme, specifically addressed to EAL students, can bring out ways in which the two fields relate. Academic literacies and EAL/ EAP draw upon the ethnography of communication tradition, the latter particularly through development of the concept of 'communicative competence'. Leung (2005), one of the tutors on the WP programme, has argued that the interpretation of 'communicative competence' in the CLT tradition has frequently been reductionist and based upon abstracted contexts and idealized social rules rather than the more open and broader social perspective evident in ethnographic research (cf. Dubin 1989). We can, then, see the Widening Participation Programme as a case study for exploring the relationship between theory and practice in these fields as well as contributing to the larger story regarding applications of new literacy theory to educational practice.

learning empowerment through training in ethnographic research (LETTER)

A further example of such theory/ practice relationship is to be found in a programme I describe below that involves support for adult literacy training and learning. It also brings together social practice theories of literacy and of numeracy with practical work in the field of learning and teaching in the Global South and as such provides a further pointer to future directions in the literacy field.

Learning Empowerment through Training in Ethnographic Research (LETTER) is a development project that concentrates on literacy and numeracy learning. It aims to help adult trainers and course organizers to gain first-hand experience of ethnographic-style approaches to local literacy and numeracy practices to support learning and teaching (Street et al. 2006). The project starts by working with the trainers of those who teach in adult and non-formal education programmes – the facilitators and teachers – so that the trainers can train them to adapt these approaches to their own local situations.

The project is based on recent understandings of literacy and numeracy as social practice. If 'New Literacy Studies', as we have seen, assumes that both literacy and numeracy have many different cultural and social uses and meanings in different contexts then it follows those preferred by some teachers and educational policy makers and planners are only a few amongst many. These are often different from those currently held by the literacy and numeracy learners themselves. Recent studies in formal education have laid stress on the importance of schools understanding the home-based learning of the pupils; the LETTER Project similarly argues that it is very important for all those who are engaged in adult and non-formal education to discover and understand the home and community experiences and practices of literacy and numeracy of the learners – what has been termed their 'funds of knowledge'. The LETTER workshops aim to train trainers in ethnographic-style methodologies in discovering these local literacy and numeracy practices. They then pass these methodologies on to literacy and numeracy facilitators and teachers.

From this perspective, those engaged in numeracy and literacy learning programmes start by listening to and exploring local views as a means of building upon what the learners bring. During this project, those training the facilitators are helped to develop ethnographic-style methods – not to be anthropologists doing 'an ethnography' but to adopt an 'ethnographic perspective'. The Project then moves into its second phase, exploring how to use such findings for the development of new and more adult-appropriate curricula and teaching–learning approaches.

The LETTER project was first developed as a collaboration between an NGO in the United Kingdom, Uppingham Seminars (Convenor Alan Rogers) that has experience in working with literacy and numeracy as a social practice, and Nirantar in India, an NGO with experience of working especially with rural *dalit* women extending their numeracy, literacy, and other communication skills aimed at their increasing empowerment. The project draws on the expertise and experience of a number of UK facilitators, my own in ethnography and literacy (cf. Heath and Street 2008), Alan Rogers in adult education and course development (Rogers 2005 2008), and Dave Baker in numeracy and learning and teaching (Baker 2005).

The longer-term aim of the project is for the participants to gain first-hand experience of ethnographic-style approaches to local literacy and numeracy practices to support teaching and learning in these areas, and to produce some form of training guide to the methodologies so that they themselves can diffuse these approaches more widely.

The project works through a sequence of workshops that aim to train the participants in ethnographic approaches to researching the literacy and numeracy practices of the learners and their communities. They are practical workshops with fieldwork conducted during each workshop. During the first workshop, the participants design a small piece of original research that will be conducted in their own home context between the first and second workshops. They then write up these case studies with the support of the LETTER training team (by email and correspondence). Participants then report on their case studies to the later workshops which will help them to identify ways of using this material in developing curricula and teaching–learning approaches for their learners. The links here, then, between new approaches to literacy, learner-centred views of learning and ethnographic understandings of context provide profound challenges to dominant approaches to adult literacy training, that has been more rooted in top down, autonomous perspectives that pay little attention to learners' prior knowledge.

multimodality

Definitions of 'literacy' have now to take account of new modes of communication, what Kress refers to as 'multimodality' where a mode might be linguistic, visual, kinaesthetic, and so on. Educators in particular have been concerned to describe and analyse the implications of new modes and new media, such as computers, mobile phones, and so on, for how we help children learn. One common assumption is that young people today are generally ahead of the older generation with respect to the technical skills of using new technologies and communicating in new ways via them; but what then should teachers be adding to this, what do learners 'need' in addition to what they have learned in peer and auto-didact ways, how might teachers bridge the generational knowledge forms that learners and tutors range over? Snyder, Jewitt, Kress, Abbott, Street, and others are developing a set of terms for describing these situations and a set of arguments for developing

policy. As educators they are concerned with not only the technical
skills needed for handling new communications media but also the
meta knowledge for recognizing these skills and media and for integrating them in meaningful ways.

Users shift between modes and media according to what Kress terms
'interests' – what some authors refer to as 'orchestrating' modality.
Therefore understanding these choices and their implications becomes
as important with respect to these new media as they have always
been for communicative competence in print and other more traditional media. For Kress and others the central point remains that we
are 'meaning makers' and that modes and media are resources which
we take hold of and use to make new meanings – education, then, is
about helping learners develop the knowledge as well as the skills we
need regarding these processes. An aspect of this field that links closely
to the issues raised earlier in this chapter is how we take account of the
cultural and social dimensions of such processes. Although communication on the Internet, for instance, may be 'international', we have
still to take account of the fact that communicators come from specific
cultural and linguistic backgrounds and ask how does this affect their
interaction? We can't assume that because the means of communication
are now cross-cultural, the meanings are necessarily so. Hawisher and
Selfe (2000) in an edited volume bringing together authors from many
parts of the world, set out to 'resist a romanticised and inaccurate vision
of global oneness and instead celebrate the dynamic capacity of the new
self-defined literacy communities to challenge the global village myth'.
Likewise Blommaert argues that '[t]he transfer of linguistic signs does
not entail the transfer of their functions and values' (Blommaert 2004)
and he uses examples from asylum-seekers in Belgium to show how the
judgement of the value of official documents rests on power relations.
How might the ethnographic approaches to literacy signalled above
contribute to our understanding of the role of literacy and modality in
these new contexts and media of communication?

Kress and Street (2006) have recently raised the issue of how these
approaches can 'speak to each other', how New Literacy Studies and
Multimodality as fields of study can gain from each other's insights?
One starting point is to consider what is meant by the term 'literacy':

> For instance, in both approaches there is a worry about the stretch-
> ing of the term *literacy* well beyond the NLS conception of *social prac-
> tices of representation* to become a metaphor (and often much less
> than that) for any kind of skill or competence. One needs to ask

whose interests are advanced and in what ways by the use of labels such as 'palpatory literacy' (skills in body massage), 'emotional literacy' (skills in affective massage?), 'cultural literacy' (skills in social massage?), and so on. Of course, one clear effect of such moves is that where 'a literacy' is identified, those with an interest in finding the corresponding illiterates are never far behind with their remedies. But even such uses where some aspects of literacy practices are involved – computer literacy, visual literacy – bring their own problems, not least of them the blunting of analytic and theoretical sharpness and power. Where there is a label there is already an answer; and where there is an answer, any need for questions has stopped. More significantly perhaps, there is the question of 'complementarity'. This poses quite simply as a yet thorny question: where does the 'reach' of one theory stop – or, maybe better, begin to attenuate, 'fizzle out'. (Kress and Street 2006: vii–viii)

The question, then, arises of what are the limits and boundaries here and what does NLS not address that, for instance, a social semiotic theory of multimodality can better handle? Whose tools are better suited to different aspects of the broader task? The question of 'complementarity' addresses itself to that – not a matter of mere eclecticism, but of compatible competences. NLS and multimodality, in this sense, are well placed to explore each other's strengths and weakness, to develop a conversation that facilitates new growth and more powerful tools.

The kind of questions this approach opens up for those interested in education and its role in these new times include the following: What is a mode, how do modes interact, how can we best describe the relationship between events and practices, and how do we avoid becoming the agents producing the new constraints of newly described and imposed grammars? These questions are different from those often being asked in schools but they may be more relevant to the age we live in than the kind of questions that arise from the autonomous model of literacy. The features of the autonomous model were rooted in assumptions about technological determinism that the ideological model and new social practice approaches to literacy have challenged and discredited. Yet, we now find the same array of distorting lenses being put on as we ask, what are the consequences of the present generation of 'new technologies', those associated in particular with the Internet and with digital forms of communication? While these forms evidently do have affordances in Kress's (2003) sense, it would be misleading and unhelpful to read off from the technology into the effects without first positing the social mediating factors that give meaning to such technologies. How, then, can we take sufficient account of the technological dimension of new literacies without sliding into such determinism? On analogy with Literacy Studies, then, those working with different modes may need likewise to develop an ideological model of multimodality. Recent work by Pahl, Rowsell, Street, and others provides some ethnographic accounts of multimodal practices from such an ideological perspective.

conclusion

The three examples I have briefly outlined above suggest rich directions for the 'Futures of Literacy' in general and for future applications of 'social literacies' theory in particular. Drawing upon the strengths of that approach in terms of social theory and of ethnographic perspectives, two of the examples cited above provide concrete examples of the applications of these ideas in practice – in the past, New Literacy Studies has been criticized for being only 'for researchers' (Lillis 2003; Brandt and Clinton 2002), so the development of programmes such as these, in Higher Education and in adult literacy point forward to a wealth of exciting prospects that should both enlighten educational practice and in turn feed back into theory. And at the level of theory too there are challenging developments as those working in the frame of multimodality question the traditional dominance of language-based approaches to communication and lay out other communicative practices that need to be taken into account – visual, kinaesthetic, and so on. The implications of this will be profound and those in the field are currently struggling to come to terms with both the theoretical shift and the issue of how we label the various modes – do we call them all 'literacies' for example, as many commentators seem to be currently doing, generating terms such as 'computer literacy', 'visual literacy', and extended metaphors such as 'political literacy' and 'palpatory literacy' (massage!) where the term means little more than 'skill'. There is a danger that such a shift may take us back to earlier autonomous approaches, both with respect to the view of literacy as skill and to the notion that each communicative practice has its own 'affordances' or determinations. One of the greatest challenges that future literacy theorists and practitioners will have to face is avoiding a new modal determinism and an autonomous model of multi modality whilst at the same time taking on board the implications of a broader communicative repertoire is. I will conclude by suggesting that they might fruitfully build upon earlier phases of Literacy Studies by developing an ideological model of multimodality. This in turn might then be applied to the academic literacies in higher education discussed briefly above and to the wide-ranging adult literacy programmes in international contexts indicated by the Letter Project. The 'new' in New Literacy Studies continues, then, to be re-'newed'.

references

social literacies

Bartlett, L. and D. Holland (2002) Theorizing the Space of Literacy Practices. *Ways of Knowing*, 2(1) University of Brighton.

Barton, D. (1994) *Literacy: An Introduction to the Ecology of Written Language.* Oxford: Blackwell.

Barton, D. and M. Hamilton (1998) *Local Literacies.* London: Routledge.

Brandt, D. and K. Clinton (2002) Limits of the Local: Expanding Perspectives on Literacy as a Social Practice. *Journal of Literacy Research*, 34(3), 337–56.

Gee, J. P. (1996) *Social Linguistics and Literacies: Ideology in Discourse.* London: Falmer Press.

Heath, S. B. (1982) What No Bedtime Story Means: Narrative Skills at Home and School. *Language and Society*, 11, 49–76.

Pahl, K. and J. Rowsell (eds) (2006) *Travel Notes from the New Literacy Studies: Case Studies in Practice.* Clevedon: Multilingual Matters Ltd.

Street, B. (1984) *Literacy in Theory and Practice.* Cambridge: Cambridge University Press.

Street, B. (2003) What's New in New Literacy Studies? *Current Issues in Comparative Education*, 5(2), 12 May 2003 http://www.tc.columbia.edu/cice/. Accessed on 18 August 2009.

Street, B. and A. Lefstein (2007) *Literacy: An Advanced Resource Book.* Routledge: London English Language and Applied Linguistics.

Street, B. and N. Hornberger (eds) (2007) *Encyclopedia of Language and Education, Volume 2: Literacy.* New York: Springer.

Street, B. (2008) Ethnography of writing and reading, ch 16. In R. David Olson and N. Torrance (eds) *Cambridge Handbook of Literacy.* Cambridge: CUP.

academic literacies

Bazerman, C. (1988) *Shaping Written Knowledge: The Genre and Activity of the Experimental Article in Science.* Madison: University of Wisconsin Press.

Bazerman, C. and P. Prior (2004) *What Writing Does and How it Does It: An Introduction to Analyzing Texts and Textual Practices.* Mahwah NJ: Lawrence Erlbaum.

Boughey, C. (2000) Multiple Metaphors in an Understanding of Academic Literacy. *Teachers and Teaching Theory and Practice*, 6(3), 279–90.

Candlin, C. N. and K. Hyland (eds) (1999) *Writing: Texts, Processes and Practices* London: Addison Wesley Longman.

Cochran-Smith, M. and S. L. Lytle (1993) *Inside/Outside: Teacher Research and Knowledge*, Teachers' College, esp. chapter 1, 'Research on Teaching and Teacher Research: the issues that divide', Columbia: New York, 5–22.

Crème, P. and M. Lea (1997) *Writing at University: A Guide for Students*. Buckingham: Open University Press.

Dubin, F. (1989) Situating Literacy within Traditions of Communicative Competence. *Applied Linguistics*, 10(2), 171–81.

Ganobcsik-Williams, L. (ed.) (2006) *Teaching Academic Writing in UK Higher Education: Theories, Practices and Models*. Basingstoke: Palgrave Macmillan.

Hyland, K. (1999) Disciplinary discourses: writer stance in research articles. In C. Candlin and K. Hyland (eds) *Writing Texts, Processes and Practices* Longman, 99–121.

Hyland, K. (2001) Humble Servants of the Discipline? Self-Mention in Research Articles. *English for Specific Purposes*, 20, 207–26.

Hyland, K. (2006) *English for Academic Purposes: An Advanced Resource Book*. London: Routledge.

Ivanic, R. (1998) *Writing and Identity: The Discoursal Construction of Identity in Academic Writing*. Amsterdam: John Benjamins.

Ivanic, R. (2004) Discourses of Writing and Learning to Write. *Language and Education*, 18(3), 220–45.

Jones, C., J. Turner and B. Street (eds) *Student Writing in the University: Cultural and Epistemological Issues*. Amsterdam: John Benjamins.

Lea, M. (2004) Academic Literacies: A Pedagogy for Course Design. *Studies in Higher Education*, 29(6), 739–56.

Lea, M. and B. Stierer (1999) *Student Writing in Higher Education: New Contexts*. Buckingham: Open University Press/SRHE.

Lea, M. R. and B. Street (1998) Student Writing in Higher Education: An Academic Literacies Approach. *Studies in Higher Education*, 23(2), 157–72.

Lea, M. R. and B. Street (1999) Writing as academic literacies: understanding textual practices in higher education. In C. N. Candlin and K. Hyland (eds) *Writing: Texts, Processes and Practices*. London: Longman, 62–81.

Lea, M. R. and B. Street (2006) The 'Academic Literacies' Model: Theory and Applications. *Theory into Practice*, Fall, 45(4), 368–77.

Leung, C. (2005) Convivial Communication: Recontextualising Communicative Competence. *International Journal of Applied Linguistics*, 15(2), 119–44.

Leung, C. and S. Kimberly (2005) Nontraditional students in higher education in the United Kingdom: English as an additional language and literacies. In B. Street (ed.) *Literacies across Educational Contexts: Mediating Learning and Teaching*. Philadelphia: Caslon Publishing.

Lillis, T. M. (1997) New Voices in Academia? The Regulative Nature of Academic Writing Conventions. *Language and Education*, 11(3), 182–99.

Lillis, T. M. (1999) Whose common sense? Essayist literacy and the institutional practice of mystery. In C. Jones, J. Turner and B. Street (eds), *Student Writing in University: Cultural and Epistemological Issues*. Amsterdam: John Benjamins, 127–47.

Lillis, T. M. (2001) *Student Writing: Access, Regulation, Desire*. London: Routledge.

Lillis, T. M. (2003) Student Writing as Academic Literacies: Drawing on Bakhtin to Move from Critique to Design. *Language and Education*, 17(3), 192–207.

Lillis, T. M. and M. Curry (2006) Professional Academic Writing by Multilingual Scholars: Interactions With Literacy Brokers in the Production of English-Medium Texts. *Written Communication*, 23(1), 3–35.

Mitchell, S. (2006) Thinking Writing: News from the Writing in the Disciplines Initiative: Report on Consortium for Writing in the Disciplines Newsletter, Autumn. Language & Learning Unit, Queen Mary, University of London.

Mitchell, S. and R. Andrews (eds) (2000) *Learning to Argue in Higher Education*. London: Heinemann.

Pahl, K. and J. Rowsell (2005) *Literacy and Education: The New Literacy Studies in the Classroom*. London: Sage

Prior, P., J. Hengst, K. Roozen and J. Shipka (2006) 'I'll be the sun': From Reported Speech to Semiotic Remediation Practices. *Text & Talk*, 26(6), 733–66 (pdf).

Rowsell, J., V. Sztainbok and J. Blaney (2006) 'Losing Strangeness': Using Culture to Mediate ESL Teaching (submitted to *Language, Culture and Currciulum*).

Russell, D. (1991) *Writing in the Academic Disciplines, 1870–1990: A Curricular History*. Carbondale: South Illinois University Press.

Russell, D., M. Lea, J. Parker, B. Street and T. Donahue (2007) Exploring notions of genre in 'academic literacies' and 'writing across the curriculum': approaches across countries and contexts *The Simpósio International de Estudios de Gêneros (SIGET) IV panel on genre in Writing across the Curriculum (WAC) and 'academic literacies'* (ACLITS) Brazil, 2007.

Scalone, P. and B. Street (2006) An academic language development programme (widening participation). In C. Leung and J. Jenkins (eds), *Reconfiguring Europe: The Contribution of Applied Linguistics*. London: Equinox, 123–37.

Stierer, B. (1997) *Mastering Education: A Preliminary Analysis of Academic Literacy Practices within Master-Level Courses in Education*. Centre for Language & Communications. Milton Keynes: Open University.

Street, B. (2004) Academic Literacies and the 'New Orders': Implications for Research and Practice in Student Writing in HE. *Learning and Teaching in the Social Sciences*, 1(1), 9–32.

Thesen, L. and E. van Pletzen (2006) (eds) *Academic Literacy and the Languages of Change*. London: Continuum.

LETTER

Abadzi, H. (1996) *Adult Literacy: A Problem Ridden Area*. Washington, DC: World Bank.

Abadzi, H. (2003) *Improving Literacy Outcomes: Lessons from Cognitive Research for Developing Countries*. Washington, DC: World Bank.

Baker, D. A. (2005) Funds of Knowledge and Numeracy. *Reflect: Journal of NRDC* London: Institute of Education/NRDC.

Baker, D. A., B. Street and A. Tomlin (2003) Mathematics as Social: Understanding Relationships between Home and School Numeracy Practices. *For the Learning of Mathematics*, 23(3), 11–15, ISSN 0228–0671.

Baker, D. A. and B. Street (2004) Mathematics as Social: A Comment on Barwell. 24(1), *For the Learning of Mathematics*, 24(2), 19–21.

Blommaert, J. (2004) Writing as a Problem: African Grassroots Writing, Economies of Literacy and Globalization. *Language in Society*, 33, 643–71.

Fasheh, M. (1982) Mathematics, Culture, and Authority. *For the Learning of Mathematics*, 3(2), 1–8.

Green, J. and D. Bloome (1997) Ethnography and ethnographers of and in education: a situated perspective. In J. Flood, S. Heath and D. Lapp (eds), *A Handbook of Research on Teaching Literacy through the Communicative and Visual Arts*. New York: Simon and Shuster Macmillan, 181–202.

Hammersley, M. (1992) *What's Wrong with Ethnography?* esp. ch. 9 'Deconstructing the Qualitative-Quantitative Divide'. London: Routledge, 159–73.

Heath, S. B. and B. Street (2008) *On Ethnography: Approaches to Language and Literacy Research* (An NCRLL Volume) (available as word file).

Lareau, A. and J. Schultz (1996) *Journeys through Ethnography: Realistic Accounts of Fieldwork*. Boulder, CO: Westview Press.

Mace, J. (2005) *Outside the Classroom: Researching Literacy with Adult Learners*, esp. ch. 4, 'Research as process'. Leicester: NIACE, 75–83.

Mitchell, J. (1984) 'Typicality and the case study'. In R. F. Ellen (ed.) *Ethnographic Research: A Guide to Conduct*. New York: Academic Press, 238–41.

Moll L., C. Amanti, D. Neff and N. Gonzalez (1992) Funds of Knowledge for Teaching: Using a Qualitative Approach to Connect Homes and Classrooms. *Theory into Practice*, xxxi(2), 131–41.

Papen, U. (2005) *Adult Literacy as Social Practice: More Than Skills*, esp. ch. 4, 'Using ethnography to study literacy in everyday life and in classrooms', London: Routledge, 59–74.

Rogers, A. (2004) *Non-formal Education: Flexible Schooling or Participatory Education?* Dordrecht: Kluwer and Hong Kong: Hong Kong University Press.

Rogers, A. (2008) Informal learning and literacy. In B. Street and N. H. Hornberger (eds) *Encyclopedia of Language and Education*, second edition. New York: Springer, 133–44.

Rogers, A. (ed.) (2005) *Urban Literacy: Communication, Identity and Learning in Development Contexts*. Hamburg: UIE.

Saraswathi, L. S. 'Practices in Enumeration by counting and computation of sets of objects in rural Tamil Nadu: implications for adult education programmes'. Unpublished and will be available from the workshop organisers.

Street, B. (1999) Meanings of culture in development. In A. Little and F. Leach (eds) *Schools, Culture and Economics in the Developing World: Tensions and Conflicts*. New York: Garland Press.

Street, B., D. Baker and A. Tomlin (2005) *Navigating Numeracies: Home/School Numeracy Practices*. London: Springer ISBN: 1–4020-3676–0 Vol. 4 of series on Leverhulme Numeracy Research Programme (selections from theory and conclusions).

Street, B., D. Baker and A. Rogers (2006) Adult Teachers as Researchers: Ethnographic Approaches to Numeracy and Literacy as Social Practices in South Asia. *Convergence*, xxxix(1), 31–44.

Swain, J., E. Baker, D. Coben, D. Holder and Newmarch, B. (forthcoming) *'Beyond the Daily Application': Making Numeracy Teaching Meaningful to Adult Learners*. London: National Research and Development Centre for Adult Literacy and Numeracy, http://www.nrdc.org.uk. Accessed 18 August 2009.

Unesco (2006) EFA Global Monitoring Report Unesco@: Paris, esp. chapter 6, 'Defining and conceptualising literacy', 148–59.

multimodality

Abbott, C. (2000) *ICT: Changing Education*. London: Routledge.

Cope, B. and M. Kalantzis (2000) *Multiliteracies: Literacy Learning and the Design of Social Futures*. London: Routledge.

Emmison, M. and P. Smith (2000) *Researching the Visual*. London: Sage.

Hawisher, G. E. and C. Selfe (2000) *Global Literacies and the World-Wide Web*. London: Routledge.

Heller, S. and K. Pomeroy (1997) *Design Literacy*, esp. Intro, ix–x; 'Dust Jackets', 257–8; 'Typography for children'. NY: Allworth Press, 108–11.

Jewitt, C. (2005) Multimodality, 'Reading' and 'Writing' for the 21st Century. *Discourse: Studies in the Cultural Politics of Education*, 315–31.

Jewitt, C. (2006) *Technology, Literacy and Learning: A Multimodal Approach*. London: Routledge.

Kress, G. (2003) *Literacy in the New Media Age*. London: Routledge.

Kress, G. and B. Street (2006) Multi-modality and literacy practices. In K. Pahl and J. Rowsell (eds) *Travel Notes from the New Literacy Studies*. Bristol: Multilingual Matters.

Kress, G. and T. van Leeuwen (1976) *Reading Images: The Grammar of Visual Design*. London: Routledge.

Kress, G. and T. van Leeuwen (1996) *Reading Images: The Grammar of Visual Design*, esp. intro, 1–14 and chapter 1. London: Routledge, 15–42.

Kress, G. and T. van Leeuwen (2001) *Multimodal Discourse: The Modes and Media of Contemporary Communication*. Arnold: London.

Kress, G. and B. Street (2006) Multi-modality and literacy practices. In K. Pahl and J. Rowsell (eds) Foreword to *Travel notes from the New Literacy Studies: Case Studies of Practice*. Clevedon: Multilingual Matters, vii–x.

Kress, G., C. Jewitt, J. Bourne, A. Franks, J. Hardcastle, J. Jones and E. Reid (2005) *English in Urban Classrooms: A Multimodal Perspective on Teaching and Learning*. London and New York: Routledge/ Falmer.

Pahl, K. (2007) Creativity in Events and Practices: A Lens for Understanding Children's Multimodal Texts. *Literacy*, 41(2), 81–7.

Rowsell, J. (1999) 'Towards a Model of Text Production', Chapter 1 of PhD thesis 'Publishers' texts and new curricula for ESL students in UK and Canada'.

Snyder, I. (ed.) (2002) *Silicon Literacies Communication, Innovation and Education in the Electronic Age*. New York: Routledge.

Street, B. (1999) New Literacies in Theory and Practice: What Are the Implications for Language in Education? *Linguistics and Education*, 10(1), 1–24.

Street, B. (2006) 'New literacies for new times' 'invited address'. In J. Hoffman and D. Schallert (eds) *55th yearbook of the National Reading Conference*. Oak Creek, Wisconsin: NRC Inc, 21–42.

Tutle, E. (1997) *Visual Explanations: Images and Quantities, Evidence and Narrative*. Cheshire, Connecticut: Graphic Press.

2
understanding textual practices in a changing world

david barton

literacy as social practice

To address questions about the future of Literacy Studies, this chapter first gives a brief overview of some of the theoretical framing provided by Literacy Studies and then reviews the evidence from detailed ethnographic studies of literacy in different contexts, from research carried out at Lancaster in England and more broadly. The chapter discusses two common findings from the range of studies which have been undertaken: the crucial role of mediators, mentors, brokers, networks and sponsors; and how particular practices have different significance and meaning in different domains of life. Looking at the future of Literacy Studies, the chapter further points to the significance of literacy in an increasingly textually mediated social world, including how texts are cultural artefacts and can be traced across contexts to link the local and the global; and how textual meaning-making is increasingly multimodal with electronic texts having growing importance. Finally, some future directions for the field are suggested.

The overall argument is that we live in a textually mediated social world, where texts are part of the glue of social life. Understanding what people do with texts, including both page-based and screen-based texts, and what texts do to people are essential for understanding contemporary social change. Language and literacy are at the heart of much of current social change because language and literacy structure knowledge and enable communication. Literacy Studies provides a powerful lens for examining changing social practices, such as the impact of new technologies and the phenomenon of the overwork culture. It provides a powerful lens because literacy is bound up in identity, in power and in how we can act in the world. By examining the changing role of texts we uncover the central tensions of contemporary change: new literacy practices offer exciting possibilities in terms of access to knowledge, creativity and personal power; at the same time the textually mediated social world provides a technology of power and control, and of surveillance. Literacy Studies provides a window for both the humanizing and the brutalizing possibilities of contemporary change.

The field of Literacy Studies has come into being in the past 20 years. In general terms, it is an approach to the study of reading and writing which starts out from what people do in their lives. It starts from people's social practices, noting that many of these involve texts of some sort, that in carrying out many activities in life people use texts. This means that literacy is a component of most social practices. Paying attention to aspects of literacy in a practice is particularly important at a time when social life is changing rapidly. The way into examining and understanding these practices is through the study of particular events. (This social practice approach to literacy has been laid out in more detail elsewhere, for example in Barton 2007.)

In any situation we see a range of literacies, that is, configurations of literacy practices, acting together. In particular domains of activity, such as the home, school or workplaces, we see common patterns of activity and we may wish to contrast the ways literacies are used in these different domains. Starting from particular domains is a useful way of seeing how different domains interact and overlap and how there is much hybridity and fusion. The borders, transitions and the spaces between domains are then very salient: they are significant, for instance, in understanding children starting out at school, students moving from school to college or how education might support – and challenge – workplace practices.

The view of literacy as being part of social practices which are inferred from events and mediated by texts requires a certain methodology. It is a methodology of attention to detail and it draws heavily on ethnographic approaches. It involves the examination of particular events to understand broader practices. Researchers integrate a variety of methods including observation, interviews, the analysis of texts, the use of photography and more. Researchers have been innovative in developing methods which are ethical, responsive and collaborative. As with all research, there is a close link between theory and methodology and each informs and constrains the other. The methodology of Literacy Studies also provides units of analysis: The concept of literacy event provides a starting-point for analysing interactions, whilst the concept of literacy practice provides a way of bringing in broader cultural and structural aspects. Concentrating on specific domains of life, the detailed, multimethod, collaborative and responsive methodologies provide ways of carrying out research. Juxtaposed with discourse analysis, these are powerful ways of researching and analysing texts and practices.

For anyone carrying out empirical research it quickly becomes apparent that defining the limits of what counts as literacy activity and what counts as a literacy event or a literacy practice is not straightforward. First in many situations text and talk are mixed up, especially with new technologies, and all activity is very multimodal with language and image intertwined. Events are nested within each other with micro and macro events; they are chained together in sequences and they are networked across contexts.

Researchers have approached this work with different starting points. In my own work I have started out from individuals acting in everyday contexts. Others start out from institutional contexts such as education or workplaces. Many researchers are interested in the educational implications. Starting from everyday practices also reveals everyday ways of learning which are important in classroom contexts. This can be seen as a set of steps in research, that the focus needs to start with practices, before moving to learning, and only then on to teaching, as discussed below. In detailed ethnographic studies, researchers draw out the complexities people reveal about their lives. To understand change in people's lives, we work with concepts of learning based on participation and interaction, as discussed in Tusting and Barton (2006).

Literacy Studies offers a particular discourse, a way of talking about literacy; this is based upon a theory of literacy as social practice and can be developed into a social practice pedagogy. It can be used to challenge contemporary discourses about the changing workplace and about education, which often draw upon a narrow skills discourse and the deficit discourse of blame. To engage with current issues of literacy a social practice approach needs to be interdisciplinary and it needs to be a critical endeavour, developing an engaged ethnography.

the lancaster approach to literacy research

In line with the spirit of this volume, I will first provide an overview of some studies which have been carried out at Lancaster in England. Early sets of studies identified themes that have been important throughout our research, the significance of writing (Barton & Ivanic 1991) and the relationship between research and practice in adult literacy education (Hamilton et al. 1994). A key empirical study was the *Local Literacies* research (Barton & Hamilton 1998) where we studied the role of reading and writing in the local community of the town in which we lived. The study identified key areas of everyday life where reading and writing were significant for people and it contrasted these vernacular literacies, which were often voluntary, self-generated and learned informally, with more dominant literacies which were often more formalized and defined in terms of the needs of institutions.

This research also demonstrated the importance of social networks and relationships in these practices, with literacy being used for social communication. People drew upon these social networks to help them with particular literacy requirements. So, for example, we saw the ways in which literacy is significant in terms of local democratic participation, underpinning political participation at the local level and also offering ways into more formal political organizations. This data shows the importance of literacy as a communal resource, rather than just as an attribute of individual people. Literacy was used by people to make sense of events in their lives and resolve a variety of problems, such as those related to health, to their jobs, to their children's schooling and to encounters with the law. Often this involved confrontation with professional experts and specialized systems of knowledge, and people often drew upon their networks for support and knowledge, thereby becoming expert in a particular domain and becoming a resource for other community members themselves. Literacy was also used for personal change and transformation, both within and outside education-related domains, for accessing information relating to people's interests, for asserting or creating personal identity and for self-directed learning.

Further examples of local and community literacy research can be found in the later edited volume *Situated Literacies* (Barton et al. 2000), which brought together a number of studies of reading and writing in a variety of different local contexts, informed by the same theoretical perspective outlined above. The studies in this collection show how qualitative methods and detailed local studies can deepen a theoretical understanding of literacy. A study of the literacy practices of young people in prisons by Anita Wilson demonstrated the role of literacies in the struggle against institutionalization and 'losing your mind'. She has worked for many years as a prison ethnographer. She identified the importance of literacy in attempts to maintain an individual identity within a bureaucratic controlling institution, and how people used literacy to construct a 'third space' between prison and outside.

This resistant use of literacy contrasts with work by Kathryn Jones with bilingual Welsh farmers at an auction market, where literacy inscribed people's lives into a broader social order; this showed how the local and the global are linked by textual activity. Jones focuses on the process of filling in a particular form, showing how the individual farmers are incorporated into the agricultural bureaucratic system through a complex process of locally situated talk around texts and the interweaving of spoken Welsh with written English. (A wide range of further studies in multilingual literacies is reported in Martin-Jones and Jones 2000.) A study by Karin Tusting on the role of literacy practices within a Catholic congregation shows how literacy is used to manage time in a variety of ways: how literacy artefacts are produced within a preparation class both as tangible evidence of commitment through showing investment of significant amounts of time and to serve as a permanent historical record of a fleeting set of events; and how the parish bulletin is used to synchronize events in time, both locally within the parish community and globally in relation to the Catholic Church as a whole, thereby maintaining community identity. She frames this within social theories of time. As a set of studies, these investigations show how aspects of social theory can be combined with a Literacy Studies approach to make links between local and global phenomena. The studies also identify distinct practices in different domains of life.

studies of education

Literacy Studies research in the field of education has also provided significant insights into the structure of practices. Extensive research in Further Education colleges in England and Scotland takes our understanding forward in a distinct way: The *Literacies for learning in Further Education* research identifies different literacies being drawn upon in further education classes. Students are learning the reading and writing demands of the vocations they are training for, such as catering, construction or hairdressing, the literacies of particular workplaces. At the same time there are particular ways of reading and writing which help students in their learning – the literacies for learning. These literacies for work and literacies for learning exist alongside other distinct forms of reading and writing associated with assessment and, increasingly, with accountability, as in the record-keeping they have to do. This work demonstrates the different literacies which students have to grapple with simultaneously (see Ivanic et al. 2008 for further details) and identifies a phenomenon which is significant in other domains.

Studies of the literacy practices of everyday life can provide data, methods and theories for educational practice. They provide data about how and what people read and write in their everyday lives which can inform the educational curriculum (Barton et al. 2006). In terms of methods, such studies provide ways of getting students to investigate and reflect upon their own practices as a way of engaging them in their work; for example, in the uses of photography or keeping literacy diaries (see Barton 2001 and Ivanic et al. 2008). The theory of literacy as social practice offers educational practitioners a language to talk in when discussing literacy issues. And the studies of educational provision for adults in England which we carried out enable us to move towards developing principles of a social practice pedagogy, that is, ways of teaching adults which are based upon a social practice view of literacy (Appleby & Barton 2007; Fowler & Mace 2005; Tett et al. 2006).

In moving from a focus on everyday life to a focus on educational practice, educators and educational policy-makers sometimes find it frustrating that researchers studying everyday life do not immediately provide 'solutions' for educational problems. However, there is a set of steps: first, there is a need to understand what people do, their practices; then it is essential to see how people learn; and only then can we turn to questions of how to teach, or how to support learning. These are the steps we followed in the study of adult literacy students referred to above: first we aimed to understand their lives, then we turned to how they learned to participate in literacy practices, both in everyday settings and in formal educational settings, and only then did we work with teachers to see how to support the students in their learning (see Barton et al. 2007). Other work in educational contexts has been concerned with the development of writing and identity in educational contexts (Ivanic 1997, this volume; Clark & Ivanic 1997) and work applying a social practice view to understanding learning and people's lives in adult literacy education (Papen 2005) and in teaching English to speakers of other languages – ESOL (Pitt 2005), as well as research on policy (Hamilton & Hillier 2006).

More recent directions include making links with work on communities of practice (Barton & Tusting 2005). Another direction has been work on spelling and orthography as social practices (Johnson 2005; Sebba 2007). Research on literacy and creativity (Papen & Tusting 2006) again shows the value of this approach, examining individual creativity in everyday literacy practices. And work in new arenas shows the affordances of new technologies (Lee 2007).

studies of literacies in a range of contexts

So far I have focused on studies carried out at Lancaster. However, across the world there have now been a broad range of studies across different domains of activity and it is possible to draw out common themes from the research. This is not the place for a review of such studies, but to provide a flavour of recent research I will mention just a few recent publications (for an earlier overview of such studies, see Barton 2001). People have been carrying out research utilizing the theories and methodologies of Literacy Studies and complementing these with different frameworks, including discourse analysis, textual analysis, narrative analysis and aspects of social theory. They work in different contexts including all areas of education, specific workplaces and particular communities and may focus on childhood, teenagers, gender, multilingualism, new technologies or other issues. Many studies focus on the links between home communities and schools.

Cruickshank (2006) is a good example of a study which mixes the ethnographic approaches of Literacy Studies with discourse analysis, focusing on teenagers' use of technology and the links between home and school and the study identifies the importance of networks, mediation and roles. Purcell-Gates (2007) provides a useful set of case studies, covering home, school, young people, across cultures, immigrant experiences, ways in which literacy is multiple and is looking for 'new pedagogies for new literacies' (p. x), meaning in this case new social practices from a range of cultures, and not particularly new technologies. The studies in Street (2005) also cover many educational sites. The set of studies in Anderson et al. (2005) covers links between families, communities and schools. The studies reported in Lewis et al. (2007) start from socio-cultural theory and explore notions of activity, community and history. Lankshear and Knobel (2006) and Knobel and Lankshear (2007) cover new literacies as new technologies in a critical way. They are mainly interested in the school non-school divide, and most of the studies they cover are about way of incorporating technologies into school practices. A recent special issue in *Language and Education* edited by Snyder and Prinsloo (2007) looks at digital literacies in different domains of life across different parts of the world (including South Africa, Brazil, Australia and Greece).

Another recent study is concerned with applying Literacy Studies to adult literacy education. Branch (2007) provides a challenge for Literacy Studies arguing that although Literacy Studies has emphasized what people do with literacy: 'teaching literacy practices means hoping as well that literacy will do something to people, to our students. Thus, the focus on local definitions of literacy ... remains inadequate to help teachers understand and analyse what they hope to accomplish by teaching, and what they hope their students will accomplish by learning, particular literacy practices' (p. 8). Branch aims to move Literacy Studies 'toward the rhetorical construction of the future world, those literacy practices are designed to facilitate' (p. 37). This parallels our work on the *imagined futures* of adult literacy students (Barton et al. 2007) and the repeated calls by Kress (1995) to consider the future for which those in education are being prepared.

Cherland and Harper (2007) talk in terms of advocacy in relation to literacy education (a term which is not common in the UK) and, like Branch, they provide a challenge to Literacy Studies: 'The assumption that most researchers of situated literacies make is that once we see differently, we will act differently. ... But that is a problematic assumption. We often see and understand, but then do not know how to act. If we are to change the world through literacy education, we will need to find new ways to work in classrooms and new forms of research to inform our best efforts' (p. 128).

To give an example of a study outside of education, there is a tradition of South American research on the centrality of the written word in indigenous cultures and Wogan (2003) brings a social practice approach to this work. He sees the value of Literacy Studies being that it now provides 'a well established tradition of ethnographic research. ... Twenty years ago, in the absence of such research, a study like mine would have not been conceived. ... I focus on identity categories and state and church documentation. ... Other studies do not fully explore the perspectives of ordinary non-elite groups' (p. 66).

Such research tends to be detailed studies of particular groups of people in particular sites. The references so far give a hint of the range and diversity of them, and several further studies are covered in other chapters of this book. There has now been such a wealth of studies that it is possible to look across them and see common themes and repeated findings and at the same time to see how meaning of reading and writing is tied to specific practices. This is all leading to new understandings of the nature of reading and writing.

from networks to sponsors

Here I will focus on one repeated finding which has been identified across studies; that is, the role of other people in a person's literacy practices. Studies repeatedly point to the significance of other people. Early on Barton and Padmore (1991) identified the importance of people who acted as 'guiding lights'. These mentors were individuals, such as relatives or neighbours, who had supported and inspired people in their literacy endeavours; they were especially important when people were making changes in their lives. Researchers also talked of the networks of support which people were located in (Fingeret 1983) and which they drew upon. Within these networks it is possible to identify people acting as mediators, mentors, brokers and scribes. Different researchers have focused on different aspects and highlighted different terms (some of which is covered in other chapters of this volume) and the terms have different ideas of support in them. A crucial distinction here is between doing an activity on behalf of someone and the idea of supporting them to do the activity themselves. So a travel agent may fill in a form for someone else, whereas a teacher may help a student fill it in themselves and ensure that they learn how to do it. Mace (2002) also talks of scribes, people who specifically write for others, linking up the activities of people as diverse as clerks, lawyers and literacy teachers, showing the ways in which they act as scribes for others and how such support is a common everyday activity.

It is important not just to identify reading and writing as something which individuals do. Rather, groups of various sorts may use reading and writing in different ways. It is much broader than this and Deborah Brandt (1998, 2001 and this volume) talks of the role of individuals and institutions acting as sponsors of literacy practices and as supporters and facilitators for people. The idea of sponsors makes it clear that we are talking about both individuals and institutions. This idea also enables us to see how the texts come from somewhere and go somewhere, and that we need to study literacy across contexts. It is useful to look at this historically, seeing how the church, for example, has acted as a supporter of literacy practices over the years, or how in contemporary life, business, publishers or governments support particular practices. These sponsors support specific views and advocate for these views. Brandt's approach is important in understanding ways in which reading can be promoted and supported. The concept of sponsorship also links to the idea of funds of knowledge in a community which people can draw upon (Gonzales et al. 2005). Taken together these ideas can help show the different ways in which families, household, neighbourhoods and communities may support and be sponsors of literacy. Brandt's work is most valuable in drawing together these ideas, both to understand the complexities of the influences on people's literacy and also the role of teachers in educational situations (1998: 183).

different meanings in different domains

Returning to the notion of there being different literacies for different purposes in different contexts, it is probably useful to have a range of examples at this point. A good example of specific workplace practices can be seen in Wenger's description of an insurance claims office which was the basis for his study of communities of practice (Wenger 1998, as discussed in Barton & Hamilton 2005). His vignette of a day in the life of office workers (pp. 18–34) provides a clear example of specific practices associated with this sort of workplace at a certain point in time. The writing, for example, was often the filling in of forms and using pre-written paragraphs. It was routine and repetitive. The writing can also be seen as collaborative, where several people were involved in the writing at different stages and there was no identifiable author. Similarly, the range of reading activities in the workplace was formulaic, limited and constrained. In terms of the language used, this workplace had its own specific discourses, ways of talking and writing, including a specialized vocabulary, such as 'a pre-exist', 'junk claims', and so on. Many of the workplace practices were those identified as being related to the new work order by Gee et al. (1996), where literacy was used for close monitoring and self-regulation.

These are typical workplace literacies. They can be contrasted, for example, with the domain of education, where such activities of sharing, copying and collaborating are tightly controlled and policed and often punished as plagiarism. When constructing a business letter, the idea of taking existing 'boiler plate' paragraphs from elsewhere and altering and combining them into a new letter is a totally reasonable and common practice in the workplace. The idea of changing someone else's text is central to text producing organizations such as banks and other businesses. However, 'patchwriting' (Howard 1999) in education, where a student takes a paragraph from elsewhere and alters a few words and phrases has the completely opposite values associated with it; it becomes a crime, policed by electronic plagiarism detection systems and it may lead to a student being excluded from higher education.

Often when people talk about reading or writing, they have one very specific form in mind, but this differs from domain to domain. What seems to be the same activity, such as copying and pasting from the

Internet or commenting on someone else's work has to be understood in terms of the social practices which it forms part of. Only then can we understand the meaning of an activity. This is important when trying to understand plagiarism at a time of technological change. Another example related to the academic world is the issue of citation, where what is required in newspapers, on Wikipedia, or in a political statement differs markedly from what is required in academic writing.

The use of texts changes in importance over time. We see differences across domains and these need to be understood within contemporary social change. The rapid spread of Internet form-filling is a good example. Forms are a special type of structured writing. They are important today for booking a flight or a train trip or buying a book or paying for a hotel. They also appear in classrooms and may be important in maintaining a portfolio of work or doing an exam. They are probably much more important now in everyday contexts. Nevertheless, the values around them are subtly different at different times. We know on the Internet when accuracy and truth is important and where invention and fantasy is reasonable: giving our name and details to the online bank is different from giving details to people in the chat room. Confirming in an online form that we have read the terms and conditions is often an inaccurate convenience.

Recent Lancaster research, mentioned earlier, has peeled this away further and shown how different literacies for different purposes interact within one context. So, our work in college-based vocational courses has identified literacies for learning, literacies for assessment and workplace related literacies all being enacted at the same time (Ivanic et al. 2009). This becomes complex and we see tensions where the same text is serving different purposes, such as the individual learning plans which are common in English education; here a range of potentially conflicting purposes are invested in one text (as in Hamilton 2009; Burgess 2008). We have also seen how students in college come across writing demands which are unlike writing practices they have participated in elsewhere and certainly unlike their everyday writing practices. When examining the dynamics of literacies in a particular context, identifying different sponsors and their aims enables us to see the pressures which support and hinder different practices. Part of this is seeing where a text has come from and where it is heading.

agency and sponsorship

If our aim is to understand the changing significance of literacy in the contemporary world, we need first to understand some properties of texts which enable them to travel across contexts, and then to see how texts fare in the changing world. There is greater understanding of texts and how they function, and how a written text is different from other artefacts. Texts act as cultural artefacts – as agents with sponsors. Texts are things and this 'thingness' is important as we investigate and come to understand the virtual world and its relation to the physical world. Wenger (1998) identifies four characteristics of 'things' (or reifications in his terms): their succinctness and power to evoke meanings; their portability across time, physical space and context; their potential for physical persistence or durability; their focusing effect, drawing attention to specific features or distinctions within social reality. It is useful to think of texts in these terms and, in fact, when Wenger and others (such as Latour) focus on things, they are often talking primarily about language-laden texts (see Barton & Hamilton 2005). Texts are a special sort of reification and compared with other objects are generally strong on all four of these characteristics.

Texts also have agency; that is, they act as people, on behalf of people and in place of people. Where Latour and others question the basic division of people and things, this helps us see that texts act as people in interactions: texts have agency. They act as agents by having sponsors. Often these sponsors are institutions and deploying texts is one of the ways in which institutions act as people. An example of this is the way in which Literacy Studies contributes to studies of social interaction in the classroom; Literacy Studies adds the point that much interaction in classrooms are mediated by texts: texts are used as fixed points and in many ways texts act 'as a person'. Texts are used to coordinate activities and to regulate behaviour (see, for example, Pitkanen-Huhta's work (2003) in an English as a foreign language classroom). The idea of sponsorship, again, enables us to see more about the life of texts, where they originate and where they are going.

future directions

Finally, I would like to identify two key foci for future work in understanding the role of texts in contemporary society. First, our work has critical engagement with public discourses, especially the discourses of educational change. Given the way that new communications technologies have affected the nature of the literacies which people engage in, there are significant implications for education. Throughout the world, educational innovation is one of the central ways for governments to respond to rapid social and technological change. Policies emphasizing the improvement of literacy, numeracy and language skills of adults and young people (as in the Skills for Life Strategy in England) are examples of this. Through our work in education, we have a critical engagement with the discourses of educational change implicit in these policies. Through detailed ethnographic studies, we draw out the complexities people reveal about their lives which challenge the equation between 'skills' and 'employability' implicit in much policy discourse. Broader notions of literacy and learning are needed. To understand change in people's lives, we work with concepts of learning based on participation and interaction. One point of tension is where the constant deficit discourse of 'literacy crisis' in public discussion is in conflict with the 'creativity and possibilities' promises in other parts of the knowledge economy discourse. To engage with these educational issues a social practice approach to literacy needs to be interdisciplinary, engaged and critical. Pedagogical thinking needs to consider how students' uses of reading and writing are changing and needs to change, both to reflect the different practices people are participating in and to enable critique.

Second, literacy can be a powerful lens for examining changing social practices, including the impact of new technologies, the growing audit culture and the growing textualization of life. Engagement with texts of various kinds is central to such phenomena. We can examine the reality of these phenomena in people's lives, and see how the activities are located structurally. Issues of power and identity are highlighted. Using literacy as a lens and with ideas of networks and sponsors we are able to link up activities across contexts. Texts are the threads joining contexts. If we want to address current social issues as diverse as migration, health care, environmental issues and overwork culture, Literacy Studies can provide the lens for understanding these issues. For instance, in drawing attention to the general role of other people and networks of support it reveals structures of social interaction, emphasizing the importance of mediators, brokers and sponsors of literacy. It draws attention to how people learn in everyday settings as a step towards understanding more formal and institutional learning. In relation to globalization, the examination of literacy practices provides a way of interrogating the complex changes in specific sites, tracing links between local and global practices and documenting local forms of appropriation and resistance. The tools of Literacy Studies are also useful when studying how people across the world engage in web-based literacy events.

The range of studies, the developments of theory and methodology and the links to practice over the past 20 years are evidence for the success of Literacy Studies. These studies have been used to challenge myths about literacy and an important role for this ethnographic data has been as providing a critique. At the same time, it offers a set of concepts, such as *networks, brokers* and *sponsors* which are useful in understanding literacy. Even the basic concepts of *literacies* or *practices* have been powerful in the ways in which they have enabled people to reconceptualize literacy. The approach of Literacy Studies is close to data, but at the same time it is theorizing by providing concepts and linking to broader theories. It is good at individual descriptions and how to locate them in broader issues. In drawing attention to the role of the written word, Literacy Studies treads a line between a narrow skills approach which cannot locate literacy in anything broader and more general approaches to social practice which do not draw attention to the role of language and textuality. However, in the links to policy and to public discourses, we see not only the success but also the failure of Literacy Studies, so far. Policy and public discussion of literacy issues, in England at least, is still mainly focused on skills, on reading and on a deficit view of literacy. There is much to do to challenge these dominant discourses. The richness of work in Literacy Studies should enable us to locate current obsessions around literacy in broader frameworks and to challenge the shallowness of the skills vision – especially their lack of interest in the creative, the political, the liberatory, the aesthetic, or the personal possibilities of acts of reading and writing.

note

I am grateful to Mary Hamilton, Carmen Lee and Uta Papen for comments on an earlier version of this paper.

references

Anderson, J., M. Kendrick, T. Rogers and S. Smythe (eds) (2005) *Portraits of Literacy across Families, Communities, and Schools: Intersections and Tensions.* Mahwah, NJ: Lawrence Erlbaum.

Appleby, Y. and D. Barton (2007) *Responding to People's Lives in Adult Literacy, Language and Numeracy Teaching.* Leicester: NIACE.

Barton, D. (2001) Directions for Literacy Research: Analysing Language and Social Practices in a Textually-mediated World. *Language and Education,* 15, 92–104.

Barton, D. and M. Hamilton (1998) *Local Literacies: Reading and Writing in One Community.* London: Routledge.

Barton, D. and M. Hamilton (2005) Literacy, reification and the dynamics of social interaction. In D. Barton and K. Tusting (eds) *Beyond Communities Of Practice: Language, Power and Social Context.* Cambridge University Press, 14–35.

Barton, D., M. Hamilton and R. Ivanic (eds) (2000) *Situated Literacies.* London: Routledge.

Barton, D. and K. Tusting (eds) (2005) *Beyond Communities of Practice: Language, Power and Social Context.* Cambridge: Cambridge University Press.

Barton, D. and R. Ivanic (eds) (1991) *Writing in the Community.* Newbury Park, CA and London: Sage.

Barton, D. (2007) *Literacy: An Introduction to the Ecology of Written Language,* second edition. Oxford: Blackwell.

Barton, D., R. Ivanic, Y. Appleby, R. Hodge, and K. Tusting (2007) *Literacy, Lives and Learning.* London: Routledge.

Barton, D. and S. Padmore (1991) Roles, networks and values in everyday writing. In D. Barton and R. Ivanic (eds), 58–77.

Branch, K. (2007) *Eyes on the Ought to Be: What We Teach When We Teach about Literacy.* Cresskill, NJ: Hampton Press.

Brandt, D. (1998) Sponsors of Literacy. *College Composition and Communication,* 49, 165–85.

Burgess, A. (2008) The Literacy Practices of Recording Achievement: How a Text Mediates between the Local and the Global. *Journal of Education Policy,* 23(1), 49–62.

Cherland M. R. and H. Harper (2007) *Advocacy Research in Literacy Education.* Mahwah, NJ: Lawrence Erlbaum.

Clark, R. and R. Ivanic (1997) *The Politics of Writing.* London: Routledge.

Cruickshank, K. (2006) *Teenagers, Literacy and School: Researching in Multilingual Contexts.* London: Routledge.

Fingeret, A. (1983) Social Network: A New Perspective on Independence and Illiterate Adults. *Adult Education Quarterly,* 33, 133–46.

Fowler, E. and J. Mace (eds) (2005) *Outside the Classroom: Researching Literacy with Adult Learners.* Leicester: NIACE.

Gee, J., G. Hull and C. Lankshear (1996) *The New Work Order: Behind the Language of the New Capitalism.* London: Allen and Unwin.

Gonzalez, N. E., Moll, L. and Amanti, C. (eds) (2005) *Funds of Knowledge: Theorizing Knowledge in Households, Communities and Classrooms.* Mahwah, NJ: Lawrence Erlbaum Associates.

Hamilton, M., D. Barton and R. Ivanic (eds) (1994) *Worlds of Literacy.* Clevedon: Multilingual Matters.

Hamilton, M. and Y. Hillier (2006) *Changing Faces of Adult Literacy, Language and Numeracy: A Critical History.* Stoke on Trent: Trentham Books.

Hamilton, M. (2009) Putting Words in Their Mouths: The Alignment of Identities with System Goals through the Use of Individual Learning Plans. *British Educational Research Journal,* 35(2), 221–42.

Howard, R. M. (1999) *Standing in the Shadow of Giants: Plagiarists, Authors, Collaborators.* Stamford, Conn: Ablex.

Ivanic, R. (1997) *Writing and Identity.* Amsterdam: John Benjamins.

Ivanic, R., R. Edwards, D. Barton, M. Martin-Jones, Z. Fowler, B. Hughes, G. Mannion, K. Miller, C. Satchwell and J. Smith (2009) *Improving Learning in College: Rethinking Literacies across the Curriculum.* London: Routledge.

Johnson, S. (2005) *Spelling Trouble? Language, Ideology and the Reform of German Orthography.* Clevedon: Multilingual Matters.

Knobel M. and C. Lankshear (eds) (2007) *A New Literacies Sampler.* New York: Peter Lang.

Kress, G. (1995) *Writing the Future: English and the Making of a Culture of Innovation.* Sheffield: National Association for the Teaching of English.

Lankshear, C. and M. Knobel (2006) *New Literacies: Changing Knowledge and Classroom Learning,* second edition. Maidenhead: Open University Press.

Lee, C. K. M. (2007) Affordances and Text-Making Practices in Online Instant Messaging. *Written Communication,* 24(3), 223–49.

Lewis, C., P. Enciso and E. B. Moje (eds) (2007) *Reframing Sociocultural Research on Literacy: Identity, Agency, and Power.* Mahwah, NJ: Lawrence Erlbaum.

Mace, J. (2002) *The Give and Take of Writing: Scribes, Literacy and Everyday Life.* Leicester: NIACE.

Martin-Jones, M. and K. Jones (eds) (2000) *Multilingual Literacies.* Amsterdam: John Benjamins.

Papen, U. (2005) *Adult Literacy as Social Practice – More Than Skills.* London: Routledge.

Papen, U. and K. Tusting (2006) Literacies, collaboration and context. In J. Maybin and J. Swann (eds) *The Art of English: Everyday Creativity.* Basingstoke: Palgrave Macmillan, 312–59.

Pitkanen-Huhta, A. (2003) *Texts and Interaction: Literacy practices in the EFL Classroom.* Jyväskylä: University of Jyväskylä.

Pitt, K. *Debates in ESOL Teaching and Learning: Cultures, Communities and Classrooms.* London: Routledge.

Purcell-Gates, V. (ed.) (2007) *Cultural Practices of Literacy: Case Studies of Language, Literacy, Social Practice, and Power.* Mahwah, NJ: Lawrence Erlbaum.

Sebba, M. (2007) *Spelling and Society: The Culture and Politics of Orthography around the World.* Cambridge: Cambridge University Press.

Street, B. (ed.) (2005) *Literacies across Educational Contexts.* Philadelphia: Caslon.

Snyder, I. and M. Prinsloo (2007) Young People's Engagement with Digital Literacies in Marginal Contexts in a Globalised World. *Language and Education,* 21(3), 171–9.

Tett, L., M. Hamilton and Y. Hillier (eds) (2006) *Adult Literacy, Numeracy and Language: Policy, Practice and Research.* Milton Keynes: Open University Press.

Tusting, K. and D. Barton (2006) *Models of Adult Learning.* Leicester: NIACE.

Wenger, E. (1998) *Communities of Practice: Learning, Meaning, and Identity.* Cambridge and New York: Cambridge University Press.

Wogan, P. (2003) *Magical Writing in Salasaca: Literacy and Power in Highland Ecuador.* Boulder, CO: Westview Press.

3
writing over reading: new directions in mass literacy

deborah brandt

In 1982, Henry Leonard was hired as a special collections archivist at a university library, where he prepared exhibit notes and composed occasional letters to researchers inquiring about the rare books under his care. By 2005, he was director of web services for the same library, writing 800-word essays and fictionalized blogs to serve as conceptual portals to digitized materials. 'The idea,' he said, 'is to get what we have into people's living rooms.' Leonard writes more often, in more genres, and toward more venues than he did 25 years ago. But more profoundly, through his work, he is changing an institution that was designed to think like readers into one that thinks like a writer. 'Instead of collections,' he observed, 'now we think about audiences.' In the process, Leonard's own literacy—including the relationship between his reading and writing—is undergoing significant transformation.

As the nature of work has changed—toward making and managing information and knowledge in globalized settings—intense pressure has come to bear on people's scribal skills. More and more people around the world are spending more and more time in the posture of a writer. This shift represents a new direction in the history of mass literacy, one with serious social, political, and cultural implications. What happens when writing (and not just reading) becomes the grounds of mass literate experience, when more and more people 'think about audiences' as part of their daily, routine engagement with literacy? How does a societal shift in time and energy away from reading and toward writing affect the ways in which people develop their literacy and understand its value? More profoundly, how does a rivalry between mass writing

54

and mass reading create tensions in societies that were founded on the premise that readers would be many and writers would be few?

Until now writing has played second fiddle to reading, a more minor strain in the history of literacy. But as it has risen in prominence (not because of new technology but along with it), it is bringing challenges to reading-based understandings of literacy that tend to dominate thinking in theory, research, and policy. As will be explored further below, mass reading and mass writing have developed differently, especially in terms of their social rationales and in terms of the cultural forces that have sponsored and sanctioned them (Furet and Ozouf 1983; Monaghan 2005). Although reading and writing are typically taught together in school, studied together, and treated as similar underlying or mutually dependent processes (even to the point that one is sometimes used to prove or measure the achievement of the other), their different cultural origins remain consequential to the ways that they are accessed, practiced, and experienced as part of ordinary life. As I hope to show, it is the radical differences between writing and reading—particularly the cultural and political heritages of each—that must be better apprehended to understand literacy as it is going forward. Attunement to differences between reading and writing is important for literacy researchers, who are used to focusing on the interrelationships and similarities between the two. This awareness is especially important for observers of networked communication, who, in their quest to identify formidable forces in the shaping of our communicative futures, rarely attend to the history of mass literacy and the relationships between reading and writing that are found there.

Before proceeding, a few definitions are in order. In this chapter, *mass* literacy refers to the nearly universal participation in meaning-making based on encoded symbols (i.e., alphabets or characters) as well as the systems and expectations that grow up around this phenomenon. Mass literacy is stratified in terms of access and reward and various in practice, value, and impact. According to most observers, the United States had become a mass literate society by the latter half of the nineteenth century (even as great discrepancies by race, region, ethnicity, and occupation remained). However, at the time, mass literacy was presumed to be a reading literacy (and often still is today). *Mass writing* refers specifically to nearly universal access to and routine activation of writing systems and to expectations that grow up around this phenomenon. (It is not meant to refer merely to writing in groups nor to written messages geared to mass audiences.) Like mass reading, mass writing is highly stratified in terms of access and reward and various in practice, value, and impact.[1] As I will argue further below, mass writing is a more recent social achievement than mass reading and is in a period of especially intense development and change right now. Finally, another key term in this chapter is literacy *sponsorship*, by which I mean forces that promote, withhold, or otherwise exploit literacy and gain advantage by it in some way (see Brandt 1998).

In calling this chapter 'Writing Over Reading', I wish to bring attention to the rivalry between writing and reading as discrete literate practices, their different social, economic, and legal statuses, and the growing ascendancy of writing due to recent changes in forms of labor in many developed societies. Mass reading emerged gradually through the eighteenth and nineteenth centuries largely through the sponsoring agents of church and state, institutions that understood the power of books to enculturate and instantiate shared belief and so established systems of schooling with reading at their center. By the late nineteenth and early twentieth centuries, these large-scale institutional efforts had produced such a surplus of reading literacy that it could be captured easily for other purposes (including, eventually, writing). A robust consumer market grew up around recreational reading, while the broader economy came to rely tacitly on people's capacity to read as a mechanism for instruction, organization, advancement, and control.[2]

In the initial projects of mass literacy, however, writing had held no great sway. Harder to teach, messy to learn, not as suitable a vehicle for religious or social control, and especially dangerous in the hands of the oppressed, writing emerged separately from reading and more slowly through the eighteenth and twentieth centuries.[3] It was promulgated not through church and state but through artisanship and commerce. First linked not with spiritual salvation but with apprenticeship, not with reading but with mathematics, writing as a productive vehicle for craft knowledge, record-keeping, and communication at a distance kept the wheels of commerce and administration turning.[4] In comparison to reading, it offered a clearer path to upward mobility (Furet and Ozouf 1983; Laqueur 1976). The imperative for mass writing emerged with industrialization, which ramped up the scope, pace, and technologies of written communication, bringing into existence expanding tiers of writing-intensive workers, including secretaries, managers, and government bureaucrats (Beniger 1986; Yates 1989, 2005). This trend only intensified in the latter half of the twentieth century as many Western economies shifted to the mass production of information and knowledge as things in themselves that could be made, bought, and sold. This transformation compounded the need to record and communicate at many more levels of production—putting keyboards and computer terminals into virtually all work settings. Today, writing serves not merely as a chief mode of production but a chief product as well, engaging millions of workers at various levels in composing, processing, distributing, and organizing written symbols for large portions of the workday, often in high-stakes contexts (Brandt 2005; Cortada 2004). By the end of the twentieth century, change in work—enhanced by computer technology and the Internet—was creating a surplus of writing literacy, much like the reading surplus of a century before. As home computers have been mass marketed and access to the Internet has broadened, writing is becoming a widely practiced recreational and consumer activity and a gateway to other literacy-based practices. In and out of the workplace, the demand for writing and the opportunities for authorship have never been as acute as they are now.

This ascendancy of writing does not diminish reading, necessarily, but it does re-position it. More and more people read at the screen, from the posture of the writer, with hands on the keyboard. Increasingly people read to inform their own writing. Increasingly people write to (and with) other people who write (Barlow 2007; Lenhart et al. 2004; Rainie 2005). Acts of reading are now more routinely embedded in acts of writing: writing occurs 'over' reading.

The title of this chapter signals not only the rivalry between writing and reading but also their critical sequencing in the history of mass literacy. Mass writing as a societal achievement is arriving after and on top of the achievement of mass reading and is necessarily influenced by and accountable to that chronology. Reading, associated early on with proper conduct and right belief, as well as the exercise of civic rights and duties, still enjoys a nearly sacred status in many societies. It is nearly universally regarded as wholesome and uplifting, an avenue to moral development and responsible citizenship, just as the inability or refusal to read is still regarded often as a road to ruin (Graff and Duffy, 2008). But in the moral universe of reading, writing holds a lesser status. Writing has never been central to doctrines of salvation or assimilation. Compared to reading, writing has been regarded alternatively as crass and mercantile or rebellious and suspect, and the democratization of writing has been far less promoted or sanctioned by the state. As I will explore further below, to the extent that writing garners moral or civic standing, it is indirectly through the prestige or goodness of reading. Writing is good to the extent that it demonstrates what reading teaches: rule abiding conduct. Good writing is correct writing. And writing is good to the extent that it uplifts readers—indeed, the more uplifting for readers, the more highly regarded the writing. Writing is seen to be in the service of reading. The role of writing in edifying (or even entertaining) those who undertake it is a weaker concept in the history of mass literacy, as is the view that reading might function in the service of writing.[5] Relatedly, writing tends to be protected politically and legally only indirectly, through the constitutional protections of an informed (i.e. reading) citizenry (Brown 1996; Zimmerman 2004). In short, at least until now, writing has taken its character from the ideological arrangements of a reading literacy. In these arrangements, readers are presumed to be many and writers presumed to be few. But if we are at a moment when writers are becoming many—when reading is being 'overwritten' for the first time in the history of mass literacy—then the status of both may be up for grabs. At the least, the rise of mass writing in the twenty-first century will bring to the foreground literacy's minor strain. The crass, the commercial, the rebellious and suspect may finally put pressure on the moral order of reading with potentially significant implications for society and the future of literacy.

I was driven to investigate the divergent cultural legacies of reading and writing when their potent differences first presented themselves to me, as a surprise, in the course of doing life-history research in the United States in the early 1990s, a project that gave rise to *Literacy in American Lives* (2001). In interviews with 80 people from all walks of life born between 1895 and 1985, I asked them to recollect how they learned to read and write (anything) and how they used writing and reading across their lifetimes. As significant memories surfaced, we focused on concrete details including where a literacy event took place, who was present, what was present in terms of materials, and what motivations or feelings surrounded the event. Across age, race, gender, and class, the nature of these reading-writing memories were palpably divergent. With exceptions, of course, scenes of early reading could be remembered vividly, and the memories were for the most part pleasant: Early reading events typically were described as taking place in pleasurable family settings, with adult endorsement and often as part of shared family rituals or in socially sanctioned places like libraries or houses of worship. They were often embedded in feelings of personal achievement or the affirmation of relatives or teachers. People could routinely remember the first words or first lines of a text that they were able to read on their own (including in cases where learning to read came hard). A reverence for reading pervaded these memories, even those connected to more scattered social circumstances. I interviewed one man who, as a teenager in the 1940s, went on the road as an itinerant laborer, spending nights in makeshift, communal camps along railroad tracks, where he did not always feel safe. He said he always made sure to carry a book among his belongings. 'If you were reading,' he told me, 'people generally left you alone.'

Overall, memories of writing were starkly vaguer, mixed in with other activities like drawing, playing, or parental work or bill paying. Even more dramatic, many early-writing memories were associated with pain, guilt, humiliation, secrecy, and isolation. Early self-sponsored writing was often remembered to have occurred alone or in lonely places, for instance, in a hospital bed or in an abandoned garage. Early-writing acts often took forms that challenged family relationships or domestic decorum: angry notes to siblings or parents, scrawls on walls or doors, forgeries, profanities, and secret codes. In these memories, writing was often hidden: under mattresses, in ceilings, in well-guarded journals, or destroyed altogether to avoid detection. Periods of self-sponsored writing tended to flourish either during difficult periods, such as social estrangement, military service, divorce, death of a loved one, incarceration, or discrimination, or during highly intense emotional periods like adolescence or courtship or during bursts of political activism or after a brush with death. Self-sponsored writing could be associated with positive emotions such as romantic or familial love or the urge to record memoirs, especially late in life, or to maintain important social relationships, or to express creativity. And writing was regarded as extremely valuable to the people I interviewed. At the same time, however, writing was recalled as the cause of great humiliation or punishment: the note confiscated in school, the violated diary, the censored student newspaper, or, in one case, a low-graded school essay dropped unintentionally on the school bus floor, then picked up by a bully and read aloud to the jeers of other children. In comparison to reading, writing was more volatile, more apt to lead to trouble or to be associated with troubles or ambivalence. In an interesting contrast to the itinerant mentioned above, one person I interviewed who hitchhiked around the country as a youth in the 1960s recalled how one evening he settled into a booth in a rural diner and pulled out his travel journal to make his daily entry. But he was forced to put his journal away after being verbally accosted by uneasy patrons who wanted to know if he was a government spy.

Strong psychological and social differences between reading and writing also surfaced in accounts by parents recalling the early literacy experiences of their children or children recalling the literacy of their parents. Parents expressed greater obligation and confidence in teaching young children to read at home. But beyond the matters of forming letters or printing names, parents were much less likely to have taught writing explicitly to their children, either because they lacked confidence or because they associated writing with natural creativity or privacy and not to be forced. On their part, children recalled their parents' reading primarily as a form of relaxation or worship or as part of secular family rituals into which children were easily drawn. However, except for collaborative letters to relatives or the obligatory thank-you note, children were less asked or invited to write or to share in any writing by their parents. Parents' writing was associated mostly with work or household management and often went on over the heads of young children or took place in areas of the home that were off-limits to children. Several people I interviewed were surprised later in life to learn that their parents had kept journals or had written stories or poetry in private—activities that had remained invisible to them while they were growing up. In one particularly illuminating read-write memory, a young woman who had grown up on a struggling dairy farm in the 1980s said she was unnerved when she picked up the daily newspaper to read and saw her father's troubled budget calculations penciled in the margins.

It was not surprising, then, that among the people I interviewed, an identity as a reader seemed easier to come by than an identity as a writer. Many people described themselves as 'quite a reader,' or 'reading all the time' or from 'a family of readers.' Hardly anyone claimed the identity of 'writer,' including one well-respected, published poet. Several people who took a serious interest in literary writing in their youths said they were actively dissuaded from it by relatives or else gave it up because of a lack of encouragement from any source. Several people I talked with had private writings stolen, destroyed, or tampered with by disapproving others.

To sum up, the sharp cultural dissociations between reading and writing, noticed by Furet and Ozouf in their study of mass literacy in eighteenth- and nineteenth-century France, remained surprisingly resonant in accounts of middle-class and working-class Americans in the final decade of the twentieth century. These differences suggest a lingering influence of divergent traditions and ideological legacies (at least in how writing and reading are framed in memory) that can be traced back to the earliest sponsoring agents of mass reading and writing. Especially pronounced is the residual reverence for reading left over from Christian evangelism and the ingrained moral obligation of parents, particularly mothers, to teach children to read.[6] Such reverence and obligation did not extend to writing, which held a more ambiguous status in household literacy practices, associated much more with making a living or else with creativity, autonomy, resistance, or a privacy that could border on secrecy.

As I mentioned before, confronting the cultural dissociations between reading and writing is not to deny their obvious interconnections and co-dependencies. There can be no writing without reading, because writers read their own texts in progress. And obviously there can be no reading without writing, as acts of writing create objects for reading. At a deeper level, the relationship between reading and writing sustains the intersubjectivity so central to literacy. Acts of writing are propelled by projecting language toward imagined others—to those who will be reading—just as the interpretive work of reading is enhanced by understanding that texts have been written by someone (Brandt 1990; Salvatori 1986). Educational research and practice have well documented the similar constructivist cognitive processes that underlie writing and reading as well as the ways people coordinate read-to-write activities and the ways they learn to write through reading and vice versa (Flower et al. 1990; Haas and Flower 1989). As social practices, writing and reading help each other make sense.

However, reading and writing (along with the study of them) always take place within profoundly tacit cultural regimes, including, as I have been suggesting, long-standing patterns of sponsorship which, across time, have influenced how reading and writing stand in relationship to each other. Of course, these tacit cultural regimes are subject to change. My life history interviewing ended in 1995, at a time when few of the people I talked with owned home computers or had access to the Internet either at work, school, or home. Many dramatic changes in communication practices have occurred since then, including a rapid drop in book-reading (*Reading at Risk* 2004) and a growing public visibility of writing. Personal computers, with their prominent keyboards and screens, are now positioned in a majority of American homes and in many households it is common to see preschool children perched on the laps of typing adults, transfixed by what the fingers make appear on the screen. Undoubtedly more intergenerational teaching and learning of writing is going on now than my earlier research turned up, if only because the young must teach the old how to use new writing technologies! People also write more in public areas now, carrying laptops into coffeehouses or airports or logging on to the Internet at kiosks in libraries or Internet cafes. This is a change with potentially significant implications for the writing-reading relationship.

In any case, for most of the history of mass literacy, reading has been the more subsidized and more amplified partner. Literacy has been practiced mostly as a few-to-few or few-to-many form of communication. Now, writing is becoming much more broadly subsidized and dramatically more amplified than in the past. Writing is rising in social use in large part because of the inexpensive ease of written communication and because of the new markets mass writing opens up. Many-to-many forms of communication are becoming more routine as part of work and leisure. No generation has written or read under this set of conditions before. Needless to say, then, the ascendancy of writing provides a wide frontier for the future of Literacy Studies.

However, such studies must be keen to histories and legacies of reading and writing differences. In the following pages I want to call attention to particular differences between (mass) writing and reading that have, in my view, been under-researched by literacy scholars and yet could have broad implications for literacy going forward. These differences have been implied in the foregoing discussion but receive more in-depth attention here.

writing has more direct transactional value than reading

As was mentioned, mass writing has its origins in the world of work, particularly in craft cultures, which used writing to codify and preserve specialized knowledge, as well as commercial cultures, which used writing for record-keeping and communication. Writing became a preferred mode for the delivery of professional services and an organizational tool for both private and public bureaucracies. As the economy has shifted increasingly to information and knowledge, writing is now a thing itself: a chief form of knowledge-making and a direct grounds for competition and profit , even as it continues to serve as a central medium for important productive processes, such as publicity, communication, and coordination. Overall, the role of writing in the creation of economic wealth, the recognition of writing as a form of labor, and the status of texts as transactional commodities all give writing a unique status among the so-called language arts (Brandt 2007). While reading is a skill central to modern work and a skill into which much time and effort may be invested in the workplace, it just does not operate economically in the same way as writing. Reading is not readily perceived as a form of labor in itself. (No job descriptions will be found for 'technical reader' or 'speech reader' or 'freelance reader' in the employment ads.) And, in fact, the fruits of reading only become visible and redeemable when rendered as output, typically, in writing. Writing is the means by which literacy as a skill is transacted.

The transactional value of writing and its status as a commodity have been mostly missing from theories of composition and studies of writing development, perhaps because student writers have been the main subject of study or because the utilitarian and mercantile are generally *devalued* in the humanities, where most research on writing occurs. Interestingly, the eschewing of the worldly and practical is exactly what separated writing from reading in eighteenth- and early nineteenth-century education in England, the United States, and elsewhere. Writing was evicted from Sunday School classes despite its popularity, dissociated from Greek and Latin in the grammar school and often relegated to separate instructional sites (Laqueur 1976; Monaghan 2005). Today, in the United States, for instance, writing instruction still finds difficulty fitting into the K-12 curriculum, and in higher education is often carried out on the periphery.[7]

In any case, if mass reading has been implicated in the making of believers, citizens, consumers, and learners, mass writing has been implicated in the making of goods and services. To understand the development of writing literacy is to understand how it has been organized around production processes. This gives it a distinctive character, particularly in the way that writing literacy has been an object of private and not just public investment.

This level of investment came clear to me in a new set of interviews I have been conducting over the past two years among workaday people who spend at least 30 per cent of their time on the job writing in some form. In the interviews, I ask people how they do their workplace writing, how they learned to do it, and how it affects other areas of their lives. So far I have talked with 45 people in an array of occupations in the private and public sectors. It is not unusual in contemporary workplaces where writing is a chief product or at least a chief means of generating revenue or reputation to find spaces given over especially for writing: a sound-proofed room in a law office for the preparation of briefs; an entire (secured) floor for policy writing in an insurance company; a technology-rich area for writing reports in a police station. The more writing employees do (or the more important their writing is perceived to be), the more privacy they usually enjoy. As important deadlines arrive, uninterrupted time for writing is blocked out. In these

cases, phone calls are diverted or 'do not disturb' signs go up or, in some
cases, writers leave the premises entirely to find more contemplative
conditions. Such organizational investment of time and space does not
appear to extend to reading (save for reading that prepares for or accom-
panies writing). For its part, professional reading occurs in catch-as-
catch-can circumstances, during spare minutes or in down production
times or during unpaid hours.

Workplaces , especially larger ones, also make significant investments
in the teaching and learning of writing. While instruction sometimes
takes the explicit form of classes, seminars, or workshops, most literacy teaching and learning occur informally, peer-to-peer, supervisor-
to-supervised (or, on occasion, the other way around). The accounts of
people I am interviewing are rife with incidents of teaching and learning
writing on the job, including being coached by more experienced personnel, receiving oral or written feedback on their writing, talking about
their writing with others, or having their writing edited and returned
for change or correction. They in turn often serve as teachers of writing
in their organizations, officially or unofficially. Especially impressive
is the level of teaching and learning that appears to be accompanying
transformations and innovations in computer-based communication.
These new ways of writing rely heavily (and remarkably successfully) on
peer-to-peer knowledge-sharing and demonstration.

People who are responsible for particularly high-stakes writing (for
instance, legal briefs or project proposals) also report receiving a lot of
assistance, not only in the form of collaborators who take on chunks of
the work but also in the form of figures who make the writing better by
smoothing out, correcting, or troubleshooting works in progress. It was
not uncommon among those I interviewed to work with peers, subordi-
nates, or supervisors who served as editors, proofreaders, fact checkers,
writing coaches, or even, when conditions necessitated, ghostwriters.
If we add in 'IT' departments as units that, in part, work to develop
and sustain technical skills of writing literacy in workplaces, the investment in teaching and promoting writing in non-school settings could
well exceed expenditures for instruction of writing in school. In my
research, except for the occasional mention of a speed-reading class,
I can find no comparable forms of explicit teaching, learning, or assisting
around acts of reading in professional jobs. People in writing-intensive
positions are expected to know how to read. Reading per se is not a direct object of evaluation or intervention among supervisors or peers.[8]
Undoubtedly, it is the status of writing as both a recognized form of
labor and a high-stakes product that justifies direct interventions into

employees' writing literacy and makes it acceptable for even high-level personnel to need or ask for assistance and correction.

The modern workplace as a school for writing is little acknowledged or understood in the field of Literacy Studies, nor is the role of the workplace in contributing to literacy stratification and inequity in society. In the workplaces of the Knowledge Economy, writing know-how is a critical resource. As such, it is developed, sustained, renewed, and amplified as a by-product of production. This means that opportunities for learning and receiving assistance (not to mention access to powerful communication technologies) depends on one's location in the production process—with people in the higher-echelons more likely to have more access and more help than those in lower-echelons.[9] Workplaces manufacture and support literacy unequally as a matter of course—making workplaces quite different in doctrine from the evangelizing church or the common school which, ostensibly at least, offered literacy to all. The tightening association between socioeconomic status and literacy, the growing gaps in wealth between the literacy-haves and the literacy have-nots, stems in part from the patterns of access and investment that accompany the role of writing in economic production.

The transactional value of writing arises, then, from its functions (productive), its forms (tangible and material), and its reliance through history on strong sponsoring intermediaries (patrons, publishers, employers) who subsidize writing, administer its distribution, and expect returns on it. These conditions have made writing amenable not only to private investment and intervention but also to a status as intellectual property, a system of ownership that typically includes sponsors along with creators. In *The Future of Creativity,* when Lawrence Lessig (2004) discusses his hopes for a 'read-write' future, his concern is that such a future is jeopardized by what he sees as increased corporate claims of private ownership over forms of cultural production, including writing. Just at a time when technology is creating conditions for mass public expression, including the capacity for creators to reach audiences without intermediaries, there has actually been a radical expansion of copyright protections that, according to critics, is dampening popular expression and making public sharing more difficult (Benkler 2006; Litman 2006). Critics see the problem as originating in the greed of major media corporations who feel their empires threatened not only by new technologies but also by the noncommercial ethos of many digital innovators and users. But cultural tensions surrounding mass expression on the Internet are deeper and older than that, harkening back to the early formations of literacy itself and its role in both private

and public domains. As one of the first technologies of cultural production, writing developed in contexts of commercial production and
transaction, under the aegis of publishers and other for-profit sponsor;
it was around writing that legal concepts of copyright emerged in the
first place. Authorship served as a mechanism for handling the transactional value of writing (Heymann 2005; Woodmansee 1984). Now, as
writing ascends as the literacy skill most associated with digital media,
its foundations in commercial sponsorship and its status as intellectual
property will continue inexorably to trail along with it. Writing on its
own has little tradition—legal or otherwise—as a public good. Whether
that can change is left to be seen—and studied.

writing is more regulated and surveilled than reading

This claim may seem paradoxical at first glance in countries with strong
free-speech traditions. However, from the earliest days of the American
Republic, for example, it has been believed that for democracy to thrive,
citizens need access to a vibrant 'marketplace of ideas,' broad and unfet-
tered contact with a variety of views and opinions. Freedom of the press
especially became a cornerstone of social thought and constitutional
law (Brown 1996; Bunker 2001; Sunstein 1995). Yet in the United States,
first amendment protections are rationalized on behalf of a reading
public who need access to written (and other kinds of) material to carry
out civic rights and duties. It has been around the needs of readers to
read, not writers to write, that American first amendment traditions
have formed. Throughout the history of mass literacy, for a variety of
reasons, writing per se has been more tightly controlled relative to reading. Whereas the power of print to create shared belief made the broad
dissemination of reading attractive to central authorities, writing in
the wrong or unknown hands was feared for the very same reasons.
Churches and Sundays Schools that provided reading instruction as
alms resisted calls to include writing instruction as part of their mission. Reading has not been free of regulation, censorship, and suppres-
sion, but the role of writing in dissent and sedition, its capacity to take
on the form of forgery, anonymity, or secret code, its insistent capacity
to give material form to self-assertion, all have made writing particularly dangerous in contexts of oppression. Harsh sanctions against literacy in slave communities were directed most strongly toward writing,
which could be used practically to forge travel passes to freedom and
ideologically to embody the very personhood that slavery was meant to

deny. The association between writing and regulation is especially pronounced in law, where writing is treated as premeditated action, as in libel, slander, or plagiarism, and can be subpoenaed and used as incriminating or exculpatory evidence. Although distribution or possession of some kinds of reading materials may be against the law, the act of reading itself cannot be used to commit a crime in the way that writing can. As I mentioned above, when I interviewed late twentieth-century Americans about their memories of writing, their accounts were rife with evidence of how a legacy of control, resistance, and surveillance functioned at the micro-sociological level. Within families, rebellion motivated a lot of ordinary writing and the discovery of writing could lead to recrimination, punishment, and remorse.

In the workplace, the regulation and surveillance of writing is growing, in part because of the high stakes accruing to writing and in part because new technology makes it easy to track computer and Internet activity (D'Urso 2006; Townsend and Bennett 2003; Wallace 2004). Software programs, with names like eSniff, Spector, or Surveillance Anywhere, promise to track or scan employees' every electronically encoded act. Email is now more heavily monitored than phone use. In the United States, government email is in the public domain and can be obtained by the press or other interested parties under various 'sunshine' acts or freedom of information legislation. In both the public and private sectors, employees who must use the Internet as part of their regular work will often find employer controls blocking free movement and expression. A survey by the American Management Association found 46 per cent of companies had taken action against employees for unacceptable use of email or the Internet (Wallace, 234). Despite employees' concerns about privacy at work, employers say such monitoring is necessary not only to promote productivity but also to avoid legal liability. According to Townsend and Bennett, U.S. courts have recognized few rights to privacy or free speech for people on the job.

Particularly as written products have become a chief vehicle for economic trade and profit-making, they also have become a vehicle for potential errors, impropriety, and even crime. This has led to greater oversight of document creation by government and professional regulators. My interviews with workplace writers were peppered with references to such overseers as the Federal Drug Administration, Securities and Exchange Commission, the National Association of Securities Dealers, the Health and Life Compliance Association, the National Credit Union Association, the State Insurance Commission, the Federal Housing Administration, the Department of Financial Institutions,

and the Internal Revenue Service, among others, all of whom provide
rules regarding the language and make-up of written documents or
require oversight in the handling of writing. Quite a few of the writers
I interviewed consulted routinely with in-house lawyers in the course
of composition. A branch manager of a securities dealership told me
he spent hours a day scanning hundreds of emails to make sure no
improper communications were coming in or going out of his office,
a process mandated by his professional organization, the NASD. One
nurse I interviewed who helped to run drug trials at her HMO said all of
her notes and charts were scrutinized, per FDA regulations, by a moni-
tor who visited regularly from the pharmaceutical company sponsoring
the research. Several people worked in industries so highly regulated
that all texts produced in their firm—including press releases—were
considered regulated documents, requiring formal protocols in the
handling of them. Much of the regulation of workplace writing stems
from the government's role in protecting the rights and safety of consumers, ranging from their right to clear and non-deceptive contract
language to truth in advertising to the production of data that adheres
to scientific and professional standards.

Research is needed to see whether monitoring or regulation of workplace writing affects the general scribal habits of people subjected to
it. A few of the people I have interviewed said they internalized curbs
and controls as part of their writing processes and in some cases felt
the influence lingering in their broader literate practices (for instance,
taking greater care with language generally or reading with greater scrutiny). More fundamentally, however, the surveillance of the everyday
output of mass writing stands in marked contrast to the broad constitutional protections that have accrued around published print, especially
newspapers, books, and periodicals. In the United States, for instance,
no government agencies oversee or regulate the writing of journalists,
novelists, or poets, for whom first amendment rights are secured by a
long tradition of case law.

These different legal climates around workplace writing and published
writing lead to two different outcomes: strong government protection
of mass reading and strong government regulation of mass writing.
These differences can be explained, of course, by differences in purpose, setting, and genre between the two kinds of writing. But together
they speak to how deeply reading-writing relationships are implicated
in long-standing political and economic traditions. Where writing has
been *protected* by law, it has been indirectly through the protections
afforded to the reading public. In the United States and other societies,

reading has been linked to the rights and duties of citizenship; it is through the rights of readers that freedom of expression has found its most secure rationales in case law. Freedom of the press, a cornerstone of civil liberties, functions for the sake of readers, not writers. Even intellectual property and copyright law, for that matter, have found their rationale through the needs of readers: government provides incentives and rewards for creative and intellectual work to insure that the minds of its citizens are nourished and replenished.

At the same time, where writing has been *regulated* by law, it also has been for the protection of the citizen-reader, only this time in the role of consumer.[10] Government justifies regulation and oversight of written communication to protect potentially gullible or under-skilled consumers who enter into contracts or seek professional advice or must make medical or other decisions based on what they read. Writing requires an active regulatory context because reading is integral to the consumption of many goods and services. For writers affected by these regulations, their influence can reach deeply into mental and scribal processes. In the United States, for example, the Plain English movement, first spearheaded by the federal government and now taken up by states and professional organizations, is a case in point, mandating clear, accessible language in contracts, insurance policies, product safety guidelines, and the like. At the local industry level, these mandates are often translated into specific, in-house rules that, for instance, mandate limits on the number of words per sentence or the number of syllables per word. One insurance writer explained to me that he no longer required checking his work with an industry-mandated software program for Plain English compliance because he had managed so thoroughly to internalize the rules.

It is hard to fault efforts to protect consumers and promote clarity in language. It is hard to fault employers trying to avoid trouble from employees' unauthorized writing. But the fact remains that everyday writers at work find regulation and surveillance penetrating deeply into their cognitive and linguistic processes in ways that are just not—and cannot—be experienced in reading. Given the way that literacy has been integrated into political and economic ideologies, legal protection for mass reading is strong and legal protection for mass writing is weak. Writers in the service of readers do not hold ground in free-speech traditions nor are the needs of writing citizens taken up as a concept by government or courts. In neither public nor private domains are there traditions for scribal citizens.

conclusion: the future of mass literacy

Digital technologies as catalysts of change are receiving much attention in literacy and communication studies. These technologies are seen to afford unprecedented range, intensity, and variety in meaning-making and communication and stand to transform, if not undo, literacy as we have known it. But sneaking up along with new technologies over the past several decades—much less noticed but no less momentous and, in some ways, more profound—has been the ascendancy of writing, a second stage of mass literacy arriving some one hundred years after the first. For the first time in history, writing is joining reading as the basis of mass literate experience. Through most of this chapter I have tried to show how until now writing, as a practice and as an ideological construct, has been positioned, somewhat precariously, within a read-only literacy, within the presumption that readers would be many and writers would be few. Writing has derived its rationales, its value, its legal protections, and its opportunities through the arrangements of mass reading. But if now fortunes are reversing (as difficult as that may be even to contemplate) and writing is becoming the more promoted, the more valued, and the more catalytic partner in mass literacy, the more amenable to the economic and technological conditions of these times, then reading may find itself precariously positioned in the future of literacy. A few trends deserve watching: (1) What will happen to reading as it is taken up in acts of writing more regularly? What kind of reading is reading in the service of writing? Also, what will happen to writing as it becomes more regularly directed to other writers? (2) What values will adhere to literacy as is treated more and more as what Zimmerman calls 'speech goods,' as more of its practices are corralled by commercial sponsorship and treated as intellectual property? Will the rights of readers and writers be redefined through the commercial legacy of a writing literacy? What legal traditions might develop around scribal citizenship and why? These will be questions pertinent to the future of Literacy Studies.

notes

1. For a recent discussion of the difficulties of defining literacy and a defense of keeping the definition narrow, see Vincent (2003).
2. For broad, useful histories of mass literacy in the U.S., see Gordon and Gordon (2003); also Kaestle et al. (1993) For an excellent treatment of literacy and mass education, see Kaestle (1983). For more regional treatments,

see Amory and Hall (2007); Gilmore (1989). For generally useful critical perspectives, see Graff (1995).

3. Access to writing was especially marked by gender and race. See Cornelius (1991), Monagham (2005), Williams (2005).

4. Furet and Ozouf (1983) and Monaghan (2005) have paid most systematic attention to the early sponsorship of writing. For a fascinating view of the role of writing in developing craft knowledge and the ideologies of those origins, see Long (2001). Also see Stevens (1995).

5. There are some situational exceptions: literary writers who learn from their predecessors by way of reading or students who are assigned reading to inform their writing. But I speak here of broad cultural ideologies of reading and writing. For some exceptional studies that pay serious attention to the effects of writing on the writer, see Charon (2006), Gerber (2006), Miller (1998).

6. For useful recent treatments of mothers and literacy, see Arizpe, Styles and Heath (2006), Robbins (2004).

7. Monaghan and Saul 1987; Miller 1993. For a rare treatment of writing pedagogy in the common school, see Schultz (1999). And for a critique of writing pedagogy in higher education, see Smith (2004).

8. To the extent that reading is part of learning a job, learning new procedures, or keeping up with current information, it contributes undoubtedly to work performance that could become part of a general evaluation review. My point is, however, that among information workers I have interviewed, reading is not singled out for review, comment, or intervention in the way that writing is, nor do peers or supervisors teach each other how to read in any explicit way. Reading is a concern in adult basic education and is often tied to job requirements.

9. For a look at how writing is linked to employment and promotion, see *Writing a Ticket to Work or a Ticket Out* (2004).

10. For a fascinating treatment of how different kinds of readers are constructed by the courts, see Lidsky (2007).

references

Amory, H. and D. D. Hall (eds) (2007) *A History of the Book in America. Volume 1: The Colonial Book in the Atlantic World*. Chapel Hill: University of North Carolina Press.

Arizpe, E., M. Styles and S. B. Heath (2006) *Reading Lessons from the Eighteenth Century: Mothers, Children and Texts*. Staffordshire UK: Pied Piper Publishing.

Barlow, A. (2007) *The Rise of the Blogosphere*. Westport, CT: Praeger.

Beniger, J. F. (1986) *The Control Revolution: Technological and Economic Origins of the Information Society*. Cambridge, MA: Harvard University Press.

Benkler, Y. (2006) *The Wealth of Networks: How Social Production Transforms Markets and Freedom*. New Haven: Yale University Press.

Brandt, D. (1990) *Literacy as Involvement: The Acts of Writers, Readers, and Texts*. Carbondale: Southern Illinois University Press.

Brandt, D. (1998) Sponsors of Literacy. *College Composition and Communication*, 49, 165–85.

Brandt, D. (2001) *Literacy in American Lives*. New York: Cambridge University Press.

Brandt, D. (2005) Writing For a Living: Literacy and the Knowledge Economy. *Written Communication, 22*, 166–97.

Brandt, D. (2007) 'Who's the President?' Ghostwriting and Shifting Values in Literacy. *College English, 69*, 549–71.

Brown, R. D. (1996) *The Strength of a People: The Idea of an Informed Citizenry in America*. Chapel Hill: University of North Carolina Press.

Bunker, M.D. (2001) *Critiquing Free Speech: First Amendment Theory and the Challenge of Interdisciplinarity*. Mahweh: Erlbaum.

Cornelius, J. D. (1991) *'When I Can Read My Title Clear': Literacy, Slavery and Religion In the Antebellum South*. Columbia: University of South Carolina Press.

Charon, R. (2006) *Narrative Medicine: Honoring the Stories of Illness*. New York: Oxford University Press.

Cortada, J. W. (2004) *The Digital Hand: How Computers Changed the Work of American Manufacturing, Transportation and Retail Industries*. New York: Oxford University Press.

D'Urso, S. (2006) Who's Watching Us at Work? Toward a Structural-Perceptual Model of Electronic Monitoring and Surveillance in Organizations. *Communication Theory, 16*, 281–303.

Flower, L., V. Stein, J. Ackerman, J. Kantz, K. McCormick and W.C. Peck (1990) *Reading To Write*. New York: Oxford University Press.

Furet, F. and J. Ozouf (1983) *Reading and Writing: Literacy in France from Calvin to Jules Ferry*. New York: Cambridge University Press.

Gerber, D. A. (2006) *Authors of Their Lives: The Personal Correspondence of British Immigrants to North American in the Nineteenth Century*. New York: New York University Press.

Gilmore, W. J. (1989) *Reading Becomes a Necessity of Life*. Knoxville: University of Tennessee Press.

Gordon, E. E. and E. H. Gordon (2003) *Literacy in America*. Westport, CT: Praeger.

Graff, H. J. (1995) *Labyrinths of Literacy: Reflections on Literacy Past and Present*. Pittsburgh: University of Pittsburgh Press.

Graff, H. J. and J. M. Duffy (2008) The literacy myth. In B. Street and N. H. Hornberger (eds), *Encyclopedia of Language and Education, Volume 2*, second edition. London: Springer.

Haas, C. and L. Flower (1989) Rhetorical Reading Strategies and the Construction of Meaning. *College Composition and Communication, 39*, 167–83.

Heymann, L. A. (2005) The Birth of the Author: Authorship, Pseudonymity and Trademark Law. *Notre Dame Law Review, 80*, 1377–448.

Kaestle, C. (1983) *Pillars of the Republic: Common Schools and American Society, 1780–1860*. New York: Hill and Wang.

Kaestle, C., H. Damon-Moore, L. C. Stedman and K. Tinsley (1993) *Literacy in the United States: Readers and Reading since 1880*. New Haven: Yale University Press.

Laqueur, T. (1976) *Religion and Respectability: Sunday Schools and Working Class Culture, 1780–1850*. New Haven: Yale University Press.

Lenhart, A., D. Gallows and J. Horrigan. *Content Creation on Line.* Pew Center for the Study of the Internet and American Life. Available at www.pewinternet. org/PPF/r/113/report_display.asp. Last accessed on 7/16/2007.

Lessig, L. (2004) *Free Culture: The Nature and Future of Creativity.* New York: Penguin.

Litman, J. (2006) *Digital Copyright.* Amherst, NY: Prometheus Books.

Lidsky, L. B. (2007) Authorship, Audiences, and Anonymous Speech. *Notre Dame Law Review, 82,* 1537–1604.

Long, P. O. (2001) *Openness, Secrecy, Authorship: Technical Arts and the Culture of Knowledge from Antiquity to the Renaissance.* Baltimore, MD: Johns Hopkins University Press.

Miller, S. (1993) *Textual Carnivals: The Politics of Composition.* Carbondale: Southern Illinois University Press.

Miller, S. (1998) *Assuming the Positions: Cultural Pedagogy and the Politics of Commonplace Writing.* Pittsburgh, PA: University of Pittsburgh Press.

Monaghan, E. J. (2005) *Learning to Read and Write in Colonial America.* Amherst: University of Massachusetts Press.

Monaghan, E. J. and E. W. Saul (1987) The reader, the scribe, the thinker: a critical look at the history of American reading and writing instruction. In T. S. Popkewitz (ed.), *The Formation of School Subjects.* New York: Falmer Press, 85–112.

Rainie, L. (2005) *The State of Blogging.* Pew Center for the Study of the Internet and American Life. Available at www.pewinternet.org/PPF/r/144/report_ display.asp. Last accessed on 7/16/2007.

Reading at Risk: A Survey of Literary Reading in America (2004) National Endowment for the Humanities, Research Division Report #46. Available at http://www. nea.gov/pub/ReadingAtRisk.pdf. Last accessed on 7/16/2007.

Robbins, S. (2004) *Managing Literacy, Mothering America.* Pittsburgh, PA: University of Pittsburgh Press.

Salvatori, M. (1986) Italo Calvino's *If on a Winter's Night a Traveler:* Writer's Authority, Reader's Autonomy. *Contemporary Literature, 27,* 182–212.

Schultz, L. M. (1999) *The Young Composers: Composition's Beginnings in Nineteenth-Century Schools.* Carbondale: Southern Illinois University Press.

Smit, D. W. (2004) *The End of Composition Studies.* Carbondale: Southern Illinois University Press.

Stevens, E. W. Jr. (1995) *Grammar of the Machine: Technical Literacy and Early Industrial Expansion.* New Haven: Yale University Press.

Sunstein, C. R. (1993) *Democracy and the Problem of Free Speech.* New York: Free Press.

Townsend, A. M. and J. T. Bennett. (2003) Privacy, Technology and Conflict: Emerging Issues and Action in Workplace Privacy. *Journal of Labor Research,* 24(2), 197–205.

Vincent, D. (2003) Literacy Literacy. *Interchange,* 34(2–3), 347–57.

Wallace, P. (2004) *The Internet in the Workplace: How New Technology Is Transforming Work.* New York: Cambridge University Press.

Williams, H. A. (2005) *Self Taught: African American Education in Slavery and Freedom.* Chapel Hill: University of North Carolina Press.

Woodmansee, M. (1984) The Genius and the Copyright: Economic and Legal Conditions of the Emergence of the 'Author'. *Eighteenth Century Studies*, 17, 425–48.

Writing a Ticket to Work or a Ticket Out. National Commission on Writing (2004). Availalble at http://www.writingcommission.org/prod_downloads/writing-com/writing-ticket-to-work.pdf. Last accessed on 7/16/2007.

Yates, J. (1989) *Control through Communication: The Rise of System in American Management.* Baltimore, MD: Johns Hopkins University Press.

Yates, J. (2005) *Structuring the Information Age.* Baltimore, MD: Johns Hopkins University Press.

Zimmerman, D. L. (2004) Is There a Right to Have Something to Say? *Fordham Law Review*, 73, 297–375.

4

literacy practices, text/s and meaning making across time and space

catherine kell

There is little doubt that the New Literacy Studies (NLS) has achieved a paradigmatic shift in the study of literacy. While this shift has been slower to take effect in literacy pedagogies and policies, there is more and more evidence that the key tenets are circulating right at the level of teachers in their classrooms, as well as at the level of policy-makers in the corridors of power. In this chapter I aim to confirm the achievements of the NLS, while pointing to some tensions which have arisen in relation to its theoretical framework, in particular, the concept of literacy practices and the analytical relation between literacy events and literacy practices. With reference to data from my own ethnographic projects on literacy, I explore these tensions. I outline an approach I developed which focus on the movement of meanings across contexts and I explore the concepts of literacy events and practices in this movement, which I call *transcontextual*. I will also touch on the analytical move from the description of literacy events to the analysis of literacy practices. Both these 'moves' are related to the issue of scale.

I argue that this work is relevant to a discussion about the future of Literacy Studies for two main reasons. The first relates to the idea of transcontextual analysis and it is to do with the need in the contemporary period to find ways of describing and modelling 'flows' (Appadurai 2000; Harvey 1996) – the epiphenomena of the hyper-mobility of people, objects and information crossing borders and boundaries in the late-modern world. Such mobility foregrounds questions about the placing of people, their practices, processes and products; as well as the channels through which these become *attenuated* across space and time.

The second relates to the idea of trans-scale analysis and is to do with the ways in which we (writers and researchers) analyse and generalize from such crossings to make claims about literacy and categories such as identity, gender, power and social structure. Theories of the situated nature of learning and communication have been prominent since the 1970s and continue to be. More recently, theories about globalization and about information jostle with the earlier, more established ones which are about particularization and the local. I believe that as researchers and academics we are at a point of crossing ourselves, and that these two currents in theory have led to confusing conflation between categories of analysis, and therefore to our ability to make warranted claims about literacy in relation to inequality, power and perhaps globalization. I believe this is particularly evident in work on 'new literacies' and technologies.

Ethnography provides an important point of reference as we, ourselves, grapple with this crossing at the level of theory. In addressing the two issues set out above I will argue, in line with the approach to ethnography taken by Burawoy (1998), that it is important to seek 'not confirmations [of our favourite theory] but refutations that will inspire us to deepen that theory' (1998: 16). I draw on data from two ethnographic studies of literacy which I did in South Africa. One was undertaken in a shanty-town in the early 1990s and the other was a lengthy ethnography of literacy practices (1998 to 2001) undertaken in a participatory development initiative (which I have called Khayalethu).

new literacy studies: literacy events and practices

The key tenets of the NLS paradigmatic shift continue to be seen as, first, the dislodging of what Street (1984) identified as the 'autonomous model of literacy' (drawing as it did on a binary divide between literacy and orality, with the accompanying arguments about the consequences of literacy); second, the conceptualization of literacy as social practice; and third, the emphasis on the need for any claims about literacy to be based on an understanding of its contexts of use and acquisition, gained primarily through ethnographic research.

The concepts of literacy events and literacy practices were central to this work. As explained in other chapters in this book, Street extended Heath's (1983) identification of 'literacy events' to 'literacy practices'; thus enabling the description and analysis of such events at a 'higher level of abstraction' (Street 1995: 2) concerning the social practices, conceptions and models of reading and writing, and the patterns of activity around literacy which then link to broader cultural and social issues, as well as to themes related to pedagogies.

This pair of constructs emerged in what have been called 'first generation' ethnographic studies of literacy (according to Baynham 2004, these include Heath 1983; Scribner and Cole 1981; Street 1984 amongst others). They were then central in shaping the wave of 'second generation' research studies in the NLS tradition (again see Baynham 2004), enabling researchers to generate a wide range of rigorous descriptions of the uses and meanings of literacy, in particular places and times. In many of these studies these two constructs led to the identification of multiple literacies, in line with Street's 'ideological model'. Together this set of concepts has formed an elegant and parsimonious theoretical framework for the study of literacy, with high explanatory power, valid in explorations of literacy across different time periods (for example, Baynham 2008), across different languages and in multilingual contexts (for example, Martin-Jones and Jones 2000), as well as with reference to numeracy (for example, Street, Baker and Tomlin 2005).

In this framework the concept of events is placed firmly in the realm of everyday, observable, placed moments, study-able through ethnography. Literacy practices, however, are studied either as observable patterns of behaviour across events or inferred at the level of ideological aspects through wider observation and interview data (Maybin, cited in Street 2000: 23). In a discussion of the concepts Bartlett and Holland (2002: 11) argue that Street has since indicated that the move from the study of events to the study of practices necessitates a methodological shift away from what they characterize as 'sociointeractional analysis of the moment' towards 'long term participant observation in multiple domains of activity'. In what follows I will ask whether this methodological shift is necessitated, but long-term participant observation in multiple domains is not undertaken, what warrants are there for claims to be made about practices? How and when do we know that we know enough to make claims about practices? What are the boundaries we draw to know that these are specific claims?

Over the past few years, there has also been wide uptake of the concept of literacy practices amongst researchers, teachers and policy-makers, along with the idea of multiple literacies (especially with reference to digital literacy when the term new literacies is used very widely). The concepts have become keywords, signalling rejection of the autonomous model of literacy and the embracing of the idea that literacy should always and only be viewed in context. Sometimes, however, the concept of literacy practices seems to be almost synonymous with *education*, as if there is no specificity to education beyond the literacy practices of those who participate in it. And at times the terms are used with no reference to the tradition of study from which the concept first emerged and its insistence on specificity to domain of practice rather than channel of communication; as well as with scant reference to literacy events, the ethnographic substratum from which warranted claims about practices can be made. The paired concepts have thus been split apart, and this makes it easy for *a priori* claims to be made about what literacy practices are for particular groups, and for these to be asserted rather than proved. It is easy then, for further *a priori* identification of 'literacies'.

Since about the year 2000, three broad sets of questions have been raised in relation to the theoretical framework of the NLS (Bloome et al. 2005; Brandt and Clinton 2002; Collins and Blot 2003; Kell 2008; Maddox 2007; Reder and Davila 2005 amongst others). The questions appear to cluster into three main groups: literacy practices, multimodality and multiliteracies; agency and the materiality of texts and context and the local/global (these are outlined in greater depth in Kell (2006a)). Some questions have led to the deepening of the theoretical framework of the NLS (see Street 2003b), others are still open for debate.

literacy practices, multimodality and multiliteracies

I touch briefly on this set of questions. The NLS, obviously, in its framework of literacy events and literacy practices gives priority to a linguistic frame of reference. The New London Group's now well-known paper on multiliteracies (1996) initiated a shift towards the application of the concept of literacy to channels of communication, other than or in addition to writing, such as the visual, the gestural or embodied, audio, space or combinations of these. This idea has been taken up very widely particularly in education, but it has also led to much confusion and incoherence, which has carried over to the area of digital forms of communication. Heath and Street (2008), Kress (2003), Kress and Street (2006) and Street (2003b) have all contributed to charting a path through these debates, calling attention back to the need to focus on the specifics of literacy as involving symbolic systems for representing language while stressing the need for literacy to be viewed as one amongst other modes of communication. But questions still remain. Street's initial pluralization of the concept referred to domain of practice, not to channel of communication. A shift back to the singular term loses this dimension. In addition, Kell (2004) and Prior (2005) have drawn attention as to how the work in the field of multimodality does not yet have an adequate theorization of practices.

literacy practices, agency and the materiality of texts

Up until the late 1990s most NLS research had tended to shy away from exploring the materiality of literacy. The general focus of the events/ practices framework had shifted so much towards the social that the material texts (their physical properties and means of production) which were drawn on in such events and practices, in retrospect, seemed air-brushed out of the analysis. The concept of literacy as social practice was about modelling literacy as ideological rather than autonomous. In this, although it focused on ethnographic micro data, it was address-ing macro questions. In this hugely important achievement, however, material texts became blackboxed within the term literacy, and a lot of first and second generation NLS research elided different definitions and levels of understanding of text and underplayed the variable ways whereby text is achieved, and the specificity of the semiotic resources which were drawn upon. Likewise, the concept of genre in New Literacy Studies seemed under-theorized. There may be many different reasons for this, but further discussion is beyond the scope of this chapter.[1]

Silverstein and Urban (1996), without using the word literacy, have introduced a helpful distinction between levels at which texts can be perceived and analysed. These are the idea of culture as text, entextuali-zation processes and text-artefacts themselves. The first is as a 'trope for culture', an 'autonomously meaningful object ... understood in the sense of an ensemble of shared symbols and meanings ... deprocessualised ... and able to be transmitted across social boundaries without regard for the kinds of recontextualisations it might undergo'. This description is close to Street's autonomous model. Like Street, Silverstein and Urban argue that culture as text is epistemologically suspect. They indicate that they prefer to focus on entextualization and text-artefacts, which can be observed, be seen to be produced and transformed by people in action.

Bloome et al. (2005: 6) have argued that if events are treated as the 'empirical space' within which practices come into play with each other and people are conceptualized as agents of those practices, they are also therefore 'captured by those literacy practices and by the dis-courses within which those practices are embedded'. They suggest an alternative theorization of the events as spaces in which people act on their circumstances, where literacy is conceived not as some back-ground abstraction or shared cognitively held model 'but in its doing, then people are conceptualized as creators and actors' (p. 7).[2] This point links well with Silverstein and Urban's emphasis on entextualization and text-artefacts as forms of cultural transmission in the making.

literacy practices, context and the local/global

The third set of questions is closely related. The now well-known article called *The Limits of the Local* (Brandt and Clinton 2002) questioned that an analysis of literacy practices in local contexts could provide an adequate explanation of the role of literacy in society, and of the way in which the global reaches into the local. Without wishing to revive the premises of autonomous models of literacy, they asked whether literacy, while continuing to be seen as 'local, particular, situated, human interactions' could also be seen as arriving 'from other places – infiltrating, disjointing and displacing local life'.

Street (2003a) has argued that Brandt and Clinton tended to characterize what they called 'distant' literacies as 'autonomous'. Street has always maintained (and this lies at the heart of his autonomous and ideological models of literacy) that what might be seen as distant or autonomous literacy needs to be seen as always and everywhere ideological, deeply imbued with issues of consciousness and power, identity and control. Street states that 'We need a framework and conceptual tools that can characterize the relation between local and "distant"' (2003a: 2827) and suggests that the shift from studying literacy events to conceptualizing literacy practices is one such tool. He draws on Giddens' concept of disembedding mechanisms to argue that 'literacy has the potential to disembed, to separate interaction from the particularities of locales and yet at the same time is always instantiated, its potential realized, through local practices' (2003a: 2829).

But Reder and Davila argue that 'the paired concepts of literacy events and literacy practices effectively highlight the difference between a local event and the larger forces that shape the participants in that event' (2005: 176). They argue that the concepts together provide 'an analytical space for understanding the relationship between the local and the distant but *they do not yet constitute a coherent framework for understanding this relationship*, they provide an answer as to *where* the local and the distant collide (in many everyday literacy events) but they fail to provide an answer as to *how* this interaction occurs' (ibid.: 176).

In NLS, each of the terms, local and global, has been applied to what have been called multiple literacies, and depending on one's vantage

point, global and local (as adjectives) have been characterized as hegemonic, elite, dominant or simply 'distant' (Brandt and Clinton 2002)
as opposed to vernacular/subaltern/situated (Barton, Hamilton and
Ivanic 2000; Maddox 2001), or simply local (Barton and Hamilton 1998;
Rogers 2001). However, in Kell (2006b) I argued that these descriptors
carry *a priori* assumptions about an isomorphism between spatial location and power.

Collins and Blot (2003) look more explicitly at the issue of power,
claiming that considerations of power have largely been absent from
most ethnographies of literacy which are constrained by their 'local'
framing. Blommaert (2005) adds a further dimension with his discussion of inequality in terms of space and scale, from a World Systems perspective. He argues for the importance of viewing any written texts in
relation to 'economies of linguistic resources in which function-value
allocation, stratification and determination are powerful operators'
(p. 646), and that 'any move in space is also a move across different
economies of literacy' (p. 661).

With regard to the elusive 'how', the mechanism that Reder and Davila
identify as needed in the move from events to practices and from the
local to the global: I argue that it is important not to make *a priori* value
judgements about what I would prefer to call the *not-local* as representing a 'higher scale' with an automatic association with greater power.[3]
Such a move, from the local to the 'higher scale', would conflate spatial categories with analytical categories. Haarstad and Floysand (2007)
quote Allen, who argues that there is no spatial template for power.
Instead they argue that power is a spatially mediated relational effect of
social interaction. In what follows I suggest an approach which aligns
with this idea.

In ethnographies of bounded sites, vertical analytical movement does
happen in the gradual elucidation of patterns and the linking of these
with wider social forces. But this is not spatial movement, it is an analytical process. Pahl's (2008) work provides one approach which deals
with the gradual elucidation of patterns from situated events within
bounded sites (in her case the family) and these reveal higher scale
issues (like migration). She draws on the concept of habitus, showing
that the events index habitus as they are created by it. This is a higher
scale concept, and the analytical movement in the analysis is vertical,
from events to practices to habitus and then down again. The material,
multimodal artefacts which she focuses on circulate between the levels
of events and practices and index habitus. This is one way of addressing
the 'how'.

I would like to suggest another way of addressing the 'how', which focuses on the concept of recontextualization and I will explain this below.

an ethnographic snapshot: problematizing the boundaries of context

In this section I will briefly outline the way in which these questions were thrown into relief in an early ethnography I did in a shanty-town called Masiphumelele in South Africa in 1993. The focus of the ethnography was 'literacy practices in Masiphumelele', and it was undertaken as an almost classic second generation NLS study, in which I entered a bounded field site, collected data on literacy events and grouped these into domains, weaving through it a focus on individuals and their literacy practices. One of the methods I used, however, was to trace what I called sections of 'the life histories of agenda items', in and across the three main organizations in the domain of development. Each organization had very specific and varied communicative practices which took shape in the physical space of each building and in-between each group of participants, some of whom were Masiphumelele residents and some of whom included white residents from neighbouring suburbs, local government officials, members of NGOs and so on.

These agenda items related to processes like 'establishing an office for the Civic Association', 'organising fencing for the primary school', 'getting plans designed for an informal market'. This tracing of the flow of events over time and across the meetings of the three organizations revealed a problem of studying the ideological character and context-dependence of literacy *within* discrete or bounded contexts. If I was to make claims about literacy practices on the basis of the events I was observing in these contexts, where would I draw the boundaries of the context? Which scale was I operating on and what would count as local: the three different organizations, or the boundaries of Masiphumelele itself? The kinds of questions I was asking here were later echoed by Reder and Davila (2005: 184) who argue that '[i]n building theories based on close examination and analysis of local practices NLS has not dealt systematically with what makes a context "local"', and they also ask about the spatial and temporal boundaries of context.

The analysis showed that ideological character and context-dependence were thrown into relief as and when meaning-making processes shifted from context to context. So the development issues mentioned above were *carried through* and *mediated across* these three places by people in differing participant frameworks through social practices like meetings procedures and working through agendas, as well as through material text-artefacts like lists, agendas and plans. In retrospect, I realized that the focus on process, which I was trying to achieve, was limited by my view of ethnography as place-bound, and by the need to tie the idea of literacy practices to the individuals or groups which were bounded by this place.

Some previous research has traced processes which cross contexts and the entextualization and recontextualization that takes place with each crossing (Mehan,1996; Berkenkotter and Ravatos 1998 amongst others). These have become known as 'text trajectories' (Silverstein and Urban 1996; Blommaert 2001, 2005). A clear example is provided in Blommaert (2001), in his outline of an asylum application procedure in which the asylum-seeker is interviewed and a story about the need to escape the home country is recorded by an official. This story is then taken to higher levels of the bureaucracy, being assessed by different groups of people (professional, authorities) who then write reports, recommendations and so on, until the status of the application is decided and the fate of the individual sealed. Blommaert examines what he calls the 'unequal linguistic resources' coming into play in each stage of this sequence of events.

Iedema's (1999, 2001) work on resemiotization takes a further step in examining how the shift of meanings across contexts draws on different codes and semiotic modes. He shows how this happens in the chain of events that led to the redesign and rebuilding of a hospital, from the initial verbal discussions, through to the minutes of these meetings, to the architects' plans and finally to the durable structure – the building itself. Central to Iedema's project, and with reference to Actor Network Theory, is the idea that facts are achieved through their transposition into 'successively more durable semiotics' – like printed matter, architectural design and even buildings (1999: 51) and 'unstable agreements reached in and through embodied talk are conventionally resemiotized into alternative and less negotiable semioses such as written summaries, courses of action or more durable materialities' (2001: 25). This suggests that such transpositions are irreversible, and that permanence or stability in infrastructures and environments is thus achieved.

ethnographies of processes: staying at the local

In the later ethnography of house-building in Khayalethu (1998–2001) I decided to address these theoretical dilemmas head-on, identifying sections of five processes which originated within Khayalethu, but extended way beyond its boundaries. These were as follows

1. ordering building materials

In this sequence of micro-events which stretched over a day and a half, a woman (MamaSolani) had prepared her site for building. At this point she was given a cheque by the local bookkeepers to buy materials to build her house. She then met with the builder to discuss with him exactly what she needed, went to an already built house to check on some details and then travelled eight kilometres to buy the materials in the building supply shop, where procedures were conducted through the help of a Xhosa speaker employed by the shop. She then organized for these to be delivered and returned back to the site to stick her invoices and receipts into a notebook which had been provided as part of my research project.

2. accommodating an oversized house

In this sequence a mistake was made on site and a woman (Veliswa) built a part of her house over the site boundary so that it extended into the road reserve. The roads had not yet been pegged out on the ground but had been designed on plans. Her extension became a rallying point for members of the organization who wished to resist building the small 40 square metre houses. This trajectory was traced across about four months through a number of Khayalethu meetings, meetings with City Council officials, the architect and the NGO support organization. Eventually the engineer redrew the entire plan of Khayalethu to accommodate the house.

3. recording members' 'activeness' to ensure they qualified for building sites

The term 'activeness' (in English rather than isiXhosa) was coined by the organization to find ways of increasing members' participation in development processes. Activeness was recorded through attendance at meetings, sleeping on site to prevent deliveries of building materials from being stolen and participating in the production of concrete blocks and building processes. The sequence of events identified and reconstructed how individual moments of recording became part of wider and highly contested administrative processes at higher levels, as they shifted across space, time and participant frameworks. This trajectory intertwined with the previous one and unfolded over a period of about six months.

4. writing a wrong

In this sequence, a woman called Nomathamsanqa, as a result of her disability, had been allocated a house rather than having to build her own house. There were serious problems with the house and Noma attempted to get these addressed. She unsuccessfully raised the problems verbally numerous times in community meetings. At this point she wrote a narrative in a child's exercise book about her experiences (this was part of a writing project that I had initiated in the community). This 'story' became the focus of tremendous attention in the community and much more widely, and the decision was made that she should take it and read it out aloud at a meeting of the national organization in an adjacent area. An intervening meeting took place with a provincial level structure, and the story was read out, after which she again presented it verbally at the national meeting. An immediate decision was made that a general collection of money should be made to get new materials and a builder to put the house right. The process started when she moved into the problem house and it ended when she moved back into the rebuilt house, altogether this took about six months and shifted across organizational structures, participant groups, neighbourhoods and buildings.

5. attempting to establish an office for the civic association

This sequence was identified and reconstructed from the earlier ethnography in Masiphumelele. It involved a diverse group of people attempting to gain access to a government building which they hoped could act as an office for the local Civic Association. The trajectory wound its way through a series of meetings held within different organizational structures at different levels and scales. One of the sequences of events in the overall trajectory involved the 'occupation' of a building by a group of people, and this was viewed as a mode of communication comparable with spoken or written language. This process unfolded over about six weeks.

transcontextual analysis: a language of description

Latour talks about an 'Ariadnes's thread', a thread 'of networks of practices and instruments, of documents and translations' that allow us to pass from the local to the global (Latour 1993: 121, quoted in Brandt and Clinton 2002: 346). The threads can be traced in the above examples, and they do involve documents, translations, practices and instruments. But how do we pin them down to study and make claims about them? And can we really prove that they allow us to pass from the local to the global? I will explore these questions in what follows.

Each of the above sequences was constituted of flows of events designed by people with intentions towards particular goals. Noma's purpose was to put right the problems with her house and the injustice she felt she had experienced; MamaSolani's purpose was to order materials so that she could proceed with building her house; the office group's purpose was to establish a space from which the residents could undertake their important work. The data demonstrates the importance of studying movement beyond the 'single instance' if meaning-making of this type is to be analysed. It is in the process of recontextualization, of shifting from context to the next, that other entities such as power become thrown into relief. A person can act and feel powerful in one context at one point in time using one mode of communication, but not in another. I argued that a viable unit of analysis to pin down this 'flow' is the *meaning making trajectory*, with reference to the idea of text trajectories (Silverstein and Urban 1996; Blommaert 2001), and 'human, material and discursive trajectories in a nexus of practices' (Scollon 2003).

Each of these was reconstructed, one by one, from the mass of ethnographic data that I had accumulated. My initial focus was on literacy events on site, but as I proceeded with the ethnography I found that literacy events were a very small part of these sequences, and that I needed to focus on any events related to the trajectory (which may or may not involve any written texts). The first step in this reconstruction involved simply describing the sequence of events, checking to see if there was sufficient data to link the events in meaningful ways. These were 'emic' descriptions.

At the same time, I kept the three tensions around the NLS, described above, in mind. The data for each trajectory cast light on each of these tensions. I felt that I could not work directly from this data to make claims about literacy or literacy practices, and I was drawn to Burawoy's (1998) approach in his extended case study method, which he presents as a form of 'reflexive science' in which he argues for the refinement and elaboration of theory. Burawoy argues for a set of extension processes. These are extending from the observer to the participant; extending observations over space and time; extending out from process to force and extending theory, which together lay the basis for theoretical refinement. He states that generality cannot be directly inferred from data but that through these extension processes 'we can move from one generality to another. We begin with our favourite theory but seek not confirmations but refutations that inspire us to deepen that theory'.

Each of these sequences was transcontextual, unfolding over space and time. But in order not to conflate context with higher scale analysis, I needed to separate analytically these emic descriptions from the conceptual categories I was working with, which I saw as etic. In this work I tried to reach inside the relation between events and practices theoretically and methodologically, seeking warrants for claims to be made about this relation and therefore about the relation between the observed and the invisible, the empirical and the theoretical. I aimed to add to the set of tools available for understanding this relation, in the form of a language of description (Bernstein 1996: 135–141). The key purpose for me in focusing on a language of description involved finding conceptual terms and relations that enabled principled extensions of the analysis of ethnographic data across scales, and that could be applied in further cases of research, beyond the specificities of what I observed in the ethnographic sites.

This is what Bernstein claims is important in the idea of a language of description. The 'internal language of description' (which I have portrayed as the 'etic') is 'the syntax whereby a conceptual language is created. The external language of description refers to the syntax whereby the internal language can describe something other than itself' – this is what is seen as the emic. The crucial point that Bernstein makes is that a concept should not be known or recognized by its apparent outcomes, it should be known by 'how it comes to be' not by 'what it does'. According to Bernstein:

> if an internal language is a condition for constructing invisibles, external languages are the means of making those invisibles, visible ... A language of description constructs what is to count as an empirical referent, how such referents relate to each other to produce a specific text, and translates those referential relations into theoretical objects. (p. 136)

My understanding of Bernstein's argument is that there needs to be a 'model'. Without modelling what members are doing in a specific culture, the researcher 'is marooned in the specific contexts and their enactment, fixed in their spatial and temporal frames' (p. 137). I therefore sought to find a set of conceptual relations which were derived from the analysis of the data, but which had generality. I wanted to avoid, on the one hand, what Blommaert has called *prima facie* ethnographies (2005: 51); and on the other, the making of claims about social structure and practice on the basis of single-instance situational data without principled warrants for making such claims.

The elements in the language of description suggested ways of addressing the three tensions in the NLS's theoretical framework described above: materiality and agency, contexts and the local global, multimodality. Each of these is described by elements and sub-elements, and each is nested within the higher level element.

These sequences were mapped across time and space (a detailed explanation of this is presented in Kell 2006), with each needing to be seen as a small thread in relation to wider sets of trajectories operating on different scales. Within a trajectory, each time the meaning-making process shifted across participant framework and/or space and time, the new 'context' that thus emerged was called a strip (adapted from Goffman 1981: 10). A strip could consist of a sequence of events separated over time as long as the participant framework and the space in which they took place remained constant. The boundaries of a strip would be reached, when new participants entered or departed the space, or the gathering as a whole took place in a new space and/or point in time. This approach enabled bigger 'chunking' of data, and the studying of larger social processes than, for example, turn-taking in conversation or single utterances, as is the case in much linguistic anthropology or applied linguistic research.

The spatial reach and the temporal length of the trajectories and their strips were scale-sensitive. Many of the strips consisted of immediate face-to-face conversations, but as the meaning-making process shifted across space and time, people and their material texts literally moved sometimes across the whole city. Nomathamsanqa physically carried her story in the exercise book over to the adjacent area to go to the national meeting; Deborah, the engineer, physically carried the plan on which she had sketched the oversized house back to her office in the city centre where she reworked the whole plan, after several intervening meetings in different parts of the city. During this process additional texts like a set of national building regulations were implicated, and local struggles at Khayalethu around road widths were evident in the actual events of the trajectory. Often material texts acted as what I called 'joins' (following Smith 1999) as recontextualizations took place, carrying the meaning across and being transformed themselves.

The second problem related to specifying local contexts and the related difficulties in making inferences about literacy practices. In the language of description this required careful definition at a very micro-level of each context at which meaning was sufficiently entextualized for it to be carried over to further contexts, to be recontextualized. One of the achievements of interactional socio-linguistics has been to show at the micro-level how context is created moment by moment as people act together. So it is the people acting together that form the basic unit of analysis. The idea of action is important since it connects with the focus on agency, and trajectories of meaning making discussed above. Engestrom (1996: 35), drawing on activity theory, defines contexts as activity systems. While this is a powerful unit of analysis, I also wanted to capture the micro-analytical dimension at the level of face-to-face interaction and turn-taking, and for this reason, I chose the idea of *participant frameworks* (Goodwin 1990). These are conceptualized as being *placed within* activity systems as a way of refining the concept of context as produced interactionally, as contextualization. This allowed me to view the way in which actors or agents carry their purpose across contexts, each of which may include very different groups of participants. I argued that this unit of analysis allows for more fine-grained explorations which are less value-laden and spatially bounded, than for example, the concept of communities of practice (Lave and Wenger 1991).

With regard to the issue of the limitations placed by the linguistic frame of reference, the concept of mediational means (as integral parts of activity systems) provides a wider frame of reference than literacy and signals the shift from linguistic frameworks to frameworks of multimodality and semiotics. Semiotic resources relating to literacy (as a sub-group of mediational means) can include

- capabilities – either individual or distributed across individuals; and especially in the case of literacy, involving coding, pragmatic, semantic and critical dimensions
- technologies – for example, in the case of literacy, a pencil or a computer
- artefacts – for example, in the case of literacy, recognized genres can be seen as conceptual artefacts, or material artefacts like scraps of paper with notes on them (in order for meaning to be realized such artefacts draw upon both capabilities and technologies).

Each of these takes shape differently in different semiotic modes, like the linguistic mode of speech or writing, and the visual, aural, gestural or spatial modes. What is it about the context of any one communicative event that makes one semiotic mode more *appropriate* in terms of fit between function and form? With reference to literacy, Luke and Freebody (1999) suggest that literacy capabilities involve first the breadth of an individual's or community's repertoire of literacy practices; second the depth and degree of control exercised by an individual or community in any given literacy activity and third the extent of hybridity, novelty and redesign at work. The approach outlined here enables these capabilities to be viewed in situated ways moment by moment as the actor, within particular participant frameworks, draws upon semiotic resources, operating under conditions of choice and constraint. These are historically conditioned rather than determined. The importance of studying mediational means as elements of activity systems is that they are not tools unless they have been put to some use, and the uses of a single material thing may differ over time and across different contexts.

Nomathamsanqa's trajectory which involved writing a story about her problem house, shows that people can draw on many modes of meaning making, but that these are contingent and emergent, related to the extent of hybridity, novelty and redesign. While the spoken mode in trajectory four did not achieve Nomathamsanqa's aims in the earlier events, the writing of the story certainly did. But it was only when the group that I had initiated discussed the idea of writing stories that Noma saw this opportunity. The lack of breadth of written resources available in the wider community played a role in the fact that her story was viewed so powerfully. Noma's entextualization carried weight because of this history. But it was the text-artefact as it was recontextualized that indexed this history.

Table 4.1 outlines the elements in the language of description showing how each was 'nested' in the higher level element. More detailed description and justification for these elements can be found in Kell (2006a,b; 2009a,b).

what the language of description enabled me to say about literacy

Although this research was methodologically orientated, it did enable me to make some claims about literacy which I believe are relevant to the future of Literacy Studies. The value of ethnography is that it clarifies the issue of point of view and ensures that this is always made explicit in research and writing. Ethnography is an attempt to understand and communicate 'insider perspectives'. So, unlike Latour's Ariadne's

Table 4.1   Elements of language of description nested in higher level elements

Key problem	Conceptual shift	Element in LoD
1. Single-instance data (events)	To meaning making as flow across time, defined in terms of	Sequences of events Nodes Strips Trajectories
2. Boundaries of context and need to make inferences about literacy practices	To contexts as activity systems, defined by	Actors and purposes Participant frameworks mediated by: 1. rules 2. division of labour and:
3. Linguistic frame of reference	To multimodality, conceptualized as one set of	3.mediational means including semiotic resources: -modes -media -artefacts -technologies

thread which allows us to pass from the local to the global, I argue that we cannot ever definitively say what is global but that we can perhaps say what is 'not-local' when we understand and make explicit the point of view of 'local'. It may then be possible to collect data starting from 'local' and extend to further 'not-locals'.

The method described here enables a view of flows or vectors, made up of crossings from one local to another not-local (depending on the perspective taken) rather than from the local to the global. Such crossings are enabled by sequences of chained entextualizations and recontextualizations. As we trace these threads we as researchers may follow a process and a set of actors far away from where it all started but it will not necessarily result in global (unless we work with different order categories and this is where slippage and conflation of levels and terms occurs). In this way Appadurai's (2000: 5) 'vectors' and 'flows' can be appreciated not as abstract concepts but as situated chains of human activity. This approach implies what Engestrom called 'a radical localism' (1999: 36).

At the same time, through the development of the language of description I was able to work in a way that I felt gave me warrants to make higher-level claims. In a sense, I first worked horizontally, following the thread from place to place. While doing this I suspended my wish to imagine I was working at higher scale levels (global?), and the way in which I worked analytically at higher levels (vertically) was through the development of the language of description which translated between the emic data and the theoretical framework of the NLS, which I hoped to deepen.

I have pointed to what I called 'joins' (drawing on Smith 1999) in this chaining, some of which were physical texts like a story book, a list, a plan. Some were verbal performances, which in the performing, became decontextualized and therefore more mobile. Some enabled the projection from the local to other participant frameworks in other trajectories in which some participants had more power and influence. Some involved transduction (Kress 2003) or resemiotization (Iedema 2001), in which a verbal performance was turned into a written story, a list became a set of building materials, or an extension to a building was turned into the redrawing of an entire plan for the area. The semiotic modes themselves had little to do with determining such transformations, but the social conditions at the point of joining had everything to do with them.

In the crossing between contexts some patterns could be observed. I argued that some of these joins were reified, others were naturalized and I will explain this further, with reference to those that were printed texts (see also Kell 2006a, for an in-depth discussion of this).

Wenger (1998) outlines a definition of *reification*, which he sees paired with *participation*. This idea has been taken up quite widely and also used in the field of Literacy Studies. Reification, in his meaning, is about 'producing objects that congeal experience into 'thingness''. Wenger sees this production of 'thingness' as a natural and necessary part of human activity, while participation is all about experience and somehow prior to the producing of such objects. Harvey (1996: 81) also uses the term: 'reifications of free-floating processes are always occurring to create permanences in the world around us'. I preferred to stay with a more Marxian and critical definition of reification, which carries connotations of fetishism and alienation.

In contrast, Bowker and Star (1999) use the terms *membership* and *naturalization*. In elaborating their theory of objects or things (I would include written texts as well), they note that 'something only becomes an object in the context of action and use, it then becomes as well something which has the force to mediate subsequent action' (p. 298). They define naturalization as meaning 'stripping away the contingencies of an object's creation and its situated nature. A naturalized object has lost its anthropological strangeness' (p. 298). We can think of a reified object as the opposite of a naturalized one, as an object which has not lost its anthropological strangeness, nor had the contingencies of its creation stripped away.

In the 'joins' across contexts that made up the trajectories, some texts were reified and some were naturalized. In the 'ordering building materials' trajectory, the texts that formed the joins were all naturalized – they did not index conflicted processes or intense struggles like all others did. As these texts were recontextualized they entailed and presupposed the contexts from which they had come and the conditions that the participants in each context anticipated. However, most of the other joins in the other trajectories were reified. They were emergent and contingent and carried a sense of being fetishized. For example, there was no standardization in these texts: Noma's story was unique; Veliswa's extension was the result of a mistake; Nomhle's record-keeping of activeness was not recognized by the Housing Association officials. Sometimes a join was reified by the absence of a text.

I asked myself whether there should have been more standardization to the joins that made up the trajectories other than MamaSolani's one (ordering building materials)? Bowker and Star (1999) explore the relation between standardization and symbolic violence. In MamaSolani's case, standardization worked to her advantage, despite the fact that she herself did not read or write any of the texts that formed the joins. However, I believe that the other trajectories characterized by reification demonstrate that a lack of standardization created more space for the play of power and the exercise of symbolic violence. The exclusions that occurred in these trajectories were significant and at times, devastating personally.

A further claim that I felt I could make is related to the idea of irreversibity. In the comparison of the five trajectories, recontextualization did not necessarily lead to more durable and irreversible (Latour 1987; Reder and Davila 2005) forms of meaning making. There were few uniform administrative processes, few institutionalized networks which were regulated through material texts involving naturalized sets of procedures. Rather there were unstable, precarious agreements reached temporarily in which material texts were often reified, involving huge amounts of energy, emotion and often misunderstandings and mistakes. This contrasts with the process described by Iedema (1999) with regard to the chain of events that led to the redesign and rebuilding of a hospital, from the initial verbal discussions, through to the minutes of these meetings, to the architects' plans and finally to the durable structure – the building itself. Central to Iedema's project, and with reference to Actor Network Theory, is the idea that facts are achieved through their transposition into 'successively more durable semiotics', like printed matter, architectural design and even buildings.

The method of reconstructing trajectories for analysis has shown that in some cases in Khayalethu and Site 5 resemiotization did lead (as claimed by Iedema 1999, 2001) to more durable forms of semiosis, but in many other cases, it did not. I claim therefore that a modernist teleology is implied in Iedema's approach, which does not hold in contexts which are characterized by severe poverty, inequality and disrupted lives. According to this teleology, in Khayalethu, the architects' design should have led to the production of a house, for example. But it often didn't. So in Khayalethu we had, for example,

- A plan became a house (sometimes it did).
- No plan became a house (often houses were built without plans; the builders were simply asked to copy and adapt other houses, even though this was very difficult).
- A house became a plan (Veliswa's house led to the redrawing of the overall plan and the re-submission to the Council).
- A house became no plan (in-between the building of Veliswa's extension and the resolution the plan was 'in abeyance').
- No plan (nearly) became no house (Veliswa was asked to remove her extension, because it threatened the plan).

The research of Iedema and Blommaert discussed above was conducted in highly industrialized countries and bureaucratized societies. Sequential recontextualizations in these cases followed well-worn paths like rivers that have carved out their patterns on the sub-strata. The stages along these paths did represent more durable and less negotiable forms of meaning making, for example, even as they perhaps naturalized symbolic violence. The kinds of spectacular, emergent and contingent processes characterizing Noma's trajectory, or the recording activeness one, were not evident. Although in Noma's case the trajectory did lead to a more durable form of meaning making (i.e. her house was rebuilt), in many other cases the opposite occurred.

What was uncovered in this research resonates with Rampton's claim that

> System and coherence lose their compelling force when their status as culturally specific values becomes clearer and when analysis moves into the gap between relatively stable groupings, where regularities and conventions are much less certain. (Rampton, 2000: 2)

conclusion

In this chapter I have provided a method for transcontextual analysis. In the process I have shown how I started with the concepts of literacy events and literacy practices, but questioned them. In following the threads of meaning making and focusing on the joins between one local and another not-local, I moved across space and time. To make claims at a higher analytical scale I needed to develop a language of description that separated the emic and the etic. The language of description was tied back to questions about the concept of literacy practices in relation to transcontextual analysis. The concept of practices works well in spatially defined ethnographic sites and the analytical work derived from these, but that it needed further exploration when it comes to examining 'flows'. I developed a method for examining these, in a context that is not normally associated with the 'hype' of globalization (a shantytown on the edges of a city in South Africa), but used this to explore this tension around the local and the global in relation to literacy.

The method allowed me to make some claims about literacy. Entextualization occurs within interactive and participant frameworks and the text-artefacts thus created (which may be non-linguistic or non-print) form joins between one context and another. The sub-elements of strips and nodes were not addressed in this chapter, but in Kell (2006a, 2009) I show how these elements permit chunking of data at a bigger scale than the situated moment, as well as a focus on how different moments offer the opportunity for new semiotic means to be drawn on, in order that people may project their meanings beyond their immediate 'local'. Joins can be reified or naturalized. When they are reified they may index creativity and emergence as well as struggles and lack of standardization. When they are naturalized, their effects seep into the infrastructure and connect contexts in predictable ways that involve standardization.

This view enables us to think about literacy as part of wider information ecologies, but its positioning in the dynamic of the trajectory and the participant frameworks means that we never lose the view of literacy as always instantiated and never autonomous.

postscript

In a further ethnography (for which I am currently analysing the data, July 2008), I am studying the literacy practices of Open Source computer programmers as they work on building a piece of educational software from distributed sites in New Zealand, engaging with users all over the world who are testing it and adapting it as it is being built. There are interesting similarities between the house-building process observed at Khayalethu and the software building process in that both are highly participatory, have very flattened working relationships which attempt to be democratic and have very provisional, emergent and negotiable working processes and practices. I am finding that there is much less of a distinction between transcontextual analysis and trans-scale analysis in this case. I suspect that there are two main reasons for this. These are, first, the fact that the instantaneity of digital communication means simply that transcontextual analysis is trans-scale (in that a person in a small town in New Zealand is communicating with people in Germany, Peru and South Africa in (almost) the same situated moment through Internet relay chat. Second, material text-artefacts are less important in the joins, since all communication takes place through digital text. Contextualization cues, rather than joins, may become the focus even though communication is written rather than spoken, the approach would be analogous with interactional sociolinguistic and conversational analytical work. A new language of description may have to be built, but it will draw upon the methods described here.

notes

1. Over the past few years materiality of texts has been addressed by, for example, Ormerod and Ivanic (2000). Kress focuses on the materiality of "the stuff" through which humans make meaning (2003:13). In Pahl and Rowsell (2006), the introduction written jointly by Kress and Street brings together NLS and multimodality, while Pahl (2008), and Stein and Slonimsky (in Pahl and Rowsell, 2006) explore multimodal texts and three-dimensional artefacts.
2. This is not to assume an unbridled sense of agency. Of course, at the same time that people act with and through entextualization processes, they are also acted upon and positioned by texts in literacy events. For example, answering yes to the question in an official form 'Have you had any criminal convictions?' when you have had criminal convictions.
3. It may well be that this is the case, but it is a case that needs to be proved not assumed or asserted.

references

Appadurai, A. (2000) Grassroots Globalisation and the Research Imagination. *Public Culture*, 12, 1–19.
Bartlett, L. and D. Holland (2002) Theorising the Space of Literacy Practices. *Ways of Knowing Journal*, 2(1), 10–22.

Barton, D. and M. Hamilton (1998) *Local Literacies*. London and New York: Routledge.

Barton, D., M. Hamilton and R. Ivanic (eds) (2000) *Situated Literacies: Reading and Writing in Context*. London: Routledge.

Baynham, M. (2004) Ethnographies of Literacy: Introduction. *Language and Education*, 18(4), 285–90.

Baynham, M. (2008) Elite or powerful literacies? Constructions of literacy in the novels of Charles Dickens and Mrs. Gaskell. In M. Prinsloo and M. Baynham (eds) *Literacies, Local and Global*. Amsterdam: John Benjamins, 173–92.

Berkenkotter, C. and D. Ravatos (1998) Voices in the Text: Varieties of Reported Speech in Psychotherapists' Initial Assessments. *Text*, 18(2), 211–39.

Bernstein, B. (1996) *Pedagogy, Symbolic Control and Identity: Theory, Research, Critique*. London: Taylor and Francis.

Blommaert, J. (2001) Investigating Narrative Inequality: African Asylum Seekers' Stories in Belgium. *Discourse and Society*, 12(4), 413–49.

Blommaert, J. (2005) *Discourse: A Critical Introduction*. Cambridge: Cambridge University Press.

Bloome, D., S. Carter, B. Christian, S. Otto and N. Shuart-Faris (2005) *Discourse Analysis and the Study of Classroom Language and Literacy Events: A Micro-ethnographic Perspective*. Mahwah, NJ and London: Lawrence Erlbaum.

Bowker, G. and S. L. Star (1999) *Sorting Things Out: Classification and Its Consequences*. Cambridge MA and London: The MIT Press.

Brandt, D. and K. Clinton (2002) Limits of the Local: Expanding Perspectives on Literacy as a Social Practice. *Journal of Literacy Research*, 34(3), 337–56.

Burawoy, M. (1998) The Extended Case Method. *Sociological Theory*, 16(1), 5–32.

Collins, J. and R. Blot (2003) *Literacy and Literacies: Texts, Power and Identity*. Cambridge and New York: Cambridge University Press.

Engestrom, Y. (1996) Developmental studies of work as a test-bench of activity theory: the case of primary care medical practice. In J. Lave and S. Chaiklin (eds), *Understanding Practice: Perspectives on Activity and Context*. Cambridge: Cambridge University Press, 64–103.

Engestrom, Y., R. Miettinen and R. Punamaki (eds) (1999) *Perspectives on Activity Theory*. Cambridge: Cambridge University Press.

Goffman, E. (1981) *Frame Analysis*. Oxford: Blackwell.

Goodwin, M. (1990) *He-Said-She-Said: Talk as Social Organisation among Black Children*. Bloomington: Indiana University Press.

Haarstad, H. and A. Floysand (2007) Globalisation and the Power of Rescaled Narratives: A Case of Opposition to Mining in Tambogrande, Peru. *Political Geography*, 26, 289–308.

Harvey, D. (1996) *Justice, Nature and the Geography of Difference*. Malden, MA and London: Blackwell.

Heath, S. B. (1983) *Ways with Words: Language, Life and Work in Communities and Classrooms*. Cambridge: Cambridge University Press.

Heath, S. B. and B. Street (2008) *Ethnography: Approaches to Language and Literacy Research*. New York: Teachers College Press.

Iedema, R. (1999) Formalising Organisational Meaning. *Discourse and Society*, 10(1), 49–65.

Iedema, R. (2001) Resemiotisation. *Semiotica*, 137(1/4), 23–39.

Kell, C. (2004) Review Essay: 'Literacy in the New Media Age' by Gunther Kress. *E-Learning.* 1(4).

Kell, C. (2006a) Crossing the margins: literacy, semiotics and the recontextualisation of meanings. In K. Pahl and J. Rowsell (eds), *Travel Notes from the New Literacy Studies.* Clevedon, Buffalo, Toronto: Multilingual Matters, 147–69.

Kell, C. (2006b) 'Moment to Moment: Contexts and Crossings in the Study of Literacy in Social Practice'. Unpublished PhD Dissertation: Open University, Milton Keynes.

Kell, C. (2009a) Making things happen: meaning making, agency and literacy in housing struggles in South Africa. In K. Basu, B. Maddox and A. Robinson Pant (eds) *Literacies, Identity and Social Change: Interdisciplinary Approaches to Literacy and Development.* London and New York: Routledge.

Kell, C. (2009b) Weighing the scales: recontextualisation as horizontal scaling. In M. Baynham, J. Collins and S. Slembrouck (eds) *Globalisation and Language Contact: Spatiotemporal Scales, Migration Flows, and Communicative Practices.* New York: Continuum.

Kress, G. (2003) *Literacy in the New Media Age.* London and New York: Routledge.

Kress, G. and B. Street (2006) Multimodality and literacy practices (Foreword). In K. Pahl and J. Rowsell (eds), *Travel Notes from the New Literacy Studies: Instances of Practice.* Clevedon: Multilingual Matters, vii–x.

Latour, B. (1987) *Science in Action: How to Follow Scientists and Engineers through Society.* Cambridge MA: Harvard University Press.

Lave, J. and E. Wenger (1991) *Situated Learning: Legitimate Peripheral Participation.* Cambridge: Cambridge University Press.

Luke, A. and P. Freebody (1999) *Further Notes on the Four Resources Model.* Accessed at http://www.readingonline.org/research/lukefreebody.html on 15 October 2008.

Maddox, B. (2001) Literacy and the market: the economic uses of literacy among the peasantry in North-West Bangladesh. In B. Street (ed.) *Literacy and Development: Ethnographic Perspectives.* London and New York: Routledge.

Maddox, B. (2007) What Can Ethnographic Studies Tell Us about the Consequences of Literacy? *Comparative Education, 43*(2), 253–71.

Martin-Jones, M. and K. Jones (2000) *Multilingual Literacies: Reading and Writing Different Worlds.* Amsterdam: John Benjamins.

Mehan, H. (1996) Beneath the skin and the ears: a case study in the politics of representation. In S. Chaiklin and J. Lave (eds), *Understanding Practice: Perspectives on Activity and Context.* Cambridge: Cambridge University Press, 241–68.

New London Group (1996) A Pedagogy of Multiliteracies. *Harvard Education Review.* 66: 60–92.

Pahl, K. (2008) Habitus in children's multi-modal text-making: a discussion. In M. Prinsloo and M. Baynham (eds), *Literacies, Local and Global.* Amsterdam: John Benjamins.

Prior, P. (2005) Moving Multimodality beyond the Binaries: A Response to Gunther Kress' 'Gains and Losses'. *Computers and Composition, 22,* 23–30.

Rampton, B. (2000) Continuity and change in views of society in applied linguistics. In Trappes-Lomax (ed.) *Change and Continuity in Applied Linguistics.* Clevedon: Multilingual Matters, 97–114.

Reder, S. and E. Davila (2005) Context and Literacy Practices. *Annual Review of Applied Linguistics*, 25,170–87.

Rogers, A. (2001) Afterword: Problematising literacy and development. In B. Street (ed.) *Literacy and Development: Ethnographic Perspectives*. London and New York: Routledge.

Scollon, R. (2003) *Discourses in Place: Language in the Material World*. London and New York: Routledge.

Scribner, S. and M. Cole (1981) *The Psychology of Literacy*. Cambridge MA: Harvard University Press.

Silverstein, M. and G. Urban (eds) (1996) *Natural Histories of Discourse*. Chicago: University of Chicago Press.

Smith, D. (1999) *Writing the Social: Critique, Theory and Investigations*. Toronto: University of Toronto Press.

Street, B. (1984) *Literacy in Theory and Practice*. Cambridge: CUP.

Street, B. (1995) *Social Literacies: Critical Approaches to Literacy in Development, Ethnography and Education*. London and New York: Longman.

Street, B. (2000) Literacy events and literacy practices. In K. Jones and M. Martin-Jones (eds) *Multilingual Literacies: Comparative Perspectives on Research and Practice*. Amsterdam: John Benjamins, 17–29

Street, B. (2001) *Literacy and Development: Ethnographic Perspectives*. London and New York: Routledge.

Street, B. (2003a) The Limits of the Local – Autonomous or Disembedding? *International Journal of Learning*, 10, 2825–30.

Street, B. (2003b) What's New in New Literacy Studies? Critical Approaches to Literacy in Theory and Practice. *Current Issues in Comparative Education*, 5(2), 77–91.

Street, B., M. Baker and A. Tomlin (2005) *Navigating Numeracies: Home/School Numeracy Practices*. Dordrecht: Springer.

Wenger, E. (1998) *Communities of Practice: Learning, Meaning and Identity*. Cambridge: Cambridge University Press.

5
bringing literacy studies into research on learning across the curriculum

roz ivanič

In this chapter I focus on the study of literacy practices in educational settings. By this I mean not settings designed for the teaching and learning of literacy, but those where the main goal is the learning of curriculum subjects, ranging from Applied Science to Childcare. These curriculum areas may seem odd examples to those familiar with primary or elementary education or the traditional subjects of the secondary curriculum: they are examples of courses in vocational and further education.

I will propose that recent research on the uses of reading and writing to mediate learning on college courses such as these has implications not only for the post-compulsory sector but also for literacies for learning across the curriculum more generally, and for the conceptual development of Literacy Studies for the future. In particular, I will address the question how best to use the term 'literacy practice'. In Literacy Studies so far this key term has been used in at least three ways:

1. To refer to what is done with written texts, as opposed to paying attention only to the linguistic (and, perhaps, semiotic) features of the texts themselves.
2. To refer to any social practice which is textually mediated, from those which are constituted by texts, such as reading a newspaper, to those in which written language is important, but not constitutive, such as fighting racism, to those in which written language is relatively peripheral, such as dog breeding.
3. To refer to small-scale, 'micro' practices – the way in which one or a subset of the constituent elements of a practice is played out.

100

In sense (i), the term 'practice' contrasts with the term 'text'. In senses (ii) and (iii) the term 'practice' contrasts with the term 'event', meaning a culturally recognizable, habitual way of using written language. I suggest that the word 'practices' is doing too much work and that, in the future, researchers in the Literacy Studies paradigm need to specify more precisely how they are using it. In particular, constant shifts between meaning (ii) and meaning (iii) are, in my view, counterproductive and in danger of losing the valuable specificity offered by meaning (iii). To be more radical, perhaps the term 'literacy practice' should be reserved for one of the above meanings rather than being used variously for all three. Ron Scollon (2001 and elsewhere) proposes that the term 'nexus of practice' might be more useful for meaning (ii), allowing the term 'practice' to be used more consistently for meaning (iii). Mark Sebba, in his work on orthography as a social practice (Sebba 2007), uses the term 'social practice' for the most micro of practices: that of choosing the spelling 'woz' to contrast with 'was' as a means of social positioning. The research on which this chapter is based shows the potential afforded by paying greater attention to meaning (iii).

I start by tracing the relationship between Literacy Studies and education, from the conscious efforts to move literacy research out of the classroom, through insights gained from studies of vernacular literacies which have relevance for education, to the present time, when Literacy Studies has established a firm base from which to make new types of contribution to education. I then provide an overview of a major research initiative in the United Kingdom on literacy practices in relation to vocational education: the Teaching and Learning Research Programme *Literacies for Learning in Further Education* research project. This research has brought a Literacy Studies perspective to understanding the reading and writing required by vocational courses, to examining how they interface with students' vernacular literacies, and to consequent fine-tuning of learning opportunities. Drawing upon the work of this project, I will propose three new directions for Literacy Studies: bringing the lens of Literacy Studies to bear on learning and teaching, moving beyond a focus on the situatedness of literacies and redefining the term 'literacy practice' at a greater degree of delicacy than has been common in the past.

out of the pedagogic domain and back again

Recurring panics about literacy standards since the beginning of compulsory schooling have been based on tests of reading and writing as autonomous skills (as described by Street 1984), or on observations about the declining standards in the use of written language by college students. 'Literacy' was treated as the ability to read and write based solely on criteria of accuracy and correctness in conformity to linguistic conventions (as described, for example, in Ivanič 2004). Research and public interest in literacy was concerned with the reading of word lists, answers to 'comprehension questions' and scores on spelling tests. These tests were, as has subsequently been shown, privileging those who took easily to the abstracted teaching, learning and assessment of written language which was offered by school systems. No wonder social scientists wanted to dissociate themselves from 'schooling' in their conceptualization of 'literacy'.

Since the inception of Literacy Studies in the 1970s, the aim has been to show that 'literacy' is not JUST what is taught in schools. The work of Scribner and Cole (1981) and Heath (1983) showed how people who did not do well on tests of reading and writing, and people who had not been to school at all, were nevertheless using written language for everyday purposes in ways which were totally sufficient to their needs and which were culturally shaped and culturally specific. These insights have been substantiated over the past 20 years by a large number of studies showing the richness, diversity and complexity of the literacy practices in people's vernacular and working lives, as elaborated in other chapters of this book. In this work, 'literacy' is not conceptualized as individuals' ability to code and decode written language, but rather as the social uses of written language.

In view of these origins of the Literacy Studies research paradigm, countering the traditional view of literacy as what is learnt and tested in school, it is understandable that literacy researchers focused their attention on the identification and investigation of the nature of literacy practices in all domains of social life other than education. The aim was to demonstrate the worth of the reading and writing which is done as part of living, working and social participation, and this had to be researched outside school (Hull and Schultz 2002). By maintaining this focus, the research area of Literacy Studies has made a convincing case for valuing the vernacular literacy practices in people's lives rather than assessing their literacy only by reading and writing activities and tests at school. Further, Literacy Studies has shown that most children and adults are not 'illiterate' when they start school or college, but they already have a great deal experience of leading literate lives in their homes and communities. Most come to education with 'funds of knowledge' in terms of the literacy practices in their everyday lives, which might act as resources for literacy development at school or college. Some recent research in Literacy Studies has focused on how its insights can be used in literacy education, both for children (Pahl and Rowsell 2005; Luttrell and Parker 2001) and for adults (Barton et al. 2007), and in education more broadly (Gee 2003). The enormous contribution of Literacy Studies is to make educators aware that this everyday reading and writing has value and should be recognized as 'literacy', just as much as, or more than performance on reading and writing tests and activities in school.

Research in the Literacy Studies paradigm has made substantial contributions to education through its insights about literacy as a social practice in other domains. However, it can also contribute to education in another way: by going back into educational settings and studying the literacy practices which mediate learning, in the same way as it has thrown light on those which mediate home, community and workplace activities. Education is an aspect of social life which is in itself quintessentially textually mediated and ripe for investigation through the Literacy Studies approach. There has been substantial research on the literacy practices of Higher Education, and in particular on student writing as a social practice with consequences for identity. These studies have paid attention to the socio-cultural and political context of writing, particularly to epistemological differences between disciplines and fields of study (Bazerman 1981; Swales 1990; Ivanič 1998; Jones, Turner and Street 2000; Lea and Street 1998; Lea and Stierer 2000; Lillis 2001; Russell 2002). However, they have not looked at academic literacy practices more broadly: at the wide range of uses of reading and writing to mediate learning, teaching and assessment in higher education. There have also been socially situated studies of what have been termed 'curriculum literacies', mainly in Australia (see, for example, Lee 1996; Martin 1993; Wyatt-Smith and Cumming 2003; see also Unsworth 2001). However, these studies to date have focused almost entirely on the linguistic aspects of literacy practices.

The Literacy Studies research paradigm can make invisible, discounted practices visible not only in the full panoply of people's lives but also on courses of study in all disciplines and subject areas across all sectors of education. The full power of Literacy Studies theory and methodology has not been exercised to this end. The studies summarized above have focused mainly on students writing assignments in higher education, and on identifying the generic features of disciplinary texts. The multiplicity of ways in which written language mediates learning and assessment has only just begun to attract the interest of literacy researchers, for the reasons already given. In the next section, I describe in some detail a recent research project for which I was responsible which has extended Literacy Studies in this domain.

recent research on literacy practices in the vocational curriculum

The *Literacies for Learning in Further Education* (LfLFE) project[1] took up the challenge of studying the literacy practices which mediate learning across the curriculum. It aimed to identify literacy practices which enable students to succeed in learning in a wide range of courses in Further Education[2] (for an overview of the research see Ivanič et al. 2007, 2009; Pardoe and Ivanič 2007). One of its major objectives was to uncover actual and potential overlaps and connections between the reading and writing students do in their everyday lives for their own purposes and the literacy demands of their courses. It was a collaboration between The University of Stirling, Lancaster University and four Further Education colleges from January 2004 to June 2007. Six university-based researchers worked with 16 college lecturers to research their own courses and students. More than a hundred students took part in researching 32 units of study across 11 curriculum areas. To provide a basis for comparison, Childcare courses were studied in common across all four colleges. The other areas ranged from A Level Social Sciences to Painting and Decorating (for further details, see the project website www.lancs. ac.uk/lflfe).

literacy practices in college

Literacy practices in colleges can be grouped into four broad categories:

- literacies for being a student, for example registration, use of learning resource area;
- literacies for learning of knowledge, understanding and capabilities;
- literacies for assessment;
- literacies related to an imagined future, for example placements, work simulations.

The literacies for being a student are to a large extent common across courses, but the other categories vary from course to course. For example,[3] studying AS Level Media Studies involves very different literacy practices from studying NVQ Level 2 Food and Drink Service.[4]

Media Studies is what might be thought of as a textually saturated curriculum area in which students are expected to engage with a wide variety of different texts. In spite of the fact that Catering and Hospitality might seem at first sight to be a curriculum area with minimal textuality, we found that Food and Drink Service, both as a job and as a subject area, involves a wide variety of literacy practices too, but very different ones from those on a more academically oriented course such as AS Level Media Studies (for a more detailed analysis of these cases, see Satchwell and Ivanič 2007).

an example from media studies

Texts do not just mediate but actually constitute this curriculum area (for different disciplinary perspectives on the relationship between language and social life see Halliday 1978, Smith 1990). The particular unit looked at for the project was the three-month introductory unit of the AS course, which is the first year of the two-year A Level. In just one lesson, the students were required to 'read' written texts and images simultaneously, to write notes based on the teacher's explanation and with reference to paper-based texts produced by the teacher, sourced from examination board assessment criteria, from a website, and from local information relating to the college resource centre and cinemas and video shops in the towns nearby. They were expected to keep this information and refer to it as the course progressed. In subsequent sessions students were shown moving images from documentaries, advertising, news programmes, films, pop videos. After watching a clip, they were required to write notes and subsequently to develop their notes into an academic style essay, all the while being expected to translate their interpretation of the visual images into a standardized form of language espoused by the education system but frequently flouted by the very texts under scrutiny.

Media Studies as an academic subject throws into relief the complexity of the relationship between students' everyday literacy practices and the literacy practices required by their college courses and highlights the difficulty of bringing the two together. While a student may 'idly' watch pop videos or read magazines in their spare time, the same video clip or magazine article can become the focus of a literacy practice which carries the values and identities of the educational system. While the media texts they were analysing are part of the everyday world, the way in which the students were analysing them is grounded in academic terminology and the literacy practices associated with AS level study.

an example from catering and hospitality

When the Catering and Hospitality department was first approached as a subject area for inclusion in the project, the response was that there was not much literacy in Catering. However, observation of the college restaurant and kitchens – not to mention the theory classes – indicates that this is not the case. Literacy practices for both doing and learning this vocational area were invisible and therefore discounted.

Students on courses at levels 2 and 3, including the NVQ Level 2 Food and Drink Service course researched, are given a log book which has to be filled in as they fulfil different criteria for assessment. The logbook is used to demonstrate knowledge and competence for the purposes of accreditation, and hence they are in evidence throughout all activities in the restaurant and kitchens. At the same time, as part of their college course students are 'working' in the restaurant, taking orders ('writing checks'), reading and explaining menus to customers, reading booking entries in the diary, working the bar and the till, reading the whiteboard in the kitchen with details of the dishes and who is cooking what, accessing the computer for information about customers' special requirements and filling in electronic templates for customers' bills and cash summary sheets. At other times they are designing and writing menus, posters and leaflets for direct use in the restaurant. In addition, students are asked to complete assignments, such as researching how to find a job and complete a CV, culminating in a mock interview, and designing and costing a menu to fit given criteria. One student explained how he had learnt to describe the same dish in a variety of styles, ranging from a £7 meal to one for £40. This might appear to be the kind of activity required of an A Level (level 3) Media student, rather than level 2 Catering.

The fact that a large part of the students' time in Catering, even within college, is spent in a work environment means that once again the juxtaposition of different kinds of literacies is clearly in evidence. In this curriculum area, there is the requirement for formal academic literacy practices in the completion of the log book, and the less formal but equally prescriptive workplace literacy practices involved in the effective and efficient running of a restaurant.

similarities and differences across curriculum areas, levels and institutional contexts

Looking at educational contexts through the lens of Literacy Studies revealed that a great deal of the writing students do on their college courses in all curriculum areas is for assessment, rather than for learning, and that a great deal of what they were given to read merely symbolized curriculum coverage, rather than actually being used for learning (for further discussion, see Edwards and Smith 2005). A key factor which influenced students' engagement with these pedagogic literacies was the extent to which they identified with the subject positions inscribed in them (for further discussion, see Ivanič 2006). Focusing on literacy practices also showed that the demands on lower level courses are in many respects greater and more diverse than those on higher level courses, and that there is often a tension between vocational and academic goals, the former involving, for example, reading and writing associated with simulations of work tasks, and the latter usually involving writing essays and reading for factual learning. Literacies for learning differed more by level than by country or by college. While the policy contexts and working conditions differed substantially between Scotland and England, pedagogic practice was very similar in both countries, in all four colleges and across the eight Childcare units. Bringing the lens of Literacy Studies to bear on learning and teaching thus contributes to thinking on issues at the cutting edge of educational research.

literacy practices in students' everyday lives

People who enrol in college courses engage in a multiplicity and abundance of literacy practices in their everyday lives, compared with the very specific sets of practices that are valued within the context of FE. Staff and students themselves tend to talk about literacy in terms of what students CAN'T do, rather than in terms of what they CAN do. The richness and diversity of students' vernacular practices – that is, the reading and writing they do in association with activities of their own choice – counter this perception. Analysis of over a hundred case studies of the literacy practices in which students engaged by choice showed the characteristics listed in Figure 5.1.

For example,[5] Nadine's passion is following her horoscope; she follows her horoscope closely and believes in the predictions contained within them, although she recognizes that not all horoscopes are as accurate or useful as others. She reads the horoscope each evening in her local paper and thinks that this is well-written – she worries if she has not had the opportunity to look at this paper's horoscope in the evening. She doesn't like the horoscopes that appear in the national daily newspapers, although she might glance at the Daily Mail horoscopes if her mum has left the newspaper lying around. She reads the horoscopes in

❖   purposeful to the student
❖   oriented to a clear audience
❖   shared, i.e. interactive, participatory and collaborative
❖   learned through participation
❖   in tune with students' values and identities
❖   agentic, i.e. with the students having control
❖   non-linear, i.e. with varied reading paths
❖   specific to times and places
❖   multimodal, i.e. combining symbols, pictures, colour, music
❖   multimedia, i.e. combining paper and electronic media
❖   varied; not repetitive
❖   generative, i.e. involving meaning-making, creativity and getting
     things done
❖   self-determined in terms of activity, time and place

Figure 5.1   Characteristics of students' vernacular literacy practices

Cosmo Girl, although she thinks these tend to be a bit too general, and she might skim through the contents of Take a Break, Chat or other magazines which other students bring to college. Her reading is purposeful, located in time and space, and she is exercising critical agency as to its truth and value. Using the handset of her parents' television, she navigates the Sky Channels to find astrology programmes and reads her horoscope on Sky menus and using teletext. She doesn't particularly like using computers, but took advantage of an IT lesson to go online and use a search engine to find different astrology sites. These technologies add variety to her reading in terms of media, modes and reading paths. Nadine keeps a diary of the major events that happen to her – she dates these so that she can refer back to them to see patterns in her life. This writing is purposeful and generative of meaning in terms of Nadine's life and guiding passion.

College students engage not only in vernacular literacy practices – that is, those which arise from their own interests and concerns – but also in a wide range of bureaucratic, more formal literacy practices which are demanded by the practicalities of their lives. For example, Eve gave birth to her son, Alex, while at school. She is now 18 years old and lives in her boyfriend's own house with the two-year-old Alex. Eve has kept all the paperwork and books that she was given while she was pregnant, and these are stored with Alex's birth certificate, bank statements, council tax information, and other bits of bureaucratic paperwork. These practices are embedded in social action, serving essential, if imposed, purposes in the context of Eve's life. The texts are very varied in medium and mode, according to their function. She keeps Alex's 'red book' of developmental stages and health details at home by her bed and writes in this regularly to keep it up-to-date. She takes this book with her on visits to the health visitor or GP. She read the two books that her midwife gave her which explained pregnancy and birth in detail, although she skipped over the sections on breastfeeding as she found these distasteful, exercising agency over what and how she reads. Eve recently received paperwork relating to the Child Trust Fund and understands that Alex will receive a payment although she isn't sure what she should do with this – she says that she will probably give the information to her mum to sort out: a practice involving collaboration around texts. Eve is transferring Child Tax Credit from her mum's name to her own name as she now works part-time as well as being a student – she feels confident about filling in these forms as she recently sorted out the paperwork for Council Tax after moving in with her boyfriend (for further analysis of this case, see Ivanič et al. 2009, Chapter 5).

These examples bring out the variety of literacy practices in students' everyday lives, and show how analysis of these practices has provided the basis for identifying the characteristics listed in Figure 5.1.

fine-tuning literacies for learning

Understandings about vernacular and curriculum literacies such as those outlined above draw upon the fundamental insight that literacy practices are socially situated: shaped by their social context. However, the imperative to make Literacy Studies relevant to pedagogy raises the question of whether vernacular practices can be drawn upon as resources for enhancing students' success. Addressing this question demands that we move beyond identifying 'situated literacies', and look for ways of harnessing students' capabilities in other domains of practice for purposes in the educational domain.

Aspects of the literacy practices in students' everyday lives, for example, their collaborative nature, can be harnessed as resources for learning, examples of which are discussed in detail in Goodman et al. (2007), Ivanič et al. (2007), Ivanič and Satchwell (forthcoming), Mannion et al. (forthcoming), Miller and Gaechter (2006), Pardoe and Ivanič (2007), Satchwell (2007), Smith (2005) and Smith and Mannion (2006). Changes in practice which drew upon characteristics of students' everyday literacy practices tended to increase their capacity for engagement and recall and their confidence.

For example, on the Food Hygiene Practices unit of a course in Tourism and Hospitality, the lecturer was dissatisfied with the way he was teaching the topic of the construction and design of food premises.[6] He had presented the information in a Powerpoint presentation with a lengthy accompanying handout and then required the students to write an essay to demonstrate their knowledge. He observed that they were bored by the Powerpoint presentation, were not reading the handout, and were not understanding the textbook. Their essays did not display understanding, and they contained large chunks copied directly from the notes and textbook. Based on his understanding of the students' vernacular literacy practices, he made a small change in his pedagogic practice: he introduced a new activity to mediate between the students encountering of the theory and being assessed on it. He asked them to work individually or in groups and to produce a floor-plan of an imaginary kitchen, showing where different types of food would be stored. The students were able to choose the type of kitchen according to their particular interests or intended futures. The students then presented their floor-plan to the rest of the class, explaining why it was laid out as it was. In the design of this activity the lecturer drew upon the characteristics of students' everyday literacy practices in several ways. He saw it as giving the students a clear purpose for their reading and allowing them to work collaboratively. The students read what they needed to gain information, rather than sequentially. They were able to choose the media and modalities for their floor-plans, adding variety to the literacy practices on the course. They had considerable flexibility as to when, where and how they would do their work, although there was a deadline for its completion. When the students eventually had to write their assessments (which were set by the awarding body), they showed far more understanding of the material and far more engagement in the unit as a whole. This example shows how it was not so much whole practices which were harnessed for pedagogic purposes, but aspects of those practices, as we discuss further below.

consequences for theory

moving beyond 'situated literacies'

The LfLFE project had set out to identify what we called 'border literacies' – those literacy practices in which students engaged successfully in their everyday lives which might be recognized and harnessed to enhance their success on their courses.

However, it soon became clear that there was a conceptual anomaly here in that it is an established tenet of Literacy Studies that literacy practices are socio-culturally situated. That is, texts and ways of reading and writing differ from one context to another (see, for example, Barton, Hamilton and Ivanič 2000; Barton, this volume). Therefore, the idea of mobilizing practices wholesale from students' everyday lives as resources for learning in educational settings did not make sense. Literacy practices such as reading horoscopes (Nadine) or those involved in expecting and caring for a baby (Eve) depended on their location in the context of the students' lives, interests and responsibilities and were not the same as the literacy practices on their NVQ Level 1 course in Childcare. Even when, for example, computers were used in the curriculum as well as at home, they were used in different ways and, above all, for different purposes.

To resolve this anomaly, we had to reconsider the nature and extent to which literacy practices are 'situated', whether it was possible for boundaries between contexts to be permeable, and whether literacy practices which are located in one context could be mobilized to serve different purposes in another. However, we also wanted to reject the familiar and, in our view, simplistic terminology of 'transferable skills', and to think in terms of movements and flows across contexts rather than in terms of mediation, mobilization, transition and harnessing of resources. We were attracted by theorizations of boundary-crossing and border-crossing (as presented in Tuomi-Gröhn, T. and Engeström 2003), with associated notions of boundary objects. The conceptual tool of 'boundary objects' was first developed within Actor-Network Theory (ANT) (Star 1989). A boundary object is

> [p]lastic enough to adapt to local needs and the constraints of the several parties employing them, yet robust enough to maintain a common identity across sites. ... They have different meanings in different social worlds but their structure is common enough to more than one world to make them recognizable, a means of translation. The creation and maintenance of boundary objects is a key process in developing and maintaining coherence across intersecting social worlds. (Star & Griesemer 1989: 393)

In ANT boundary objects were at first conceptualized as cultural artefacts, typically but not exclusively texts. This is a promising way of expanding the 'situated literacies' approach, suggesting that texts which students used in their everyday lives – for example, weekly magazines – and/or perhaps the artefacts they used – for example computers – might fulfil the criteria to act as boundary objects. However, the difference in context between the everyday life-world and the institutionalized domain of education is too great, and these material objects on their own are not 'plastic enough to adapt to local needs and the constraints of the several parties employing them'. To take the magazines which students read outside college as an example, they belonged too much to the students' 'out-of-college' worlds to be useful for learning on their courses: the context and purposes of the classroom were too different and changed the practice of reading the magazines to such an extent that it was no longer engaging for the students. To take the other example, computers were so much changed by the way they were used in college that students' familiarity with them in their vernacular practices was not sufficient to 'cross the border' into the college uses.

The concept of 'boundary objects', and the idea of their 'creation and maintenance ... as a key process in developing and maintaining coherence across intersecting social worlds' also plays a part in the theorization of communities of practice (Lave and Wenger 1991; Wenger 1998). Boundary objects work at the edges of communities of practice and enable coordination from one community to another (1998:107). However, this way of thinking about boundary objects is not productive, as students seem more inclined to work to maintain the boundaries between everyday life and college than to attempt to achieve any coordination between them. They have neither the power to do this boundary work nor any investment in the creation of such boundary objects (for further discussion, see Edwards 2005). Nevertheless, this aspect of boundary objects is, we suggest, very relevant to literacy theory in general (see also Barton and Hamilton's discussion of the communities of practice concept of 'reification' (Barton and Hamilton 2005)).

As ANT developed, boundary objects were understood not merely as material objects, but could be 'stuff and things, tools, artefacts and techniques, and ideas, stories and memories' (Bowker and Star 2000: 298). This conceptualization made us consider that it may be not so much the artefacts, but the ways of using them – the practices – that might be mobilized from one context to another. Certainly, the practices would be changed by recontextualization in a different context – they may be differently nuanced, and/or differently valued as in the example of 'boiler-plating' discussed in Barton's chapter. However, the changes in practice which were trialled on the LfLFE project showed that there was considerable mileage in breaking down our analysis of students' everyday practices, into 'micro-practices' (as discussed in the next section) and treating these as 'boundary objects' which, while having 'different meanings in different social worlds' would have a 'structure … common enough to more than one world to make them recognizable, a means of translation'.

The tutors who were working to fine-tune the reading and writing on their courses to achieve maximum resonance with students' everyday literacy practices found that what can be mobilized from one context to another are not fully formed social practices, and not texts or technologies on their own, but aspects of the practices such as collaborativeness, or non-linear processing. That is, they were looking to configure the literacy practices on their courses in one or more of the ways in which students engaged with written language in their vernacular practices, as listed in Figure 5.1. Reproducing some of the characteristics of the reading and writing in which the students engaged successfully in their everyday lives turned these practices into resources to enhance their success on their courses (for this argument, see also Gee 2003 and 2005).

The implication of this for Literacy Studies is that 'micro-level' literacy practices can be sufficiently common to more than one context, to the extent that they can even cross domain boundaries. However, it also leads us to probe what exactly we mean by 'micro-level' literacy practices.

levels of detail in theorizing literacy practices

On the evidence of the research described above, I suggest that Literacy Studies might benefit from being more precise about the use of the term 'literacy practice'. The argument here is in three stages. First, it is useful to recognize that literacy events and practices are made up of a finite number of constituents, and that it is valuable to attempt to specify these constituents. Second, each of these constituents can be configured in infinite ways, and in turn the configurations can be combined in infinite ways. These configurations, and combinations of configurations, are what we are attempting to identify when we research literacy events and attempt to identify literacy practices more broadly conceived (that is, in meaning (ii) presented at the beginning of this chapter). Third I suggest that, for many research purposes, and particularly when looking for mobilizations from one context to another, it might be profitable to reserve the term 'literacy practice' for the culturally recognized 'micro-practices' represented by these configurations (that is, for meaning (iii) presented at the beginning of this chapter), rather than requiring it to serve as many functions as has been the case to date.

As discussed in the previous section, the evidence suggests that 'whole' literacy practices, in the sense of social practices which involve the use of written language such as applying for Child benefit, or reading horoscopes, cannot be recontextualized wholesale into educational settings because the social domain changes the practice. Nor, at the other extreme, is the current notion of 'transferable skills' satisfactory, since reading and writing are shaped by their social context. Nor, in the simplest interpretation of ANT, is it simply a question of bringing apparently 'authentic' texts from other domains into educational settings because they are no longer 'authentic' to their new context (see also Breen 1985 for this argument). to pursue our original intention of identifying ways in which students' everyday practices might be mobilized as resources for their learning on college courses, we needed a way of theorizing literacy practices which allowed us to talk about their fine detail.

The need to specify what we mean by 'literacy practices' is not confined to the issue of mobilization for pedagogic purposes across borders between domains. The LfLFE project alerted us to the desirability of refining this concept for Literacy Studies in general. The lecturers made changes to the literacy practices on their courses in the light of their introduction to a social practice view of literacy more generally and using the insights they had gained from their research into their students' everyday literacy practices in more ways than we had anticipated. As we researched these changes, we found it useful to recognize that each 'literacy practice' such as, for example, using mind maps to take notes, could be analysed according to the way in which each of a number of aspects of literacy was configured. This led to the insight, implicit in Literacy Studies but, we believe, extremely valuable to make explicit, that there are a finite set of aspects of a literacy event or literacy practice, each of which can be configured and combined in an infinite variety of ways.

The idea of identifying elements of literacy events and practices is not new. It is integral to the Literacy Studies research paradigm to ask the fundamental ethnographic wh-questions:

Who is doing what? with whom? to/for whom? where? when? how? why? and under what conditions?

The idea that a literacy event or practice can be analysed using a set of categories is implicit in Literacy Studies and has been discussed explicitly by, for example, Mary Hamilton in her article distinguishing visible and non-visible elements of literacy events. She identified these as follows.

Basic categories	Elements visible within literacy events	Non-visible constituents of literacy practices
Participants	The people who can be seen interacting with written texts	Other people or groups of people involved in the social relationships of producing, interpreting, circulating and otherwise regulating written texts
Settings	The immediate physical circumstances	The domain of practice within which the event takes place and takes its sense and social purpose
Artefacts	The material tools and accessories (including texts)	All the other resources brought to the literacy practice including values, understandings, ways of thinking, feeling, skills and knowledge
Activities	The actions performed	Structured routines and pathways that facilitate or regulate actions; rules of appropriacy and eligibility – who does/ doesn't, can/can't engage in particular activities

Figure 5.2   Basic elements of literacy events and practices
Source: Adapted from Hamilton 2000, Table 2.1 p. 17

This was a useful starting-point, and we found it useful to extend and reconfigure this list for our own purposes, using the ethnographic questions, other theoretical accounts of the constituents of a social practice and categories emerging from our data. We expanded some of Hamilton's categories, added others, and made the distinction between elements which are common to all social practices, those which are specific to literacy practices and those which are inscribed in a practice. We have presented these in different ways for different purposes (see, for example, Pardoe and Ivanič 2007; Ivanič et al. 2007, 2009; Ivanič and Satchwell 2007).

The set of elements in Figure 5.3 is an attempt to be relatively comprehensive, and it includes all elements that have at one time or another been considered salient within the LfLFE analysis; however, I do not want to propose the list as necessarily complete. It does not, for example, deal separately with elements such as institutional structures and cultural norms which shape social practices, which are extremely important but not my focus in this chapter. Several of the items in the list could be further sub-divided in the way I have indicated for 'Time'. Others might be combined to avoid repetition: for example, element (15) 'Talk around texts' is a type of Semiotic action, and therefore a sub-category of element (5). However, it is a particularly important element which is specific to literacy practices, and therefore I have mentioned it independently. I have included 'Values attitudes and beliefs' both as elements which are specific to participants and as elements which are inscribed in practices more broadly, but in a simpler presentation these might be

---

ELEMENTS WHICH ARE COMMON TO ALL SOCIAL EVENTS AND PRACTICES

1. Participants' roles, relationships and participation structures
2. Participants' thoughts, feelings and reactions
3. Participants' values, attitudes and beliefs
4. Purpose(s)
5. Activities, actions and processes (physical, cognitive and semiotic)
6. Place and space
7. Time: timing, frequency, speed and duration
8. Tools and resources

ELEMENTS WHICH ARE SPECIFIC TO LITERACY EVENTS AND PRACTICES

9. Media
10. Modes
11. Literacy-specific Artefact(s)
12. Text-type(s)
13. Content / Topic
14. Audience(s) for texts
15. Talk around texts

ELEMENTS WHICH ARE INSCRIBED IN AND PERPETUATED BY PRACTICES

16. Values, attitudes and beliefs
17. Identities / subject positions
18. Relations of power and status

Figure 5.3   Constituents of a literacy event or practice

mentioned only once. Strictly speaking 'literacy artefacts' and 'tools and resources' are the same thing, but we have found it useful to distinguish tools and resources more generally – to include such things as furniture and mixing bowls – from those which are literacy-specific such as keyboards and magazines. Some theories reduce the constituents of a social practice to a bare minimum; for example Activity Theory works with the concepts of Subject(s) (that is, human participants), Object(s) (that is, both purposes and substances being worked upon) and Mediating Means (that is, all the culturally shaped tools and artefacts which lead to the achievement of the Object(s) of the activity (for further detail, see Russell and Yañez 2003). While the Activity Theory framework has the advantage of being extremely flexible and practical, it can result in important elements being overlooked: something I have tried to avoid in the more detailed specification of constituents of a literacy practice here. The exact elements and number of elements on the list are not so important as the principle that there are a finite set of elements which constitute literacy events and literacy practices, each of which can be configured in an infinite number of ways, as discussed below.

This raises the question of whether the elements we are talking about are elements of an event or elements which constitute a practice. In my view, it is useful to treat them as both. In Figure 5.3, I have explicitly labelled the first 15 elements as constitutive of both events and practices. By this I mean on the one hand that information about these elements could be elicited for any literacy event. That is, by observation, photographic documentation, interviews, focus groups and/or the collection of documentary evidence, it would be possible to know details in some or all of these categories, and maybe others too, about any literacy event which is the object of study. On the other hand, if a literacy researcher is attempting to make claims about the nature of a 'literacy practice', in the sense of 'a general, cultural way of utilizing written language which people draw upon in their lives' (Barton and Hamilton 1998), they might also wish to specify not only the elements which constitute the practice (the first 15 in Figure 5.3) but also those which are inscribed in and perpetuated by it (the other three). To describe these elements of a literacy practice as opposed to an event, it would be necessary to provide regular and repeated evidence of their occurrence and of their occurrence in combination.

Each of these constituents can be configured in many ways, and a change in the way any one of them is configured changes the nature of the practice. In other words, each element has a potentially infinite number of 'settings' according to the particular event or practice of which they are a part. So, for example, in many of the literacy practices in which the students in the LfLFE project engaged, the reading and writing processes were non-linear: moving from one part of a text to another and reading, or writing, at variable speeds according to the part of the text. In a great deal of the reading and writing they were expected to do on their courses, however, there was an assumption that the text would be read or written sequentially. To take another example, there is a 'timing' element to every literacy event or practice, that is, decisions as to what to do when; however, the actual timing may be specific to a particular person, to a particular event or, if culturally recognized as habitual, to a specific 'practice'. I suggest that these diverse, socially situated configurations of the constituents of a literacy event or practice are what might be termed 'micro' literacy practices: literacy practices which can serve different purposes in different events, but have something in common across events (somewhat in the same way as proposed by Scollon 2001 in relation to his notion of a 'nexus of practice'). In turn, the configurations can be combined in infinite ways, and the combinations, if repeated often enough for them to become stablized, might become 'recognized for now' as literacy practices of a different order (that is, meaning (ii) presented at the beginning of this chapter) – 'macro-practices', perhaps.

The recognition that a literacy event or literacy practice can be analysed into constituent elements raises the issue of whether the term 'literacy practice' might be better reserved for these more 'micro' practices (that is, for meaning (iii) presented at the beginning of this chapter) – again, something which is pointed to by Scollon. In our research, we found that working at the greater degree of delicacy in describing literacy practices was extremely profitable.

Whatever literacy researchers decide about terminology, more important is the recognition of the value to Literacy Studies of attending to the fine detail of a literacy practice. I suggest that researchers will find it extremely beneficial to analyse literacy events and practices into constituent elements in the way discussed here. The elements identified can then be used as analytical categories for any type of data, revealing the fine detail of how each element is configured.

conclusion

The research I have been discussing here has, I suggest, significant implications for educational practice. Looking at pedagogic practices through the lens of Literacy Studies provides valuable insights into the ways in which learning, teaching and assessment are textually mediated. Combined with greater understanding of the abundance of literacy practices in the students' everyday lives and their characteristics, these insights can be used to fine-tune the students' learning opportunities. Teachers of all subjects in all sectors of education can use the insights from this project as a tool for analysing and fine-tuning the literacy practices on their own courses. In particular, these insights complement those from the programme of research conducted by the National Research and Development Centre for Adult Literacy and Numeracy (NRDC) into the embedded provision of language, literacy and numeracy learning and teaching (for details see Roberts et al. 2005 and Casey et al. 2006). The NRDC research draws attention to the value of using the actual literacy practices of vocational education to provide the basis for literacy learning and teaching. The LfLFE project provides an understanding and analysis of those literacy practices without which, I suggest, the embedding process may founder.

In this chapter I have provided a specific example of the power of Literacy Studies to make invisible, discounted practices visible: the example of the literacy practices of Further Education students in and out of college. I have argued first that Literacy Studies is now well placed to make a new type of contribution to education, bringing the lens of literacy theory to bear on learning and teaching. The research has contributed to the advancement of theory by reconceptualizing 'transfer' and 'border crossing' and by refining the concept of literacy practices. I have argued that Literacy Studies might benefit in the future from moving beyond a focus on the situatedness of literacies, and by redefining the concept of 'literacy practice' at a greater degree of delicacy than has been common in the past.

notes

1. The project was part of the Teaching and Learning Research Programme (TLRP) in the U.K., funded by the Economic and Social Research Council (ESRC), Grant no RES -139–25-0117. The research was conducted by a team which included David Barton, Angela Brzeski, Richard Edwards, Zoe Fowler, Greg Mannion, Kate Miller, Candice Satchwell, June Smith and Sarah Wilcock as well as me.
2. Further Education (FE) Colleges in the United Kingdom offer an alternative to school for 16–19 year olds and provide both vocational and academic courses. Many adult students also attend courses, both full-time and part-time. FE colleges are characterized by a particular focus on vocational education and training, and have links with workplaces.
3. The examples which follow are drawn from case studies written by Candice Satchwell.
4. NVQ stands for National Vocational Qualification, which can be studied at levels 1, 2 and 3.
5. These examples are taken from case studies written by Zoe Fowler. For other similar examples, see http://www.lancs.ac.uk/lflfe/casestudies.htm
6. This example is shown in detail on the project DVD (Pardoe and Ivanič 2007).

references

Barton, D. and M. Hamilton (1998) *Local Literacy: Reading and Writing in One Community*. London: Routledge.

Barton, D. and M. Hamilton (2005) Literacy, reification and the dynamics of social interaction. In D. Barton and K. Tusting (eds), *Beyond Communities of Practice: Language, Power and Social Context*. Cambridge: Cambridge University Press.

Barton, D., M. Hamilton and R. Ivanič (eds) (2000) *Situated Literacies: Reading and Writing in Context*. London: Routledge.

Barton, D., Y. Appleby, R. Hodge, K. Tusting and R. Ivanič (2007) *Adult Learners' Live*. London: Routledge.

Bazerman, C. (1981) What Written Knowledge Does: Three Examples of Academic Discourse. *Philosophy of the Social Sciences*, 11, 361–87.

Bowker, G. and S. Star (2000) *Sorting Things Out: Classification and Its Consequences*, Cambridge, MA: MIT Press.

Breen, M. P. (1985) Authenticity in the Language Classroom. *Applied Linguistics*, 6, 60–70.

Casey, H., O. Cara, J. Eldred, S. Grief, R. Hodge, R. Ivanič, T. Jupp, D. Lopez and B. McNeil (2006) *'You Wouldn't Expect a Maths Teacher to Teach Plastering ...' Embedding Literacy, Language and Numeracy in Post-16 Vocational Programmes – the Impact on Learning and Achievement.* London: NRDC.

Edwards, R. (2005) 'Contexts, boundary objects and hybrid spaces: Theorising learning in lifelong learning', paper presented at the 35th Annual SCUTREA Conference July 2005, University of Sussex, England, UK. Available at Education-line http://www.leeds.ac.uk/educol/documents/142037.htm. Accessed on 24 October 2007.

Edwards, R. and J. Smith (2005) Swamping and Spoonfeeding: Literacies for Learning in Further Education. *Journal of Vocational Education and Training*, 57(1), 47–60.

Gee, J. P. (2003) *What Video Games Have to Teach Us About Learning and Literacy.* New York: Palgrave/Macmillan.

Gee, J. P. (2005) Semiotic social spaces and affinity spaces: from the *Age of Mythology* to today's schools. In D. Barton and K. Tusting (eds), *Beyond Communities of Practice: Language, Power and Social Context.* Cambridge: Cambridge University Press.

Goodman, R., G. Mannion and A. Brzeski (2007) Reading, Writing and Resonance: An Experiential Workshop for Practitioners. *Research and Practice in Adult Literacy Journal*, 6, 10–14 (Special issue for RAPAL Conference 2006).

Halliday, M. (1978) *Language as Social Semiotic.* London: Edward Arnold.

Hamilton, M. (2000) Expanding the new literacy studies: using photographs to explore literacy as a social practice. In D. Barton, M. Hamilton and R. Ivanič (eds) *Situated Literacies: Reading and Writing in Context.* London: Routledge.

Heath, S. B. (1983) *Ways with Words.* Cambridge: Cambridge University Press.

Hull, G. and K. Schultz (eds) (2002) *School's Out! Bridging Out-Of-School Literacies with Classroom Practice.* New York: Teachers College Press.

Ivanič, R. (1998) *Writing and Identity: The Discoursal Construction of Identity in Academic Writing.* Amsterdam: John Benjamins.

Ivanič, R. (2004) Discourses of Writing and Learning to Write. *Language and Education*, 18(3), 220–45.

Ivanič, R. (2006) Language, learning and identification. In R. Kiely, P. Rea-Dickens, H. Woodfield and G. Clibbon (eds) *Language, Culture and Identity in Applied Linguistics.* London: Equinox.

Ivanič, R. and C. Satchwell (2007) Boundary Crossing: Networking and Transforming Literacies in Research Process and College Courses. *International Journal of Applied Linguistics*, Special Issue on New Directions in Academic Literacies Research, 4(1), 101–24.

Ivanič, R., R. Edwards, C. Satchwell and J. Smith (2007) Possibilities for Pedagogy in Further Education: Harnessing the Abundance of Literacy. *British Educational Research Journal*, 33(5), 703–21 (TLRP Special Issue).

Ivanič, R., R. Edwards, D. Barton, M. Martin-Jones, Z. Fowler, B. Hughes, G. Mannion, K. Miller, C. Satchwell and J. Smith (2009) *Improving Learning in College: Rethinking Literacies across the Curriculum*. London: Routledge.

Jones, C., J. Turner and B. Street (eds) (2000) *Students Writing in the University: Cultural and Epistemological Issues*. Amsterdam: Benjamins.

Lave, J. and E. Wenger (1991) *Situated Learning*. Cambridge: Cambridge University Press.

Lea, M. R. and B. Street (1998) Student Writing in Higher Education: An Academic Literacies Approach. *Studies in Higher Education*, 23(2), 157–72.

Lea, M. R. and B. Stierer (eds) (2000) *Student Writing in Higher Education: New Contexts*. Buckingham: Open University Press/SRHE.

Lee, A. (1996) *Gender, Literacy, Curriculum: Rewriting School Geography*. London: Taylor and Francis.

Lillis, T. (2001) *Student Writing: Access, Regulation and Desire*. London: Routledge.

Luttrell, W. and C. Parker (2001) High School Students' Literacy Practices and Identities and the Figured World of School. *Journal of Research in Reading*, 24(3), 235–47.

Mannion, G., K. Miller, I. Gibb and R. Goodman (forthcoming) Reading, Writing, Resonating: Striking Chords across the Contexts of Students' Everyday and College Lives. To appear in *Pedagogy, Culture and Society*.

Martin, J. R. (1993) Literacy in science: learning to handle text as technology. In M. A. K. Halliday and J. R. Martin (eds) *Writing Science: Literacy and Discursive Power*. London: The Falmer Press.

Miller, K. and J. Gaechter (2006) Thinking about Learning the Curriculum in Different Ways. *Broadcast*, 72, 20–1.

Pahl, K. and J. Rowsell (2005) *Literacy and Education: Understanding the New Literacy Studies in the Classroom*. London: Paul Chapman Publications.

Pardoe, S. and R. Ivanič (2007) *Literacies for Learning in Further Education: Making Reading and Writing Practices across the Curriculum More Useful for Learning*. DVD and Accompanying Booklet, Lancaster: PublicSpace Ltd and Lancaster University.

Roberts, C., M. Baynham, J. Eldred, S. Grief, J. Brittan, B. Cooper, C. Castillino, M. Gidley, P. Shrubshall, M. Walsh and V. Windsor (2005) *Embedded Teaching and Learning of Adult Literacy, Numeracy and ESOL: Eight Case Studies*. London: N.R.D.C.

Russell, D. R. (2002) *Writing in the Academic Disciplines: A Curricular History*, second edition. Carbondale: Southern Illinois University Press.

Russell, D. R. and A. Yañez (2003) Big picture people rarely become historians: genre systems and the contradictions of general education. In C. Bazerman and D. R. Russell (eds), *Writing Selves/Writing Societies Research from Activity Perspectives*. Fort Collins, Colorado: The WAC Clearinghouse and Mind, Culture, and Activity. Available at http://wac.colostate.edu/books/selves_societies/

Satchwell, C. (2007) Creating Third Spaces: Helping Further Education Students with Course-Related Reading and Writing. *The Teacher Trainer*, 21(2), 11–14.

Satchwell, C. and R. Ivanič (2007) The Textuality of Learning Contexts in UK Colleges. *Pedagogy, Culture and Society*, 15(3), 303–16 (Special Issue on *Contexts, Networks and Communities*).

Scollon, R. (2001) *Mediated Discourse: The Nexus of Practice*. London and New York: Routledge.

Scribner, S. and M. Cole (1981) *The Psychology of Literacy*. Cambridge: Harvard University Press.

Sebba, M. (2007) *Spelling and Society: The Culture and Politics of Orthography around the World*. Cambridge: Cambridge University Press.

Smith, D. (1990) *Texts, Facts, and Femininity: Exploring the Relations of Ruling*. New York: Routledge.

Smith, J. (2005): Mobilising Everyday Literacy Practices within the Curricula. *Journal of Vocational Education and Training*, 57(3), 319–34.

Smith, J. and G. Mannion (2006) 'What's "key"/"core" about literacy in FE? Authorising resonance between everyday literacy practices and formal learning', paper presented at British Educational Research Association Conference. Available on World Wide Web http://www.leeds.ac.uk/educol/documents/160853.htm. Accessed on February 2007.

Star, S. L. and J. R. Griesemer (1989) Institutional Ecology, 'Translations' and Boundary Objects: Amateurs and Professionals in Berkeley's Museum of Vertebrate Zoology. *Social Studies of Science*, 19, 387–420.

Star, S. L. (1989) The structure of ill-structured solutions: boundary objects and heterogeneous distributed problem solving. In L. Gasser and M. Huhns (eds) *Distributed Artificial Intelligence*, Vol. II. London: Pitman.

Street, B. (1984) *Literacy in Theory and Practice*. Cambridge: Cambridge University Press.

Swales, J. (1990) *Genre Analysis: English in Research and Academic Settings*. Cambridge: Cambridge University Press.

Tuomi-Gröhn, T. and Y. Engeström (2003) Conceptualising transfer: from standard notions to developmental notions. In T. Tuomi-Gröhn and Y. Engeström (eds) *Between Work and School: New Perspectives on Transfer and Boundary-Crossing*. London: Pergamon.

Unsworth, L. (2001) *Teaching Multiliteracies across the Curriculum: Changing Contexts of Text and Image in Classroom Practice*: Buckingham and Philadelphia: Open University Press.

Wenger, E. (1998) *Communities of Practice: Learning, Meaning and Identity*. Cambridge: Cambridge University Press.

Wyatt-Smith, C. and J. Cumming (2003) Curriculum Literacies: Expanding Domains of Assessment. *Assessment in Education*, 10(1), 47–59.

6
digital literacy studies: progress and prospects

mark warschauer

Information and communication technologies are transforming the way we read, write, interact, find and make use of information, and participate in public life (Coiro et al. 2008). The development and diffusion of these technologies thus present important challenges to the field of Literacy Studies.

Has our field been up to these challenges? In this chapter, I assess the theoretical and empirical work to date in examining literacy in the digital era and suggest some directions for future work. In conducting this assessment, I draw upon my earlier three-pronged framework for assessing the relationship between technology and literacy, that of *change*, *power*, and *learning* (Warschauer & Ware 2008). These points address, respectively, how literacy practices have changed, how politics and power shape these changes, and what the consequences are for literacy instruction and assessment in schools.

change: uncovering new literacies

Digital technologies have been portrayed as bringing about a 'fourth revolution in the means of production of knowledge' (Harnad 1991: 39), with the other three stemming from the development of language, writing, and print. Indeed, the changes in literacy practices occurring due to digital media use are undoubtedly the greatest since the development and diffusion of the printing press in Europe. And, in at least one sense, the current changes are even more impressive: whereas the impact of the printing press on literacy unfolded gradually over several hundred years (Eisenstein 1979), digital media has reshaped literacy within a matter of decades, at least within the developed countries and the major urban areas of other nations.

There is wide societal recognition of the importance of new technologies in daily life and learning. Yet the precise nature of digital literacies is difficult to discern for those who hold the reductionist view that literacy can only mean phonetic decoding of text from a page. The field of Literacy Studies holds a much broader view of literacy as ways of making meaning with diverse semiotic resources and is thus able to uncover 'invisible literacies' (Baynham 1995: 246). A key theoretical contribution toward making visible the new literacies of digital media use was made by the New London Group (1996), which brought together ten major literacy scholars from Australia, Great Britain, and the United States The group examined two important trends—(1) the increasing multiplicity and integration of diverse semiotic modes and (2) the growth in cross-language and cross-dialect interaction due to globalization—and situated these trends within broader changes of work, citizenship, and life in the post-Fordist economic era.

diverse semiotic modes

A member of the New London Group, Kress, has played a key role in further exploring diverse semiotic modes. He and his colleagues (Kress 2003, 1998, 1999; also see Kress, & van Leeuwen 1996, 2001) have analyzed textbooks, newspapers, signs, clothing labels, and computer multimedia to examine the grammar of visual and multimodal design. Kress points out that while language and sound are governed by sequence and time, images are governed by space, display, and simultaneity. The development and combination of modes thus results in what he terms transformation (a reshaping of resources within a mode), transduction (the shift of semiotic material across modes) and synaesthesia (the qualitatively new forms of meaning which occur through transformation and transduction).

Kress's work on multimedia has been extended through the work of Hull and her colleagues, who have promoted and analyzed digital storytelling among urban youth and adults in California. Through their fine-grained analysis of a multimedia digital story composed in an after-school community technology project, Hull and Nelson (2005) demonstrate how the combining of image and text transcends rather than combines what is possible in each particular mode. In such layering, images can work to repurpose the words they accompany, modes become progressively imbued with the associative meanings of each other, and iconic and indexical images are rendered into symbols.

Other features of digital storytelling noted in this and a follow-up study by Nelson (2006) of undergraduate second language writers include a resemiotization (repurposing semiotic relationships) through repetition (with the repeated image serving to punctuate a story or take on more complex meanings as a story evolves), an awareness of language topology (i.e. the relationship between what written language says and what it looks like), and an amplification of authorship (with digital storytellers finding a deeper meaning of what they want to say through the process of adding and combining modes). As seen in case studies conducted by Hull and Katz (2006), this process of crafting digital stories helps enable urban youth to explore and craft new forms of identity and agency.

cross-language interaction

The nature of cross-language interaction and its relationship to identity has long been an important topic in new Literacy Studies (see, e.g., Blommaert 1992; Rampton 1995). Lam illuminates this topic in the digital era by investigating the cultural and linguistic hybridity that emerge when new forms of online interaction are combined with emigration, diaspora, and global communication. In one study, she highlighted how a Chinese immigrant to the United States combined Japanese *kanji*, emoticons, and songs with the global English of adolescent pop culture in his Website and online chats about a Japanese pop star (Lam 2000). As with the digital storytellers mentioned above, this immigrant youth was able to find outlets of expression denied to him in school. A second study by Lam (2005) explored second language interaction in a bilingual chat room through the experiences of two teenage female immigrants from China in the United States The girls used a mixed code of English and Romanized Cantonese, switching back and forth from one or the other depending on interlocutor and topic of conversation. In many contexts, they preferred English, but added Chinese particles to English terms to target interlocutors who are part of their social network, signal their orientation to them, and negotiate relationships with each other. Other times, they assembled idiomatic expressions of English words and Romanized Chinese to create humor or to reflect how social relations are conducted in the Cantonese-speaking culture. All of these forms of interaction allowed the immigrant youth more possibilities to navigate between their native language and culture and those of their adopted home.

My own research on online communication in Egypt reinforces Lam's findings and conclusions. Two colleagues and I examined the online language use of a group of young Egyptian professionals in Cairo, almost all of whom had been educated partly in Arabic and partly in English (Warschauer et al. 2002). The study found that, among this group, English was used overwhelmingly in Web browsing and in formal e-mail communication, but that a Romanized version of Egyptian Arabic was used extensively in informal e-mail messages and online chats, albeit with much code-switching to English. The extensive use of English among this group reflected their elite background, their use of technology for professional purposes in a globalized economy, and the still undeveloped nature of text editors, e-mail clients, and other text software capable of handling Arabic script at the time of the study. Nevertheless, their use of Egyptian Arabic whenever possible allowed them, as in the case of the Chinese immigrants above, to express hybrid forms of communication and identity. As Lam (2006) explains in a recent theoretical overview, these new blended forms of online communication allow those who cross physical and societal boundaries to experience *transculturation* rather than *acculturation*.

new forms of social interaction

In the dozen years since the New London Group's paper was first published, the architecture of the Internet has changed substantially. Today's *Web 2.0* (see, e.g., O'Reilly 2007) allows greatly enhanced forms of interaction through blogs, wikis, social network sites, and multiplayer online games, thus reshaping traditional notions of what constitutes authorship, audience, or textual artifact (see Warschauer & Grimes 2007).

Gee and his colleagues have turned their attention to literacy practices that emerge in these new online forms. Gee's major focus has been on videogames; his influential book on the topic (2003) outlined 36 learning principles that he views as embedded in games that are often missing in schools. A particularly valuable contribution is Gee's tripartite analysis of identity; with game-players having *virtual* identities (i.e. those of their characters in a virtual world); *real-world* identities (i.e. their actual self playing a computer game); and *projective* identities. The latter refers to both how learners project their own values and desires onto the virtual character and also how they see the virtual character as their own project in the making. In a follow-up book, Gee (2004) ties the concept of identity in game-playing to a broader concept of identity in today's network society, as 'shape-shifting portfolio people ... manage their own risky trajectories through building up a variety of skills, experiences, and achievements in terms of which they can define themselves as successful now and worthy of more success later' (p. 105).

Two of Gee's former students have carried out ethnographic research on online literacy practices. Steinkuehler (2007) examined the literacy practices of participants in a massively multiplayer game called *Lineage*, both within the game's virtual world (e.g. social interaction, in-game letters, and orally delivered narratives) and beyond (e.g. asynchronous discussion on online game forums, the creation of fansites and fanfiction). She argues that youth in this and other massively multiplayer games are satisfying much of what we say we want children to be doing in schools, as expressed, for example in standards published by professional organizations. She concludes that through reading, writing, and interacting in new online spaces, youth can transform the corporate-owned culture into raw materials for telling their own stories and forging their own communities.

Black, another former student of Gee, examined (2008) the literacy practices of English-language learners on Fanfiction.net, where thousands of people around the world contribute original works of fiction related to their favorite books, cartoons, comics, games, movie shows, animation, or other media. Black focuses in particular on the experiences of Nanako, a native speaker of Chinese and immigrant to Canada. At the time of Black's research, the 16-year-old Nanako had published more than 50 fanfiction texts on the site that had received more than 6000 reviews from other readers. Black demonstrates how Nanako exploited the social, textual, and technological elements of the networked community, and in particular, the vast feedback she received to scaffold and promote her literacy development and identity and self-confidence as a writer.

In reviewing the above examples, as well as other recently published research (see, for example, collections edited by Coiro et al. 2008 and by Knobel & Lankshear 2007, and a journal issue edited by Snyder & Prinsloo 2007), we can summarize some of the strengths of the literacies studies perspective in illuminating the nature of digital literacy. First, Literacy Studies closely attends to meaning-making, rather than just text-decoding. This orientation helps Literacy Studies scholars to interpret new forms of meaning-making with diverse semiotic resources. Second, the understanding of literacy as a social process aids Literacy Studies scholars in uncovering the kinds of literacy practices that take place through complex new forms of networked communication. Third, Literacy Studies focuses on the kinds of under-recognized literacy practices that occur in home, community, and other non-school settings; this perspective enables Literacy Studies scholars to both value and understand literacy practices that are often ignored or derided in society at large, such as those carried out while playing online games.

Though there is much more terrain to explore in understanding digital literacy practices, the research to date, as reviewed above, provides a strong foundation for extending our understanding in the above-mentioned domains (e.g. digital storytelling, fanfiction, online games) and others as well (blogging, wikis, social network sites).

power: an ideological model of digital literacy

New digital literacies develop not in a vacuum but in the midst of broader social, political, and economic contexts. At the widest level, advanced capitalist countries are in the midst of a transition from industrial to postindustrial capitalism, which entails emphasis on the harnessing of information and knowledge rather than infusions of more capital and labor; a shift from material production to information-processing; a change from vertically integrated mass production to flexible and customized production by horizontal networks; and increasingly globalized organization of capital, production, management, labor, and markets (Castells 1996). This transformation means that the ability to use and adapt information technology has become 'the critical factor in generating and accessing wealth, power, and knowledge in our time' (Castells 1998).

Any examination of digital literacy needs to be understood in this context. As Street (1993) wrote in an introduction to the field of new Literacy Studies, 'Literacy practices are aspects not only of 'culture' but also of power structures' (p. 7), involving 'fundamental aspects of epistemology, power, and politics' (p. 9). The acquisition of literacy thus involves 'challenges to dominant discourses, shifts in what constitutes the agenda of proper literacy, and struggles for power and position' (p. 9). Street critiques what he refers to as the *autonomous model* of literacy, which suggests literacy functions outside of political contexts. Instead, he puts forth an *ideological model*, which emphasizes the need to carefully understand how issues of context and power shape the practice and meaning of literacy.

Almost all of the researchers cited above have attempted to challenge dominant discourses by examining, and indeed promoting, shifts in what constitutes the agenda of proper literacy. However, there is much more to accomplish in understanding how fundamental aspects of power influence the development and practice of digital literacies. For example, much of digital literacy research to date has been carried out among those who are either relatively privileged or demonstratively successful with new digital media. Gee's work on videogames is based to a considerable extent on his analysis of his own game-playing and that of his son; one wonders whether those who start out with lesser amounts of cultural, social, and human capital can exploit the learning potential of games in the same way. Lam's and Black's work is based on Chinese immigrants to North America, rather than on the larger and more marginalized Latino immigrant community. Hull's work is based in a predominately low-income African-American community and carefully documents the intersection of new media use with community members' sociopolitical reality; at the same time, it focuses on those who have taken the initiative to show up at a community learning center, persist in activities there, and successfully master a new digital genre.

Thus, in each of these studies, the researchers have taken as a unit of analysis those who have been successful in the practice of new digital literacies. In each particular case the motivation for that is well founded and the resulting scholarship is of great value to our field. Yet, taken as a whole, this body of research may present a less than complete picture of digital literacy practices today. For example, it is interesting to contrast their findings to those of a pair of sociologists who investigated *typical* digital literacy practices of diverse participants. Attewell and Winston (2003) spent several months observing and interviewing two groups of computer users at home and school. The first group consisted of African-American and Latino children aged 11 to 14 who attended public middle school; most came from poor and working-class families and all scored below grade level in reading. The second group consisted of school children from more affluent families who attended private schools.

The wealthy group studied by Attewell and Winston carried out empowering forms of communication. For example, a white, fourth-grade private school student named Zeke was a 'political junky at ten years old' (p. 124). He spent his online time reading up on the presidential inauguration, downloading video clips of politicians, and reading candidates speeches. To assist his candidacy for class president—an office that was not sanctioned officially by the teachers at his school—Zeke found a free website that allowed visitors to construct quizzes and modified it to develop an online voting system. With the cooperation of his rival for office, he told each child in his class to visit the Web page for the voting system both to read the campaign speeches that he and his opponent posted and eventually to vote.

However, the low socio-economic status group for the most part engaged in far-different activities. Typical is Kadesha, a 13-year-old African-American girl. Kadesha and her friends spent much of their online type checking out rappers and wrestlers (who they referred to as their 'husbands'), downloading their pictures as screensavers, and pasting images into reports (p. 117). They also went cyber-window shopping together, checking out everything from hot new sneakers to skateboards to Barbie dolls. The authors explained how Kadesha's ability to exploit the Internet was greatly restricted by her limited reading and writing skills:

> As image after image flashes by ... it becomes noticeable how rarely, how lightly, Kadesha settles on printed text. Like many of her friends, she reads far below grade level. So she energetically pursues images and sounds on the Web, but foregoes even news of her love interest if that requires her to read. (p. 117)

The challenge of going online with limited literacy skills followed Kadesha to school. For example, one of Kadesha's teachers brought some young professionals to class to discuss what it takes to pursue a career. The students then went online for further information. Kadesha was interested in running a bakery, but abandoned her search after continually misspelling the word bakery in the search engine and coming up with nothing. Other classmates had similar problems with this and similar online tasks; in most cases, they either didn't know how to spell the terms to be searched for or lacked the background knowledge required to make sense of search results.

It may well be the case that Attewell and Winston's sociological framework overlooked some of the particular 'funds of knowledge' (Moll et al. 2005: 72) that Kadesha and her friends brought to the task of digital literacy. Nevertheless, their account of Kadesha's limited repertoire of online abilities rings true, and it reminds one of Castells' (1996) warning of a digital future divided between the *interacting* (i.e. those with the skills and capital to shape the multimedia content of the future) and the *interacted* (i.e. those who are recipients of multimedia content created by others).

The point is not that Kadesha and her friends are automatically destined to lives of digital impoverishment. To assert that would be a simplistic determinism on a par with an equally simplistic view that computer access alone will overcome their challenges. Rather, we need to carefully analyze the constellation of conditions that contribute to or constrain the development and practice of digital literacies in particular contexts. We need to develop an ideological model of digital literacy.

I have tried to contribute to this effort. In *Electronic Literacies* (Warschauer 1999), I examined the use of new technologies for language and literacy instruction in four higher education contexts in Hawai'i. The study indicated how the social context of instruction—including the background and socio-economic status of the students, the mission of the individual college and program in serving those students, and the pedagogical beliefs and expectations of the teachers involved (which tended to reflect the broader mission)—all shaped the kinds of digital literacy that were introduced in the classroom. Working class and immigrant students in a community college English course were taught vocational skills, such as how to design brochures. Future missionaries from the Pacific Islands in an undergraduate ESL class at a fundamentalist Christian college were taught strict rules of grammar use and composition, just as they were being taught the strict scripture of the Church. International students from East Asia in a graduate program at a public research university used technology to apprentice into academic discourse, reflecting the university's scholarly approach for graduate education. Native Hawaiian students in a Hawaiian language class at the same public university used technology to express the values of their community and culture, reflecting the spirit of collective resistance that gave birth to the Hawaiian language program and the broader language revitalization movement in Hawai'i. In none of these cases were students passive recipients—they too played a role in influencing the learning environment—but again in ways that reflected broader issues of politics and power. I concluded the book by pointing out that

> [f]or students of diverse cultural, linguistic, and class backgrounds to have a voice, they need more than an Internet account. Rather, they need knowledge of the languages and discourses of power, and opportunities to critically reflect on whether, when, and how to use them, as well as opportunities to develop and use their own dialects and languages as they wish. They need access to and mastery of a variety of media, and understanding of the ways that rhetorical structure and media interact. And they need chances to read, write, and think about issues of cultural and social relevance for their lives, as they work together with others near and far to collaboratively tackle authentic complex problems. (p. 174)

In a follow-up book, *Technology and Social Inclusion* (Warschauer 2003), I examined the issue of a so-called digital divide as well as efforts around the world to ameliorate it, for example, through the development of community technology programs. Through this I developed a model of what kinds of resources are required to help promote meaningful access to and use of technology, including physical resources (e.g. computers and Internet access), digital resources (e.g. online content and tools in multiple languages and appropriate to the needs of diverse users); human resources (e.g. knowledge and skills developed through instruction emphasizing critical inquiry and situated practice); and social resources (e.g. enhanced social capital developed through in-person, online, and institutional support).

My work and that of Attewell and Winston are not inconsistent with some of the more optimistic research discussed earlier in this chapter. Kadesha's frustrations with new technology (Attewell & Winston 2003) do not contradict Nanako's successes with it (Black 2008). Problematic approaches to use of new media in a college (Warschauer 1999) do not contradict more promising approaches to use of new media in community centers (e.g. Hull 1997). However, these investigations of typical practices at home or school settings shed light on a very different reality than those cited earlier of what may be less common practices.

A challenge, then, for digital literacy scholars is how to balance these two approaches; that is, to explore the shifts in what constitutes proper literacy without downplaying the dynamics of race, class, language, and gender that constrain these shifts. This balance may be easier to achieve if one starts by examining practices common in particular communities (rather than practices by exemplary members of communities), as seen, for example, in Heath's (1983) comparative study of literacy practices in two neighboring communities in the southeast United States. Replicating Heath's approach in online research would by necessity consider virtual rather than geographic communities; nevertheless, in this realm, comparative work is also possible and would be valuable. For example, a doctoral candidate in Information Management and Systems has begun to explore how U.S. class divisions mediate youth participation in Facebook vis-à-vis MySpace (Boyd 2007). Literacy Studies scholars would have much to add to this kind of comparative research that situates online literacy practices within broader societal dynamics of race, class, and language.

As a case in point, let us consider a research agenda for an important domain that has not yet been seriously investigated by Literacy Studies researchers: the blogosphere. By mid-2007, the search engine

Technorati was tracking some 85 million blogs around the world, making blogging one of the fastest growing formats for personal writing and publishing the world has ever seen (Warschauer & Grimes 2007). A change-oriented research agenda on blogging would focus on what is new and different about this form of communication (see discussion in Lankshear & Knobel 2006). One could imagine an ethnography of blogging that would investigate the diverse semiotic resources that bloggers deploy to get their message across (e.g. postings, comments, titles, signatures, links, images, video, typography), the types of interaction that occur on well-trafficked blogs and the ways that bloggers use feedback to sharpen their writing, and the types of identity transformation that people go through as they share their voices and explore new forms of themselves in online publishing. Such a study, or collection of studies, would have value.

A research agenda on blogging that more explicitly integrated issues of power though might look different. Racial, class, gender, and linguistic dynamics within the blogosphere could be actively explored by examining, for example, differences between social participation in one popular type of blog (e.g. personal journals) vs. another (e.g. advocacy blogs). Or a particularly influential advocacy blog could be examined to see what kinds of texts or participants it privileges and what kinds are held on the margins. Or different kinds of political blogs—for example, those representing leftist vs. rightist views—could be explored to see whether they feature different types of texts or practices. Or the ways that English-language learners struggle to make their voices heard could be analyzed, either within one part of the blogosphere or comparatively in different parts. I believe that such an approach, actively incorporating issues of power as well as change, would help develop a more sophisticated understanding of how diverse individuals and groups exploit the resources of blogging in today's world.

learning: digital literacies in the classroom

A third framework for understanding technology's relationship to literacy is that of *learning*. In other words, how does the use of new media help students acquire competencies in reading, writing, and digital literacies as well as mastery of academic content?

Many of the Literacy Studies researchers cited above place particular importance on learning. The original conceptual piece by the New London Group (1996) put forth a specific pedagogical model based on design and redesign of diverse resources for meaning, incorporating situated practice, overt instruction, and critical framing. Much of the rest of the work combines descriptions of advanced types of learning with use of new media *outside* of school with laments about more restricted forms of media use *inside* of school (Black 2008; Gee 2003, 2004; Hull & Katz 2006; Hull & Nelson 2005; Lam 2003, 2005, 2006; Steinkuehler 2007; in a similar vein, see 2006; Green & Bigum 1993; Luke 2003; Seiter 2004; Vasquez & Duran 1999).

Commendably, these researchers not only *examine* literacy practices but also *advocate* for improved literacy instruction in schools, and their suggestions along these lines are valuable. However, if this goal is to be achieved—or, more specifically, if Literacy Studies researchers are to maximize their contribution toward achieving this goal—it is important to overcome two shortcomings in digital literacies research. First, while much of this research critiques schooling, relatively little of it actually takes place within schools. This is perhaps understandable, as researchers generally have easier access to abundant digital literacy sources in out-of-school environments. It is unfortunate, though, as it renders the critique of schooling as less comprehensive and nuanced than it could otherwise be.

Exceptions to this include, among others, the work of Lankshear, Snyder, and Green in Australia (e.g. 2000) and some of my work in the United States (e.g. Warschauer 2000; Warschauer et al. 2004). These case studies of technology integration and use in diverse schools reveal a number of common issues across Australian and U.S. contexts, including a tendency to emphasize technology use for its own sake, differential instruction with technology in high- vs. low-SES schools, and difficulty in integrating technology due to inflexible curricula or inadequate support structures. In contrast, my latter study in ten U.S. schools with one-to-one laptop programs found more promising results, including a more seamless integration of technology in instruction, a greater emphasis on critical inquiry, and expanded opportunities for learner-centered project work incorporating diverse modalities (Warschauer 2006). These laptop schools may not represent the norm, as school laptop programs have generally taken hold in districts with reform-oriented administrators. But it is precisely that type of nuanced understanding (e.g. of where and under what circumstances reform is more likely to occur) that is often missing in Literacy Studies discussion of technology use in schools. Further research is needed in schools, and especially studies that consider students as the primary unit of analysis, to complement the above-cited studies that primarily analyze classrooms and teachers.

Second, the field of Literacy Studies has distanced itself from any attempts at measuring the outcomes of literacy instruction. Again, this is understandable, given the emphasis of our field on literacy as a social process that is understood through its texts and practices rather than as a unitary skill that is measured by examination. But whatever is not measured in schools is not taught (see, e.g., Hillocks 2002), and if we are displeased by the current forms of measurement, we should seize the opportunity to promote new ones. This is especially the case in today's climate, when the combination of an excessively narrow approach to literacy instruction and assessment in the United States and elsewhere stands in such clear contradiction to the broad requirements of life and work in post-industrial society.

Many groups—some with more corporatist motives and some with more humanitarian ones—are thus pushing for a revised curriculum based on *21st century learning skills* (see, e.g., Eisen 2003; Jenkins 2006; North Central Regional Educational Laboratory & the Metiri Group 2003; Partnership for 21st Century Skills 2004). There is broad consensus among these groups on what kind of new skills are needed, with most including worthwhile elements similar to those put forth by the International Society for Technology in Education: creativity and innovation; communication and collaboration; research and information fluency; critical thinking, problem-solving, and decision-making, and technology operations and concepts (NETS Project & Brooks-Young 2007). But no consensus exists on how progress toward mastery of skills in these areas can be measured. The logical approach is through some sort of portfolio or performance-based assessment (see, e.g., Darling-Hammond & Ancess 1994), but recognizing that still leaves immense challenges in designing and implementing systems that can reliably assess the products or performance of millions of learners in diverse contexts.

Work on alternative forms of assessment would represent a break with tradition for the field of Literacy Studies, which has long critiqued the dominant role of school-based forms of literacy and championed more marginalized forms (see, e.g., Baynham 1995). Developing new forms of school-based assessment could thus be seen as furthering the dominance of school-sanctioned literacies. In fact, though, it would allow Literacy Studies scholars to have a voice in redefining school-based literacy and to thus help ensure that currently marginalized literacy practices become less so in the future.

Finally, it is important to note how internationalized the intersection of technology, literacy, and educational reform is becoming. The

U.S. government and other donors are making investments in educational technology in developing countries, not always based on sound understanding of local educational needs (see, e.g., Warschauer 2004). Even when such technology-based reform efforts are only inspired rather than funded from abroad, they still run the risk of running up against local educational norms (see, e.g., Fang & Warschauer 2004). This is because the significance of any technology is highly bound to particular geographic locations (Prinsloo 2005). Efforts to export educational technology to the developing world are bound to expand in the future, especially with the aggressively marketed *One Laptop Per Child* (2007) program that seeks to provide sub-$200 computers to countries in Africa, Latin America, and Asia. If and when hundreds of thousands of low-cost laptops enter schools in developing countries—where, as noted by Prinsloo (2005), relatively few youth enjoy rich experiences with technology outside of school—a host of new research questions related to digital literacy practices and outcomes will be thrust on the agenda.

conclusion

There is a long history of faith in technology as a silver bullet. Indeed, the belief that literacy (itself a technology) can automatically solve problems divorced from social context is the essence of the autonomous model of literacy that our field critiques. When put into practice, such views often contribute to a 'Sesame Street effect' (Attewell & Battle 1999), as initiatives targeted to help low-SES youth end up instead benefiting high-SES youth, due to the latter's greater amount of financial, social, and cultural capital that enables them to exploit such initiatives for their own development.

To counter such beliefs and practices, we need an ideological model of digital literacy. And we have taken important steps toward constructing that model. The historical traditions of Literacy Studies, which include an attention to diverse semiotic resources, a focus on social interaction, and a commitment to exploring non-dominant discourses, have led to groundbreaking research on the invisible forms of literacy that occur in digital domains. But research methodologies that focus on the practices of high-performing individuals may tend to overemphasize the transformative potential of new media. Increased research based on typical practice in diverse communities is required to achieve a critical balance.

Moving from theory to praxis, the confluence of economic, social, and technological changes means that educational systems in the United States and many other countries are ripe for reform, and a key element of that reform is figuring out how to better evaluate literacy practices and outcomes in technology-rich classrooms. Literacy Studies scholars have a valuable role to play here too, first by situating more of their digital literacies research inside of schools, and second by contributing their expertise to developing more authentic forms of assessment.

Vast domains of online literacy have only begun to be studied. The blogosphere, wikisphere, and huge social network sites are all fruitful terrain for future dissertations in Literacy Studies. And before those dissertations are completed, new forms of online communication will likely have appeared. The field of Literacy Studies has earned its place in the forefront of research on digital meaning-making. By firmly placing our research in the context of power and politics, both inside and outside the classroom, we can help ensure that the full potential of digital literacy is more broadly achieved.

references

Attewell, P. and J. Battle (1999) Home Computers and School Performance. *The Information Society*, 15(1), 1–10.

Attewell, P. and H. Winston (2003) Children of the digital divide. In P. Attewell and N. M. Seel (eds), *Disadvantaged Teens and Computer Technologies*. Münster, Germany: Waxmann, 117–36.

Baynham, M. (1995) *Literacy Practices: Investigating Literacy in Social Contexts*. London: Longman.

Black, R. W. (2008) *Adolescents and Online Fan Fiction*. New York: Peter Lang.

Blommaert, J. (1992) Codeswitching and the exclusivity of social identities: some data from campus Kiswahili. In C. Eastman (ed.), *Codeswitching*. Clevedon: Multilingual Matters, 124–42.

Boyd, D. (2007) Viewing American Class Divisions through Facebook and Myspace [Apophenia Blog Essay]. Retrieved 17 July 2007 from http://www.danah.org/papers/essays/ClassDivisions.html

Castells, M. (1996) *The Rise of the Network Society*. Malden, MA: Blackwell.

Castells, M. (1998) *End of Millennium*. Malden, MA: Blackwell.

Coiro, J., M. Knobel, C. Lankshear and D. J. Leu (eds) (2008) *Handbook of Research on New Literacies*. New York: Lawrence Erlbaum.

Darling-Hammond, L. and J. Ancess (1994) *Graduation by Portfolio at Central Park East Secondary School*. National Center for Restructuring Education, Schools, and Teaching, Teachers College, Columbia University: New York.

Eisen, P. (2003) Skills for a 21st century workforce: can we meet the challenge. In M. A. Fox (ed.), *Pan-Organizational Summit on the U.S. Science and Engineering*

Workforce: Meeting Summary. Washington, DC: National Academies Press, 134–47.

Eisenstein, E. L. (1979) *The Printing Press as an Agent of Change: Communications and Cultural Transformations in Early-Modern Europe.* Cambridge: Cambridge University Press.

Fang, X. and M. Warschauer (2004) Technology and Curricular Reform in China: A Case Study. *Tesol Quarterly, 38*(2), 301–23.

Gee, J. P. (2003) *What Video Games Have to Teach Us about Learning and Literacy.* New York: Palgrave Macmillan.

Gee, J. P. (2004) *Situated Language and Learning: A Critique of Traditional Schooling.* Routledge: New York.

Green, B. and C. Bigum (1993) Aliens in the Classroom. *Australian Journal of Education, 37*(2), 119–41.

Harnad, S. (1991) Post-Gutenberg Galaxy: The Fourth Revolution in the Means of Production and Knowledge. *Public-Access Computer Systems Review, 2*(1), 39–53.

Heath, S. B. (1983) *Ways with Words: Language, Life, and Work in Communities and Classrooms.* Cambridge: Cambridge University Press.

Hillocks, G., Jr. (2002) *The Testing Trap: How State Writing Assessments Control Learning.* New York: Teachers College Press.

Hull, G. A. (1997) *Changing Work, Changing Workers: Critical Perspectives on Language, Literacy, and Skills.* Albany: State University of New York Press.

Hull, G. A. and M.-L. Katz (2006) Crafting an Agentive Self: Case Studies on Digital Storytelling. *Research in the Teaching of English, 41*(1), 43–81.

Hull, G. A. and M. E. Nelson (2005) Locating the Semiotic Power of Multimodality. *Written Communication, 22*(2), 224–61.

Jenkins, H. (2006) Confronting the challenges of participatory culture: Media education for the 21st century. Retrieved 12 March 2007 from http://preview. tinyurl.com/ydvcvo.

Knobel, M. and C. Lankshear (eds) (2007) *A New Literacies Sampler.* New York: Peter Lang.

Kress, G. (1998) Visual and verbal modes of representation in electronically mediated communication: The potentials of new forms of text. In I. Snyder (ed.), *Page to Screen: Taking Literacy into the Electronic Era.* London: Routledge, 53–79.

Kress, G. (1999) 'English' at the crossroads: rethinking curricula of communication in the context of the turn to the visual. In G. E. Hawisher and C. Selfe (eds), *Passions, Pedagogies, and 21st Century Technologies.* Logan, Utah: Utah State University Press, 66–88.

Kress, G. (2003) *Literacy in the New Media Age.* London: Routledge.

Kress, G. and van T. Leeuwen (1996) *Reading Images: The Grammar of Visual Design.* London: Routledge.

Kress, G. and van T. Leeuwen (2001) *Multimodal Discourse: The Modes and Media of Contemporary Communication.* London: Arnold.

Lam, E. (2000) Second Language Literacy and the Design of the Self: A Case Study of a Teenager Writing on the Internet. *Tesol Quarterly, 34,* 457–82.

Lam, W. S. E. (2003) 'Second language literacy and identify formation on the Internet'. Unpublished doctoral dissertation, University of California, Berkeley.

Lam, W. S. E. (2005) Second Language Socialization in a Bilingual Chat Room. *Language Learning and Technology*, *8*(3), 44–65.

Lam, W. S. E. (2006) Re-Envisioning Language Literacy and the Immigrant Subject in New Mediascapes. *Pedagogies*, 1(3), 171–95.

Lankshear, C. and M. Knobel (2006) 'Blogging as participation: The active sociality of a new literacy', paper presented at the American Educational Research Association, San Francisco, April. Retrieved 10 June 2007 from http://www.geocities.com/c.lankshear/bloggingparticipation.pdf

Lankshear, C., I. Snyder and B. Green (2000) *Teachers and Technoliteracy: Managing Literacy, Technology, and Learning in Schools*. Sydney: Allen and Unwin.

Luke, C. (2003) Pedagogy, Connectivity, Multimodallity, and Interdisciplinarity. *Reading Research Quarterly*, *38*(3), 297–314.

Moll, L., C. Amanti, D. Neff and N. Gonzáles (2005) Funds of knowledge for teaching: using a qualitative approach to connect homes and classrooms. In N. Gonzales, L. C. Moll and C. Amanti (eds), *Funds of Knowledge: Theorizing Practices in Households, Communities, and Classrooms*. Mahwah: Lawrence Erlbaum Associates, 71–87.

Nelson, M. E. (2006) Mode, Meaning, and Synaesthesia in Multimedia L2 Writing. *Language Learning and Technology*, *10*(2), 56–76.

NETS Project and S. Brooks-Young (2007) *National Educational Standards for Students*, second edition. Eugene, OR: International Society for Technology in Education.

New London Group (1996) A Pedagogy of Multiliteracies: Designing Social Futures. *Harvard Educational Review*, 66(1), 60–92.

North Central Regional Educational Laboratory and the Metiri Group (2003) *enGauge 21st Century Skills: Literacy in the Digital Age*. Naperville, IL and Los Angeles: Authors.

O'Reilly, T. (2007) What is Web 2.0? Retrieved 5 June 2007 from http://www.oreillynet.com/pub/a/oreilly/tim/news/2005/09/30/what-is-web-20.html

One Laptop Per Child (2007) One Laptop Per Child (OLPC), a $100 laptop for the world's children's education. Retrieved 18 July 2007 from http://www.laptop.org/

Partnership for 21st Century Skills (2004) *Learning for the 21st Century: A Report and Mile Guide for 21st Century Skills*. Washington: Author.

Prinsloo, M. (2005) The New Literacies as Placed Resources. *Perspectives in Education*, *23*(4), 87–98.

Rampton, B. (1995) *Crossing: Language and Ethnicity among Adolescents*. London: Longman.

Seiter, E. (2004) Children Reporting Online: The Cultural Politics of the Computer Lab. *Television and New Media*, *5*(2), 87–107.

Snyder, I. and M. Prinsloo (eds) (2007) *Language and Education* (Special issue), 21(3).

Steinkuehler, C. (2007) Massively Multiplayer Online Gaming as a Constellation of Literacy Practices. *E-Learning*, *4*(3), 297–318.

Street, B. (1993) Introduction: the new Literacy Studies. In B. V. Street (ed.), *Cross-Cultural Approaches to Literacy*. Cambridge: Cambridge University Press, 1–21.

Vasquez, O. A. and R. Duran (1999) La clase Mágica and Club Proteo: multiple literacies in community institutions. In M. A. Gallego and S. Hollingsworth (eds), *What Counts as Literacy: Challenging the School Standard*. New York: Teachers College Press, 173–89.

Warschauer, M. (1999) *Electronic Literacies: Language, Culture, and Power in Online Education*. Mahwah, NJ: Lawrence Erlbaum Associates.

Warschauer, M. (2000) Technology and School Reform: A View from Both Sides of the Track. *Education Policy Analysis Archives*, 8 (4). Retrieved 28 July 2009 from http://epaa.asu.edu/epaa/v8n4.html

Warschauer, M. (2003) *Technology and Social Inclusion: Rethinking the Digital Divide*. Cambridge: MIT Press.

Warschauer, M. (2004) The Rhetoric and Reality of Aid: Promoting Educational Technology in Egypt. *Globalisation, Societies, and Education*, 2(3), 377–90.

Warschauer, M. (2006) *Laptops and Literacy: Learning in the Wireless Classroom*. New York: Teachers College Press.

Warschauer, M. and D. Grimes (2007) Audience, Authorship, and Artifact: The Emergent Semiotics of Web 2.0. *Annual Review of Applied Linguistics*, 27, 1–23.

Warschauer, M., G. R. El Said and A. Zohry (2002) Language Choice Online: Globalization and identity in Egypt. *Journal of Computer Mediated Communication*, 7(4). Retrieved 28 July 2009 from http://jcmc.indiana.edu/vol7/issue4/warschauer.html

Warschauer, M., M. Knobel and L. A. Stone (2004) Technology and Equity in Schooling: Deconstructing the Digital Divide. *Educational Policy*, 18(4), 562–88.

Warschauer, M. and P. Ware (2008) Learning, change, and power: competing frameworks of technology and literacy. In J. Leu, J. Donald, C. Lankshear, M. Knobel and J. Coiro (eds), *Handbook of Research on New Literacies*. New York: Lawrence Erlbaum Associates, 215–40.

7
shuffling towards the future: the enduring dominance of book culture in literacy education

ilana snyder

Within the broad field of Literacy Studies, some literacy researchers have had a particular interest in the connections between literate practice and the use of digital technologies, so much so, that by the late 1980s, literacy and technology studies had emerged as a discrete area of research endeavour. Since the early 1990s, the area has grown and diversified to become the multi-faceted field that it is today with research activity evident in many sites around the world.

Although the terminology predominant in the early work was different – researchers talked about computers and writing rather than technology and literacy – serious research in this area began when desktop computers made their way into schools. Researchers have challenged conventional accounts of literacy with their investigations of the new kinds of textual formations and practices associated with the use of computer and digital technologies. They have also examined the different settings in which new media are used – not only the classroom but also the workplace and other locations of everyday life.

Over three decades, researchers in literacy and technology studies have made an important contribution to our understanding of the changes to literacy practices associated with the use of new media. They have also written about the pedagogical rethinking required to integrate technology into curriculum and classroom practice effectively. Yet despite the richness of the research insights and understandings, literacy classrooms in schools remain overwhelmingly print-oriented in their approach to the teaching and learning of reading and writing. Further, even when digital technologies are used in literacy education, it is most often in traditional, print-oriented ways. As well as thinking about a way forward, my aim here is to consider some possible explanations for this phenomenon beyond those which highlight the well-rehearsed disjunction between research and practice.

My discussion begins with the trajectory of the research since its early days through to the present. Although necessarily brief, the overview presented here aims to provide a sense of the knowledge base in this area of research inquiry – what we already know about the changes to literacy practices associated with the use of new media and the directions that researchers are currently pursuing. The discussion then moves on to a consideration of why a print-oriented approach to literacy education remains dominant in schools. Taking literacy education in Australia as an example, one part of the explanation relates to literacy teachers' traditional reticence with technology. Another part relates to an enduring cultural orientation to the world of print and print literacy, which is sustained and bolstered in public discourse about books and digital technologies, particularly as represented in the Australian press. Readers are invited to consider the extent to which the case of Australia is similar to theirs and thus likely or not to be salutary.

The chapter concludes with the challenges facing researchers and practitioners. As it is no longer possible to continue with the assumption that students live predominantly in a world of print, there are important questions for curriculum development. If young people are to thrive in their post-school work and lives, school literacy curricula need to focus on enhancing both their print and digital literacy capabilities.

In addition to these educational challenges is a political one: literacy teachers and educators need to find ways to influence public discourse about these important literacy issues. If the literacy curriculum is ever to do more than shuffle towards the future, then participation in and contribution to the direction of the public debates over literacy issues are essential.

what researchers have found

All sorts of research-based claims have been made about how the use of digital technologies affects literacy learning and practices. The broad-brush stroke account that follows traces the research in the field of literacy and technology studies from its beginnings in the mid-1980s to the present. For readers wanting more detailed reports of the research, there are many available (e.g. Coiro et al. 2007; Snyder 2007a,b; Snyder & Bulfin 2007).

Intrinsic to the overview are a number of key constructs. The term 'computers' signifies the hardware and software central to the early research before the advent of the Internet. 'New media' denotes the diverse digital technologies that assume the centrality of the screen. The term 'digital literacy practices' represents culturally and socially shaped ways of using, producing and understanding information in multiple formats from a range of sources when it is presented via the electronic screens of digital technologies. Core digital literacy practices include Internet searching, hypertextual navigation, content evaluation and knowledge assembly.

the early research

The first studies were not in the tradition of the New Literacy Studies. Using mainly experimental or quasi-experimental methods, they investigated whether the use of computers improves literacy outcomes (e.g. Gould 1978). The findings were equivocal: some claimed that they improved writing quality, some that they made no difference, others that they made things worse. After three decades of this kind of quantitative research, there is still no commanding body of evidence demonstrating that students' sustained use of word processing, the Internet and other popular applications has any impact on academic achievement (cf. Snyder 2007b).

By the mid-1980s, researchers were taking account of the settings in which the computers were used, producing detailed qualitative descriptions of classroom teaching and learning (e.g. Dickinson 1986). There was a growing recognition that computers in classrooms were unlikely to negate the influence of social class on students' achievement (e.g. Hermann 1987). By the mid-1990s, the Internet and the Web had become sites for research. Informed by the understanding of literacy as a set of social practices, investigations focused on new literacy practices, identity, gender, class and access (e.g. Harraway 1992; Gerrard 1999). With an increasing affinity with a New Literacy Studies sensibility, researchers emphasized the need to teach students how to critically assess the reliability and value of the information they find on the Web by understanding its source as well as its textual and non-textual features such as images, links and interactivity (e.g. Burbules & Callister 2000; Lankshear, Snyder & Green 2000).

more recent studies

Since the late nineties, researchers have been identifying new text types, language practices, identity work and social formations as young people use mobile phones, text messaging, the Internet, instant messaging, online games, blogs, search engines, websites, email, digital video, music, imaging and more (Jones 1999; Warschauer 1999). Their digital literacy practices include word processing, hypertextual linking, participating in online discussion, social networking, using presentation software, creating webpages and assembling digital portfolios (Lankshear & Knobel 2003). Research examining the complex connections between school literacies and out-of-school literacies has provided insight for teachers about the experience and knowledge students bring to formal studies in school (e.g. Beavis, Nixon & Atkinson 2005).

Along similar lines, researchers have investigated the relationship between computer games and literacy learning (e.g. Gee 2003, 2005). Studies have demonstrated that games require complex literacies and teach a degree of multimodal, visual and linguistic sophistication, usually neglected in the literacy classroom. Research has also suggested the value such popular texts offer for consolidating and extending students' understanding of reading practices (e.g. Beavis 2002). Such studies have argued that working with computer games in literacy classrooms provides students with additional means of expression and communication to those dependent on print skills (e.g. Jenkins 2006).

Gender-based studies have revealed that computer games are one aspect of technology use where differences along gender lines are breaking down. Although most girls still do not choose technology subjects at school or in post-school study and continue to be under-represented in the IT industry, they are participating more in the culture of computer games. The assumption that the world of computer games is a male domain which emphasizes violence and sexual fantasy for boys no longer holds. The stereotypical masculine narratives of certain games are unappealing to girls, but there are now other options for them (Elliott 2007).

There is also a growing body of sophisticated computer game research which has explored both the cognitive and social implications of interactions with them. In the cognitive domain, increased decision-making speed, the enhancement of hand-eye coordination and the development of cognitive structures which operate in parallel rather than sequentially have implications for the knowledge and skills young people bring to classrooms (Carrington 2004). In the social and cultural domain, researchers have been giving attention to how games might be used in the pursuit of engaging effective learning experiences.

Researchers (e.g. Gee 2003, 2005; Jenkins 2006) have looked closely at the games environment and have argued that when children and young people play video games they experience a more powerful form of learning than when they are in the classroom. The secret is not just the extraordinary 3-D graphics but also the underlying architecture. Each level of a game pushes the user's limits, aiming to be just hard enough to be doable. However, educational games have not kept pace with the entertainment titles and so far have failed to achieve this potential.

Large-scale surveys represent another significant element of the literature (e.g. Livingstone 2002; Livingstone & Bober 2005; Snyder, North & Bulfin 2007). In these surveys, the research teams have examined the complex relationships between the media, childhood, the family and the home. Surveys have found that many young people live media-filled lives with access to an unprecedented amount of media in their homes. However, age, gender, race and class influence the amount of time young people spend using the media. Those with the poorest grades spend the most time playing video games. Television and listening to music remain important in their lives, but the Internet has surpassed television and now commands the most time. Although children and young people continue to read books, they spend less time than past generations. Some young people are concerned about their growing dependence on machines, the isolating nature of the Internet, and how technology threatens their privacy and ability to relate to others.

conclusions from the research

When considering the implications of the research findings for literacy teachers, researchers have emphasized the importance of understanding the children and young people who populate classrooms: what they do in their out-of-school lives, what captures their interest and what does not. Young people bring advanced, technology-related skills to classrooms which could be used productively for language and literacy learning. But researchers have also emphasized the great diversity in how families and young people engage with new technologies. Simply having access at home or at school does not guarantee students opportunities for literacy learning (e.g. Norris 2001; Snyder, Angus & Sutherland-Smith 2004).

Writing about the possibilities for creative changes to classrooms and schools when new technologies are used, researchers have argued that a knowledge of the history of new literacy practices is a prerequisite. Researchers have questioned the assumption that the more schools spend on technology, the better the outcomes. A similar view was once held in business and industry and, to a considerable extent, the computerization of car assembly plants increased efficiency, profits and competitiveness, making possible the dispersal of assembly work across continents. However, analyses have also demonstrated that there is not always a close association between spending on technology and increased productivity and profitability, especially it seems in the context of education (Cuban 2001).

Suggestions from the research literature for how to rethink, redefine and redesign language and literacy in the classroom to meet the needs of students in the twenty-first century include a common component: above all else, a literacy classroom for the future must involve the effective integration of print literacy and digital literacy. It should not be a choice between the world of the page and the world of the screen – literacy education needs to give attention to both. To achieve this important goal, a broader concept of literacy is required, the kind favoured by the field of Literacy Studies. Literacy practices are best understood within the context of the social, cultural, political, economic and historical practices to which they are integral. But despite the plethora of writing about the influences of digital media on literacy practices and discussions of their implications for teaching and learning, literacy education remains predominantly print-oriented.

teachers, technology and change

In the main, literacy teachers in Australia and, I daresay, further afield, have seen technology as antithetical to their concerns. Although this attitude is not shared by all, there has been a general mistrust of machines. So when desktop computers entered into education systems, touted as the new technology that would inevitably improve education, literacy teachers were reticent about exploring their potential use in the classroom. This restrained response continued through the 1980s, when computers were promoted as marvellous writing machines, tutors and drill masters. It persisted into the 1990s, when the Internet and the Web were hailed as making possible an approach to education in which students would be able to learn anything, anywhere, anytime. And it progressed into the 2000s, where the excitement has centred on the communication possibilities of Web 2.0, understood as social media such as MySpace, Facebook and Twitter. Interest in new media has slowly expanded and increasing numbers of literacy teachers, particularly the younger ones, are now using digital technologies in their classrooms, but that initial reticence persists.

As already suggested, much thought has been given in the research literature to how literacy teachers and educators might make effective use of the new technologies in their classrooms. However, the most commonly used applications in the literacy and English classroom are word processing for writing and the Internet to search for information, which is not to discount the value of both. By and large, literacy teachers at all levels of schooling have used the new technologies to continue what they have always done. Students use laptops as they would use paper notebooks. Teachers may post assignments on the Web, communicate with students by email and respond to their writing electronically, but the traditional approach of initiating a curriculum activity, setting homework and evaluating the students' work has been sustained.

My own research in Australian literacy classrooms over the past 20 years has confirmed these conclusions. In more than a dozen studies, I have examined how literacy teachers respond to policy initiatives that recommend the inclusion of computer technologies in their pedagogy and have observed that significant change in their classroom practices is infrequent (e.g. Lankshear & Snyder 2000; Snyder 1995, 1996a,b, 1999; Snyder, Angus & Sutherland-Smith 2002). These studies and many others have suggested that teachers and the institutions where they work are somewhat resistant to anything more radical than piecemeal change. The extensive research on teachers' classroom practices and their response to new ideas and ways of teaching indicate that teachers are somewhat conservative (e.g. Cuban 2001). This helps explain why literacy education remains book-oriented, with technology most often an add-on rather than integral to pedagogical practice. However, there are also the contextual and institutional realities about schools and schooling that make responding to new possibilities both difficult and unappealing. I return to these issues towards the end of the chapter.

Although teachers in some other disciplines have been more enthusiastic than literacy teachers about the promise of computers, a technological revolution in education has not happened. Despite the huge investment of governments in wiring schools, reducing the ratio of students to computers and ensuring that curriculum documents take account of new technologies at all levels of education, teaching and learning in Australian schools have not been transformed. By technologizing education, governments have aimed to make schools more efficient and productive, more connected to real life and to prepare young people for post-school employment. Without any real evidence to indicate that these goals have been achieved, governments must now be asking whether the investment in computers and other technologies has been worth the cost (Cuban 2001).

Yet no-one who attended a school in the 1950s and then visited one in 2007 could fail to notice that important changes have taken place. The point is not that schools and teachers cannot change as far as technology is concerned, but that classroom and teaching practices of the past continue due to historical legacies and a complex array of contextual factors. Incremental changes to education in response to new technologies have transpired but fundamental changes have been rare (Cuban 2001).

It seems that the provision of technology is insufficient to transform literacy education let alone equip students with the skills and agency they need to operate effectively in the post-school world of leisure, work and citizenship. Real change requires far more than simply giving schools more technological resources. The whole ecology of schooling would need to be rethought if transformation was the objective: changes in how schools are organized and funded, in how teachers are prepared and valued, and in how hardware and software are designed to meet the needs of teachers and students rather than the world of business. Without such major changes, only relatively minor shifts in classroom practice are likely to take place (Cuban 2001).

But the reality is that governments simply cannot face up to the enormity of the change required for schools to move to an infrastructure, curriculum and pedagogy that fully integrates new media. As a result, a substantive public debate over the implications the use of new media might have for 'an aging, creaky, industrial, print-based schooling infrastructure' (Luke & Luke 2001: 36) has been avoided. Rather than discussing how literacy education might change, much of the public discourse has been backward-looking, littered with nostalgic references to the good old days when things were much better in literacy classrooms. The print-media in particular has focused on an alleged crisis with students' print literacy achievement, with claims that literacy levels as measured by standardized tests have declined. Moreover, so deeply embedded within the public debates is a cultural preference for the world of print that the possibility of a significant shift towards the digital seems almost unimaginable (Snyder 2008).

book culture's remarkable endurance

A strong cultural preference for the world of print and print literacy is sustained and bolstered in public discourse. Rare is the article in the Australian print-media about books that does not assume their intrinsic cultural value. By contrast, when digital technologies are discussed, their cultural value is never taken for granted. They are either celebrated or dismissed, with anything resembling a more nuanced approach a rare occurrence.

Paeans to the book and book culture are a regular feature in the press. The reminiscences of arch-conservative cultural commentator, Christopher Pearson (2006), who writes for the Murdoch national newspaper, the *Australian*, epitomizes the genre. In response to a question, 'What turned you into a reader?', Pearson wrote 'My mind raced back to a rainy afternoon in Bellevue Hill primary school in Sydney in 1956 ... The teacher had just joined up show cards – with a C, an O and a final W and a picture of a cow – and the penny dropped'.

At age five, Pearson's 'first brush with the canon' was *The Rubaiyat of Omar Khayam*: 'I revelled in its resigned acceptance of a meaningless universe, its stoic approach to death and its celebration of the fleeting pleasures.' Exposure to the cadences of Bach, Handel and Purcell in an Anglican boys' choir 'inoculated' him 'against modernity for its own sake and anything the hit parade had to offer in the year the Beatles arrived on tour'. The local library allowed Pearson to move beyond the limitations of the school curriculum and he still looks forward to 'hours of unalloyed joy' in rereading the jokes in Evelyn Waugh. His reverence for the components of a traditional approach to literacy teaching and learning is present: the importance of phonics, the centrality of the canon and the avoidance of popular culture.

In an article in *The Age*, a newspaper with a more liberal orientation that is currently owned by a private equity group, Pamela Bone (2004) said what was implicit in Pearson's recollections: '[i]f reading declines so do we all'. Writing in response to a piece which suggested that finely honed literacy skills are simply not as important as they once were, Bone argued that only books provide the resources for exploring the meaning of life. Serious reading demands 'time and patience' and 'solitude' which is 'against the spirit of this hyperactive age'. Bone associated depth with books and superficiality with new media – her fear was an illiterate generation raised on text messaging, Internet surfing and video games.

Occasionally, an article appears in the Australian press that explores the cultural nuances of the debates. Interested in the cultural resilience of the book, Monica Dux (2006) wondered if we will ever learn to love e-books, even when the technology equals the clarity of the printed page. We still hold printed books sacred, she suggested, because of the cultural associations we have with them: pleasant memories of time spent in the unique world of reading; books as a public testament to education, wealth and social capital; books as perhaps the 'archetypal manifestation of civilized society, our most powerful symbol of culture, knowledge and freedom of expression'.

While the book is a mark of learning and culture, Dux suggested that computers carry far more ambiguous associations. Whether it is robots taking over the world or HAL the homicidal computer, technology is as likely to be a threat as a solution. But she concluded with a simple answer that resonates with the earlier discussion about teachers and change – people prefer what they are used to. Dux described a study at the University of South Australia where two groups of students – one of primary-school age, the other, adult graduate students – were given e-readers. The adults expressed mixed feelings while the children adjusted and showed as much enjoyment as they did for reading books. Already comfortable with reading from a screen, the children had no entrenched print-based literacy practices to overcome.

The lingering cultural preference for the book and print technology has been a key dimension of conservative criticism directed at English teaching and curricula in Australia. To take just one example, a question on the 2005 year 12 Advanced English exam in NSW offered students 'a choice of "texts" to analyse, including the ATSIC [Aboriginal and Torres Strait Islander Commission] site, drawing criticism that its inclusion was an insult to the classics' (Lane 2005). A state curriculum that recognized the importance of teaching students how to critically evaluate new media spaces was vehemently attacked. 'Sticking to the book' was the header for the *Australian's* editorial the next day (Editorial 2005). The editorial argued that although critical analysis should be a core component of any English course: 'Books – not blogs, not digital ephemera, but books' should be set for study.

new technologies: loving them or loathing them

Public discourse around new technologies in literacy education most often assumes polarized positions. At one extreme, there are promotions of the latest whizz-bang technology, celebrations of online life and predictions of enhanced teaching and learning when the latest technology appears. At the other, there are diatribes against computers, video games and the Internet and expressions of moral panic over the dangers for children in cyberspace. Often integral to such reports are commonsense views about the cultural importance of the printed word, the absence of any real difference between reading a book and reading a screen and the detrimental impact of old and new technologies on children's behaviour.

the enthusiasts

When *Time* magazine announced the person of the year for 2006, the shimmering cover featured a desktop computer with a mirror in place of a screen. The caption beneath read: 'You. Yes, you. You control the Information Age. Welcome to your world.' The Christmas issue honoured the individuals who are changing the nature of the information age – the creators and consumers of user-generated content who are transforming art and politics and commerce. Said Managing Editor, Richard Stengel (2006: 4), they are 'the engaged citizens of a new digital democracy'.

Twenty-seven pages of the magazine were dedicated to hyping up Web 2.0, 'the new global nervous system' that is 'changing the way we perceive the world' (Stengel 2006: 4). Web 2.0 is a term used more or less interchangeably with social media. Although networking and interacting online have been available since the Web was launched in the early 1990s, advances in technology have meant that social software tools such as blogs, wikis, social bookmarking and virtual conferencing now also allow users to upload photos, videos and music. As the extraordinary growth of Wikipedia, MySpace and YouTube has demonstrated, social media are what matters today – at least until the next best technology comes along.

Much could be said about *Time's* Person of the Year for 2006. In a period of deepening unhappiness with the Bush administration and the war in Iraq, the magazine's salute to the citizens of cyberspace seemed a curious choice. Perhaps it was intended as a confection for the holiday season, but whatever the motivation, the spread was part of a tradition of writing about new technologies which is not exclusive to the print-media. First it was hypertext, then it was the Internet and the World Wide Web, now it is Web 2.0, with really cool people talking about Web 3.0. Enthusiasts endow new media with utopian promise and discuss them in a celebratory way. The hope is social and cultural change propelled by the latest information and communication technologies.

When journalists write about new media and education, they often concentrate on how the technologies are changing schools for the better. In a longish article in the *Sydney Morning Herald*, the subject was the 'millennial generation' – computer and Internet savvy multi-taskers, born after the mid-1980s, who spend less time watching TV and more doing homework via the Internet (Friedlander 2004). The piece presented two schools, one private and one public, that have embraced digital technologies. E-learning was the slogan in both. In Australia, more than 30 per cent of students attend private, fee-paying schools. However, most of the private schools are part of the Catholic education sector where the fees are considerably lower. Successive governments on both sides of politics have provided substantial support for private schools, many would argue, at the expense of the public sector.

In the private school, total immersion had been the logic since the move to laptops in the mid-1990s. In the public school, described as 'perhaps, the most digitally advanced of all Australian schools', blackboards, rows of desks and timetables were gone and the emphasis was on doing things differently. The result, said the associate principal, was strong student motivation and one of the highest rates of attendance in the state's public schools. At least there were no claims about enhanced learning which is also often a component of such articles.

the detractors

There is another way of writing about technology in the press. Technology detractors predict the death of the book which they see as synonymous with the death of civilization. New forms of writing such as texting are dismissed as a threat to the sanctity of the English language. They associate the use of digital technologies in the classroom with the triviality and crassness of popular culture, arguing that computer games have no place in either literacy education or teacher education. The Internet is somewhere children and young people may spend time out-of-school hours, but this doesn't justify its use in formal education. The detractors also express deep concern about children's open access to undesirable resources and information via the Internet.

Part of the genre of denigrating digital technologies is to associate the use of new media with undesirable influences. When new media are portrayed in the press it is to raise people's anxiety. Such fears are not new. Since the early days of television, there has been concern about the effects of TV on children, education, literacy and culture, and recommendations made for the control of its content and for strict supervision. Each successive technology has been seen to have a negative influence on children – by sanctioning inappropriate values and by representing frightening and violent experiences (Beavis 1998). It comes as no surprise that there have been similar anxieties about children's access to the Internet, cyberspace and computer games, regarded widely as inherently dangerous unless controlled. The role of governments and schools to regulate the new technologies in the interests of vulnerable children is at the centre of public concern.

So when literacy academic, Catherine Beavis (1998), suggested that computer games could be used effectively in the English classroom, she received a lot of media attention. Like all the battles in the literacy wars, the newspaper coverage set up the parameters of the debate as simple oppositions that exploited people's anxieties: fears of illiteracy, fears of degeneration and fears of neglect of what children should be doing – playing outside, reading books and learning about civic values and Australia's cultural heritage.

Invited by the teachers' journal, *English in Australia*, to respond to Beavis's view that the use of computer games in literacy education can provide opportunities to teach important skills and knowledge, Kevin Donnelly (1998), a key conservative voice in the literacy debates in the Australian press over the past three years, argued that time spent on computer games is time not spent on more worthwhile pursuits – the study and appreciation of literature. Donnelly presented the debate as an either/or choice. He ignored the question of what it means to be literate today in contemporary political economies and cultural landscapes. He ignored what kinds of texts students need to read, manipulate and produce to participate effectively in civic life.

Donnelly concentrated on just one genre of computer games, the violent ones, and provoked the usual anxieties: their seek and destroy principle, their shallow ethical world, the absence of opportunity for reflection, the impoverished language and their emphasis on instant gratification. Clearly, computer games are not ideologically neutral nor are their values necessarily the ones parents would want their children to adopt. However, Donnelly not only ignored the range of games available but also underestimated young people's capacity to deal critically with the crude messages of certain games.

Academic, Victoria Carrington (2005), who was working at a university in England at the time, was interviewed on Australian radio about the 13-year-old Scottish schoolgirl who submitted an essay written in text using her mobile phone:

My smmr hols wr CWOT. B4, we used 2go2 NY 2C my bro, his GF & thr 3 :- kids FTF. ILNY, it's a gr8 plc'.

Translation:
My summer holidays were a complete waste of time. Before, we used to go to New York to see my brother, his girlfriend and their three screaming kids face to face. I love New York. It's a great place.

The journalist asked Carrington about textings' distinct style as compared with correct spelling and grammar, and then proceeded to link texting to youth, declining standards, poor academic achievement and social breakdown. When Carrington subsequently analysed a number of press articles discussing texting, she found that young people and standards were most often represented as needing protection from an addiction that could jeopardize their success in exams and their educational futures.

When two 16-year-old high school students were found dead in the Dandenong Ranges, east of Melbourne, the press connected their suicide to MySpace. With an image of the two girls and their last message, 'RIP Jessica & Mel' (not the girls' real names), posted on their website, the inference was that the Internet is a dangerous place for young people (Cubby & Dubecki 2007). By inserting the word 'MySpace', journalists made the story look exciting. However, all the evidence suggested that the girls didn't commit suicide because they wrote about depression on the Internet. They wrote about depression on the Internet because MySpace was a place for self-expression and communication as it is for many other young people (Hills 2007).

A degree of caution and critical perspective on digital technologies is timely and appropriate. Without doubt, technologies such as the Internet and texting enable certain undesirable social behaviours and give some people the anonymity they need to entrap the susceptible. However, children can be preyed upon in whichever places they choose for recreation and teachers can be the victims of bullying, whether on a website or in an anonymous letter to the principal (Owen 2006). History suggests that a sense of anxiety and moral panic is unwarranted as old technologies have also been used to connect children to inappropriate adult content and aggressive advertising. Risks can be exaggerated for the sake of a story but producing a moral panic doesn't inform or lead to sensible public debate or policy.

challenges and opportunities

In addition to a cultural preference for the world of print that is located deep within Australia's (middleclass) collective subconscious, there are very real systemic reasons that help explain why literacy teachers have been slow to use new media that go beyond literacy teachers' historical reticence with technology. Literacy classrooms are constrained by the static model of schools as institutions that prevents careful inquiry into the new literacies and the expansive use of new media. Teachers have little time to reflect on what they do, no matter what the proposed curriculum direction. So when they try to work with digital media in their classrooms, there is not much opportunity to build creative partnerships with colleagues and to experiment with new literacies. Imaginative uses are often limited to the technology champions who, research shows, eventually experience burn-out.

A gulf exists between the world of the literacy classroom and the world of students who are immersed in media, the Internet and video games. Problems with the infrastructure of schools also exacerbate the difficulties: the Internet may be working one day, down the next, and the computers are often not powerful enough for the use of advanced tools. Further, the schools may have constricting rules about email and Internet access which frustrate both the teachers and the students. These factors alone are enough to discourage teachers from trying to integrate digital technologies into their classroom practices even though they may be dedicated and experienced users in their private lives.

Yet teachers are still charged with the responsibility to find innovative ways to incorporate the new literacies associated with digital media into classroom practice. The skills and knowledge of print literacy are essential, but not enough to support young people's successful and participatory lives in the networked information society. Professional development programmes and pre-service and postgraduate education have a key role to play in providing opportunities for teachers to consider future-oriented classrooms underpinned by expansive definitions of literacy. When literacy is seen as a repertoire of linguistic and intellectual abilities, which learners need to function at the highest levels in a multi-media world, notions of literacy as a set of basic skills prescribed for a print-based world, seem more and more limited.

There are a number of prerequisites for productive thinking about literacy education for the twenty-first century. An essential component of all discussions is knowledge and understanding of the history of literacy. Literacy is inextricable from the changes that have taken place in communities, societies, nation states and the global domain, both in recent times and over the centuries. Literacy is also ever-changing. Today, as much as in any other historical period, new literacy practices are emerging and the concept of literacy continues to change as it has always done. Examining literacy's history provides the intellectual foundation upon which to consider how literacy education might be remade to meet contemporary material and cultural conditions.

Another prerequisite for productive thinking is recognition of the potential contribution new information and communication technologies have to make in the design of innovative approaches to literacy education. Successive advances in technology have extended the boundaries of what was previously possible and changed the ways in which literacy is socially and culturally practised. This means that it is no longer possible to continue with the assumption that students live exclusively in the world of print. Questions for curriculum development need to centre on which genres and practices should be taught in literacy classrooms and through which combination of media. Other questions relate to students' production of texts. Students are no longer just consumers and producers of print texts, decoding, interpreting and writing them; they are also consumers and producers of digital texts that they can remake and redesign. Under these conditions, the aims of literacy education need to include the provision of opportunities for students to become informed, critical users and producers of many media.

It is possible to find ways to rethink, redefine and redesign language and literacy in the classroom to meet the needs of all students, ways that succeed in integrating print with the digital effectively. Curriculum frameworks that are inclusive, imaginative, critical and rigorous become the goal. Increasingly, literacy teachers are acknowledging that media products such as film, video and computer games now have the cultural importance that was once ascribed solely to print and are also worthy of serious study. They recognize that the most effective literacy work between themselves and their students is joint and collaborative, framed around meaning making. They know that students' engagement in literacy education, both print and digital, is central to the achievement of these aims.

conclusion

Productive professional thinking and planning for the future are not enough to ensure that literacy education embraces both the world of the book and the world of the screen. As the overview of the research in literacy and technology studies indicated, many researchers and practitioners have done and are continuing to do excellent work. But the public hears little about it, rendering the possibility of a significant cultural shift in thinking about literacy education unlikely. In Australia, and I daresay in many other countries in the developed world, there is a sharp divide between the profession on the one hand and the powerful conservative politicians, policy-makers and their allies in the media, on the other. It is overwhelmingly the conservative writers and thinkers who are setting the literacy agenda and shaping public discourse on literacy matters.

The conservative critics are dismissive of contemporary approaches to literacy education which most often include the use of new media such as video games and the Internet. Their mission is greater emphasis in schools on cultural literacy, the literature of the Western canon and traditional values – looking backwards to some former golden age that probably never existed rather than forward to the challenges of the future which include rapid developments in information and communication technologies, the explosion of popular and youth cultures, changes to work, multiculturalism and globalization. A principal aim of the conservatives' attacks is to undermine confidence in contemporary approaches to literacy education and to raise public anxiety.

To enlist public support for a forward looking literacy curriculum rather than a backward-looking one, literacy educators need to get involved in the debates and contribute to the public discourse. Particular attention needs to be directed towards the untenable conditions surrounding literacy education experienced by indigenous, immigrant and poor students. Maintaining a continuing, open, public conversation about literacy education is vital to ensure that literacy curricula are creative, dynamic and responsive to new developments. Without informed public support, school-based literacy education will do no more than shuffle towards the future.

references

Beavis, C. (1998) Pressing (the Right?) Buttons: Literacy and Technology, Crisis and Continuity. *English in Australia*, 123, 42–51.

Beavis, C. (2002) Reading, writing and role-playing computer games. In I. Snyder (ed.), *Silicon Literacies: Communication, Innovation and Education in the Electronic Age* London: Routledge, 47–61.

Beavis, C., H. Nixon and S. Atkinson (2005) LAN Cafes: Cafes, Places of Gathering, or Sites of Informal Teaching and Learning? *Education, Communication and Information*, 5(1), 41–60.

Bone, P. (2004) If Reading Declines, So Do We All. *The Age* 17/12/2004.

Burbules, N. C. and T. A. Callister Jr (2000) *Watch IT: The Risks and Promises of Information Technologies for Education.* Boulder, Colorado: Westview Press.

Carrington, V. (2004) Texts and Literacies of the Shi Jinrui. *British Journal of Sociology of Education*, 25(2), 215–28.

Carrington, V. (2005) Txting: The End of Civilization (Again)? *Cambridge Journal of Education*, 35(2), 161–75.

Coiro, J., M. Knobel, C. Lankshear and D. Leu (eds) (2007) *Handbook of Research on New Literacies*. New Jersey: Erlbaum.

Cuban, L. (2001) *Oversold and Underused: Computers in the Classroom*. Boston: Harvard University Press.

Cubby, B. and L. Dubecki (2007) Tragic Last Words of Myspace Suicide Girls. *Sydney Morning Herald*, 24/4/2007.

Dickinson, D. K. (1986) Cooperation, Collaboration and Computers: Integrating a Computer into a Second Grade Writing Program. *Research in the Teaching of English*, 20(4), 357–78.

Donnelly, K. (1998) Pressing buttons ... A Reply. *English in Australia*, 123, 52–6.

Dux, M. (2006) A Little Light Reading: Will We Ever Love E-Books? *The Age*, 26/8/2006.

Editorial (2005) Sticking to the Book. *The Australian*, 22/10/2005.

Elliott, M. Education and Broadband: Serious about Games. *New Matilda*, retrieved 25 June 2008 from <http://www.newmatilda.com//home/articledetail.asp?NewsletterID=290&ArticleID=2005&email=1>.

Friedlander, J. (2004) Cool to Be Wired for School. *The Sydney Morning Herald* 16/4/2004.

Gee, J. P. (2003) *What Video Games Have to Teach us about Learning and Literacy*. New York: Palgrave Macmillan.

Gee, J. P. (2005) Learning by Design: Good Video Games as Learning Machines. *E-Learning*, 2(1), 5–15.

Gerrard, L. (1999) Letter from the Guest Editor. *Computers and Composition: An International Journal for Teachers of Writing*, 16(1), 1–5.

Gould, J. D. (1978) Experiments on composing letters: some facts, some myths and some observations. In L. Gregg and I. Steinberg (eds), *Cognitive Processes in Writing*. New Jersey: Lawrence Erlbaum, 97–127.

Harraway, D. (1991) *Simians, Cyborgs, and Woman: The Reinvention of Nature*. New York: Routledge.

Hermann, A. (1987) Ethnographic study of a high school writing class using computers: marginal, technically proficient and productive learners. In L. Gerrard (ed.), *Writing at Century's End: Essays on Computer-Assisted Instruction*. New York: Random, 79–91.

Hills, R. (2007) Blame it on MySpace. *New Matilda*, retrieved 10 June 2007 from <http://www.newmatilda.com//home/articledetail.asp?NewsletterID=315&ArticleID=2226&email=1>.

Jenkins, H. (2006) *Convergence Culture: Where Old and New Media Collide*. New York and London: New York University Press.

Jones, S. (ed.) (1999) *Doing Internet Research: Critical Issues and Methods for Examining the Net*. Thousand Oaks, CA: Sage.

Lane, B. (2005) ATSIC Website in Exam 'an Insult'. *The Australian*, 21/10/2005.

Lankshear, C. and I. Snyder with B. Green (2000) *Teachers and Technoliteracy: Managing Literacy, Technology and Learning in Schools*. Sydney: Allen and Unwin.

Lankshear, C. and M. Knobel (2003) *New Literacies: Changing Knowledge and Classroom Learning*. Buckingham, UK and Philadelphia, USA: Open University Press.

Livingstone, S. (2002) *Young People and New Media: Childhood and the Changing Media Environment*. London: Sage.

Livingstone, S. and M. Bober (2005) *UK Children Go Online: Final Report of Key Project Findings*. London: London School of Economics and Political Science. Retrieved 2 June 2005 from http://www.children-go-online.net.

Luke, A. and C. Luke (2001) Adolescence Lost/Childhood Regained: On Early Intervention and the Emergence of the Techno-Subject. *English in Australia*, 131, 35–48.

Norris, P. (2001) *Digital Divide: Civic Engagement, Information Poverty, and the Internet Worldwide*. Cambridge UK: Cambridge University Press.

Owen, M. (2006) Teachers Suffering Cyber Abuse. *The Advertiser*, 7/12/2006.

Pearson, C. (2006) Bookish since Boyhood. *The Australian*, 12/8/2006.

Snyder, I. (1995) Toward Electronic Writing Classrooms: The Challenge for Teachers. *Journal of Information Technology for Teacher Education*, 4(1), 51–65.

Snyder, I. (1996a) Integrating Computers into Classroom Literacy Practices: More Difficult Than We Imagined. *The Australian Journal of Language and Literacy*, 19(4), 330–44.

Snyder, I. (1996b) Teachers, technology and change. In G. Rijlaarsdam, H. van den Bergh and M. Couzijn (eds), *Effective Learning and Teaching of Writing: Current Trends in Writing Research*. Amsterdam: University of Amsterdam Press. 163–79.

Snyder, I. (1999) Packaging Literacy, New Technologies and 'Enhanced' Learning. *Australian Journal of Education*, 43(3), 287–301.

Snyder, I. (2007a) Critical literacy, learning and technology studies: challenges and opportunities for higher education. In R. Andrews and C. Haythornthwaite (eds), *The Handbook of e-Learning*. London: Sage, 394–415.

Snyder, I. (2007b) Research approaches to technology, language and literacy. In K. King and N. Hornberger (eds), *Encyclopaedia of Language and Education*. New York: Springer. 299–308.

Snyder, I. (2008) *The Literacy Wars: Why Teaching Children to Read and Write Is a Battleground in Australia*. Sydney: Allen & Unwin.

Snyder, I., L. Angus and W. Sutherland-Smith (2002) Building Equitable Literate Futures: Home and School Computer-Mediated Literacy Practices and Disadvantage. *Cambridge Journal of Education*, 32, 3, 368–83.

Snyder, I. and S. Bulfin (2008) Using new media in the secondary English classroom. In J. Coiro, M. Knobel, C. Lankshear and D. Leu (eds), *Handbook of Research on New Literacies*. New Jersey: Erlbaum, 809–41.

Snyder, I., S. North and S. Bulfin, 'Being digital in home, school and community'. Retrieved 18 July 2007 from http://www.education.monash.edu.au/research/projects/beingdigital/

Stengel, R. (2006) Now It's Your Turn. *Time*, Double Issue, 25 December 2006 / 1 January 2007, 4.

Warschauer, M. (1999) *Electronic Literacies: Language, Culture and Power in Online Education*. Mahwah New Jersey: Lawrence Erlbaum.

8
transnational literacies: examining global flows through the lens of social practice

doris s. warriner

In recent years, Literacy Studies scholars have been urged to provide ethnographies of literacy that illuminate how locally situated literacy practices are connected to larger sociohistorical influences, political processes, ideological questions, and material consequences (e.g. Prinsloo & Baynham 2008; Baynham 2004; Luke 2004; Pahl & Rowsell 2006; Papen 2005; Street 2003, 2004). There has been a call not only for more work that investigates the complicated relationship between the local and the global but also for empirical studies that detail 'how "distant" literacies are "taken hold" of in specific local ways, whether absorbed into previous communicative practices or used to mediate the outside and the inside' (Street 2004: 328). Coincidentally, just as New Literacy Studies scholarship is moving away from focusing exclusively on the 'local,' the anthropological and sociological study of transnationalism and transmigration has shifted from largely theoretical accounts of global flows and 'global ethnoscapes' (Appadurai 1996) to an interest in local practices and processes (e.g. Basch et al. 1994; Chamberlain & Leydesdorff 2004; Guarnizo 1994; Schein 1998; Smith 1995; Smith & Guarnizo 1998; Sorensen 1998). In turning its analytical gaze to the lived experiences of individual transmigrants, scholars of transnationalism have sought to understand the specifics of local social practice—or 'how everyday practices of ordinary people produce cultural meanings that sustain transnational networks and make possible enduring translocal ties' (Smith 2003: 468).

In a recent work (Warriner 2007a), I have argued that discussions of transnationalism are enhanced when combined with the systematic study of literacy as a social practice, in the same way that research on the locally situated nature of literacy and language learning benefits from the theoretical insights of a field long focused on the influences, processes, and 'by-products' of globalization and migration. A careful examination of transnational literacies thus provides a window into global-local interfaces, transmigrant experiences, transnational flows (of capital, technology, communication, and people) across borders, and translocal connections. Bringing together contributions from New Literacy Studies (NLS) scholarship and the study of transnationalism, the investigation of transnational literacies provides insights into the 'human face of global mobility' (Favell et al. 2006) through the lens of everyday practice. With a focus on the locally realized but globally influenced ways that individual experiences and identities are repre- sented, enacted, and transformed by specific actors living in the realm of everyday practice, this work addresses 'the condition of cultural interconnectedness and mobility across space' (Ong 1999). As such, the empirical study of transnational literacies not only represents a prelim- inary response to the call for more work on 'the various dialectical ways that such "distant" literacies are taken hold of in specific local ways' (Street 2004: 328), but it also actively challenges the many binaries and dichotomies that dominate research in both fields.

reaching beyond the 'local'

In many ways, the field of NLS remains committed to Street's conten- tion that autonomous understandings of literacy should be replaced with ideological understandings of literacy. Rather than view literacy as a skill located (cognitively) within individuals, most literacy researchers consider literacy a situated social practice that is not only influenced by local understandings and cultural norms of interaction but is also a product of ideology and power relations. In this framework, literacy is not only locally situated and context-dependent, it is multiple (as in literacies, bi-literacies, and multi-literacies).

However, even though the ideological model of literacy has been widely championed in recent decades, a few have questioned the heavy emphasis on local literacies and argued that the increased attention to multiplicity and difference 'leads us to ignore similarities' that exist across individuals, situations, and events (Bartlett 2003: 71). Brandt and

Clinton (2002), for instance, have argued that the NLS emphasis on the 'local' leaves 'global' dynamics and influences under-explored, both theoretically and methodologically:

> In truth, if reading and writing are means by which people reach— and are reached by—other contexts, then more is going on locally than just local practice. The field has learned much from the recent turn to 'local literacies.' But might something be lost when we ascribe to local context responses to pressures that originate in distant decisions, especially when seemingly local appropriations of literacy may in fact be culminations of literate designs originating elsewhere? (p. 338)

For Brandt and Clinton (2002), the social-practice perspective has under-theorized literacy's ability 'to travel, integrate, and endure'; and they urge literacy researchers to consider the 'transcontextualized and transcontextualizing potentials' (ibid.) of what are often described as local literacy practices. Interested in the ways that literacy, as a technology, has 'a capacity to travel, a capacity to stay intact, and a capacity to be visible and animate outside the interactions of immediate literacy events,' Brandt and Clinton posit a dialectical relationship between the local and the global, encouraging Literacy Studies scholars to ask of every local literacy event/practice 'what is localizing and what is globalizing in what is going on?' (p. 347). Although Street (2004) concurs that most literacy practices come from 'outside,' he maintains that the ways they are taken up (or not) by individual actors are distinct, locally specific, and often contested. He claims that 'literacy is always instantiated, its potential always realized, through local practices' (p. 326) even though the outside or the global may be 'embedded in the local' (p. 328).

Luke (2004) too addresses questions about local-global connections by emphasizing how literacy is reconfigured over distances of space and time. Focusing on 'the 'traveling cultures' of the new millennium,' he asks 'who has what kinds of access and engagements with transnational, regional and local flows of information' (p. 331) and draws attention to newer areas of focus in Literacy Studies, particularly with regard to education and schooling:

> In this regard, ethnographies of literacy must bridge not just home and school, but the local and global, and the micro and macro political-economic domains. From an educational perspective, we

need to ask…fundamental questions about which languages and literacies, sanctioned by which state educational systems and globalised institutions, have which kinds of material consequences in people's lives. (p. 334)

Like Luke, Baynham (2004) argues that it is time for Literacy Studies to turn its research lens back to questions of schooling—particularly with regard to issues of transnational movement, relations, and flows. Notwithstanding the efforts to clarify and nuance the dialectic relationship among the local, the global, the individual, and the social, theoretical (and empirical) tensions remain unresolved. As Baynham (2007) notes, we still confront the 'perennial issue of theorizing the impact of large scale social processes on small scale interaction' (p. 336), especially with regard to schooling and pedagogy.

To continue theorizing the ways in which the local and global interact—and to investigate how such interactions routinely influence discursive flows, lived experiences, and material realities—Literacy Studies scholarship must engage with new ways of investigating and representing language and literacy practices in relation to local, global, and transnational flows, events, and processes. Even though it has been useful to highlight the multiple, even contradictory ways that 'dominant, universalizing literacies can be seen on closer inspection, as profoundly local' (Baynham 2004: 289), it is also important to consider how local or 'everyday' practices intersect with the forces of history, globalization, ideology, and power. Understanding the dialectic and nested relationships that exist in the ideological-discursive-material space of transnationalism requires the careful examination of 'local' literacy practices that are interpolated by and constitutive of historical, political, economic, and social processes.

investigating transnationalism through the lens of social practice

Transnationalism has been defined as the movement of people, ideas, technology, and communication across national boundaries (Smith 2003); processes, events, flows, and relations that are 'anchored in and transcend one or more nation-states' (Kearney 1995: 548); the 'situated cultural practices of mobility' (Ong 1999); and 'highly particularistic attachments' to a locally situated space elsewhere (Waldinger & Fitzgerald 2004: 1177). According to Smith (2003), because a lot of

the literature on transnationalism has emerged out of economic sociology, it has emphasized the 'macroeconomic driving forces of global
migration' (p. 468) where transnationalism is often characterized as
a conscious effort (achieved through individual-level microeconomic
practices) to challenge the hegemonic forces of global capitalism as
enacted and dispersed by the state and its institutions. In contrast, the
approach of anthropologists and cultural studies scholars '[contributes]
to our understanding of how everyday practices of ordinary people produce cultural meanings that sustain transnational networks and make
possible enduring translocal ties' (ibid.).

As Mahler (1998) has pointed out, however, there is 'one fundamental problem besetting "transnationalism"—it is a very slippery concept'
(p. 66). This 'slipperiness' raises questions about what conceptual and
empirical approaches might be utilized to investigate not just the 'globalization of capital' or the movement of people, ideas, technology, and
goods across borders but also the 'grass-roots reaction[s],' 'particularistic
attachments,' or 'local logics' that accompany such processes. In this
chapter, my goal is to engage with and challenge this 'slipperiness' in
ways that productively contribute to the study of global-local intersections as well as the ethnographic study of literacy as a social practice.

In an effort to identify what exactly is 'new' in the study of transnationalism, Portes et al. (1999) discuss 'the pitfalls and promise of an
emergent research field' as well as the 'many contradicting claims' that
anchor our theories:

> In some writings, the phenomenon of transnationalism is portrayed
> as novel and emergent, whereas in others it is said to be as old as
> labour immigration itself. In some cases, transnational entrepreneurs
> are depicted as a new and still exceptional breed, whereas in others
> all immigrants are said to be participants in the transnational com-
> munity. Finally, these activities are sometimes described as a reflec-
> tion and natural accompaniment of the globalization of capital,
> whereas in others they are seen as a grass-roots reaction to this very
> process. (Glick Schiller, Basch, and Blanc-Szanton 1992; Basch et al.
> 1994; Guarnizo 1994; Smith 1995). (Portes et al. 1999 p. 218)

To add further complexity, Waldinger and Fitzgerald (2004) have questioned the assumed relationship between national identification processes and geographic place, arguing national affiliation(s) are always,
first and foremost, about a place (whether that place constitutes a former or current 'home'). Similarly, Guarnizo and Smith (1998) posit that

transnational identities—and the practices which constitute them—are bounded (rather than 'deterritorialized' or 'unbounded') in two senses: first, because individual understandings are 'socially constructed within the transnational networks that people form and move from;' and, second, because transnational experiences are bounded 'by the policies and practices of territorially-based sending and receiving local and national states and communities' (p. 10).

While it is clear that movement over national borders has the potential to solidify one's territorially defined identity, it is also clear that such movement disrupts an individual's or community's relationship to a geographic place or cultural space. For immigrants and refugees alike, processes of self-identification in the 'receiving' nation are largely if not primarily influenced by their prior affiliations with a particular geopolitical context—and this is true even when that territory no longer has the same political status and even when people are no longer moving regularly between two or more nation-states. When moving across borders, people create new spaces as well as new relationships. As Low and Lawrence-Zuniga (2003: 25) observe

> Globalization also radically changes social relations and local places due to interventions of electronic media and migration, and the consequent breakdown in the isomorphism of space, place, and culture. This process of cultural globalization creates new translocal spaces and forms of public culture embedded in the imaginings of people that dissolves notions of state-based territoriality. (Gupta and Ferguson 1992; Appadurai 1996)

As the study of 'transnationalism from below' (e.g. Goldring 1998; Schein 1998; Smith and Guarnizo 1998; Sorensen 1998) demonstrates, immigration processes (and the global forces that contribute to them) often break down 'notions of state-based territoriality' in the creation of new 'translocal spaces.' In this way, the 'bounded' nature of certain territorially defined identities, practices, and understandings does not prohibit individuals (or groups) from simultaneously claiming allegiance to or identifying with something 'unbound' (e.g. a diasporic identity).

Yet, even while some have attempted to confront directly the definitional, conceptual, and empirical challenges involved with trying to pin down the exact meanings of terms so widely used and contested (e.g. Kearney 1995; Kivisto 2001; Mahler 1998; Portes 2001; Portes et al. 1999; Waldinger & Fitzgerald 2004), fundamental questions remain. For instance, what is exactly meant by the term 'transnational'?

'transnational civil society'? the 'by-products of globalization'? As Waldinger and Fitzgerald (2004) note, defining transnationalism requires wrestling with historical contradictions inherent in the term itself:

> [W]hat immigration scholars describe as transnationalism is usually its opposite: highly particularlistic attachments antithetical to those by-products of globalization denoted by the concept of 'transnational civil society.' Moreover, migrants do not make their communities alone: states and state politics shape the options for migrant and ethnic trans-state social action. (p. 1177)

The examination of transnational literacies through an ethnographic lens serves to illuminate how complicated and contested such flows, processes, and relations actually are on the ground. As such, this work promises to inform debates about the exact nature of the relationship between physical space/place and national identification, a central concern not only within transnational studies but also within literacy scholarship.

Representing one effort to move beyond such dichotomous distinctions, Appadurai (1991) has shown how a particular space, and the identities associated with it, might be simultaneously deterritorialized (widely dispersed or detached from local places) *and* 'embedded in the imaginings of people.' In describing nationalism as a set of practices *and* a form of ideology, he emphasizes the ways that ideological (and hegemonic) forces that further the interests of nation-states are both sustained and contested through sets of practices that appear to be individual, local, and distinct. While discussing the idea of 'mobile sovereignties,' Appadurai (1996/2003) asserts that

> [t]he problem is not ethnic or cultural pluralism as such but the tension between diasporic pluralism and territorial stability in the project of the modern nation-state. What ethnic plurality does (especially when it is the product of population movements within recent memory) is to violate the sense of isomorphism between territory and national identity on which the modern nation-state relies. What diasporic pluralisms particularly expose and intensify is the gap between the powers of the state to regulate borders, monitor dissent, distribute entitlements within a finite territory *and* the fiction of ethnic singularity on which most nations ultimately rely. (p. 346)

This brief overview of transnational studies and some of its definitional questions and conceptual ambiguities reflects the complicated nature of what is often assumed to be a transparent model of an increasingly commonplace process (i.e. the crossing of borders).

Some transnational studies scholars (e.g. Portes et al. 1999; Sorensen 1998; Schein 1998 to name a few) have asked for more representative and descriptive accounts of 'the reality of the transnational field' including 'its internal heterogeneity' (Portes et al.: 233). I argue that the examination of transnational literacies provides a window into how global flows and transnational connections are realized within specific contexts as well as the 'transcontextualizing potentials' of those local literacy practices. To inform this research agenda, I have drawn on Gupta (2003) and Low and Lawrence-Zuniga's (2003) discussion of *translocal spaces* as spaces where literacy practices might be *embodied, inscribed, contested,* and/or *transnational*. Literacy practices are *embodied* physically, temporally, and spatially—instantiated everyday in the ways individuals orient their bodies and gazes, and influenced by scales of time (Lemke 2000) as well as the multimodal and multimedia forms of communication available. They are *inscribed* through repetition and routine, both influencing and constituting one's habitus, disposition, and tastes (Bourdieu 1984; Luke 2003); *contested* when individuals transform and/or replace them within specific contexts for particular purposes; and *transnational* in that they are inevitably implicated in global flows, processes, and relations, even while being realized (and particularized) locally.

investigating transnational literacies

By turning to the realm of everyday practice and to the role of literacy (and multimodal) practices in particular, ethnographically grounded studies of the 'situated cultural practices of mobility' are able to capture the many 'creolized articulations and syncretic practices' that emerge in various 'contact zones' (Pratt 1991, 1992); the various ways that individual identities are differentially gendered, raced, or classed across contexts; and the lived experiences and dual loyalties of those living in diaspora communities (Lavie & Swedenburg 1996: 9–14). Questions that might guide this inquiry include

1. What literacy practices do transmigrants develop while adapting to new contexts, particularly new educational contexts, and what resources are used in doing so?

2. How do transmigrants and 'transnational communities' use literacy practices to maintain and transform transnational social relations? How does their use of particular literacy practices influence their educational, social, and emotional experiences in school and classroom settings?
3. What is the role of multimodal forms of communication in fostering, maintaining, or transforming relationships (social, economic, political) across national borders?
4. In what ways do new literacy practices index (and contribute to) shifting local-global connections, shifting relations or power, and the transformation of identities—particularly in this era of increased global flows and connections?

In considering the methodological principals and approaches that might contribute to the pursuit of this research agenda, I advocate focusing not only on social practices involving texts but also on the role of multimodality and face-to-face interaction (Barton & Hamilton 2005; Rampton 2006; Wortham 2006) in constituting 'local' manifestations of transnationalism as a social process.

Within transnational scholarship, there has been a call for 'radical revisions of the ethnographic method' as well as a rethinking of what is meant by the terms 'field sites' and 'home sites,' observing that 'out there' is not always analytically (or empirically) distinct from 'home.' Others have urged a careful consideration of the ways that sites of research and writing might become usefully blurred or intermingled (Lavie & Swedenburg 1996: 18–21), while a few noteworthy studies have demonstrated the need for 'itinerant' ethnography, where 'nomad-like methods' might be considered 'the legitimate primary sources for a research that works out of whichever margins its subjects are working within' (e.g. Schein 1998: 296) and where 'an openness to others and the ability to move between different cultural milieu is practical and strategic, particularly when understood from the perspective of vulnerable individuals and groups struggling to make a living in an environment characterized by discrimination and insecurity' (Kothari 2007. 5). As Kothari has noted

> Diasporas and migrants embody both movement and rootedness and hence can reveal some of the ambiguities and ambivalences contained in contemporary debates on cosmopolitanism. Cultures travel through time and space but also exhibit enduring characteristics, and it is this combination of change and continuity that, in part, informs the blurring of the cosmopolitan/parochial divide. (p. 17)

Advocating the use of approaches that detail the ways that actual social practices are embedded in concrete daily interactions (p. 18), Kothari demonstrates in her own work with itinerant street vendors in Barcelona the value of collecting ethnographic data from the multiple places in which migrants live.

There has also been increased attention paid to the value of 'experienced-rooted analysis' (Lavie & Swedenburg 1996: 18) as well as the importance of attending to the autobiographical and the concrete (e.g. Chamberlain & Leydesdorff 2004; Chandler 1996; Hymes 1997; Lavie & Swedenburg 1996; Orellana et al. 2001; Pahl 2004; Sánchez 2007; Sorensen 1998; Warriner 2003, 2004; Wortham 2001). For instance, Low and Lawrence-Zuniga (2003) describe the ways that place is often narrated (and thus constructed, lived, internalized, or trans-formed) through writing, poetry, songs and music. Sorensen (1998) explores how Dominican migrants' narratives might be considered transnational literary products that produce particular places, even when identity narratives might be in competition, such that one's 'cultural as well as political identity are constantly negotiated and reworked in these cross-national contexts' (p. 255).

Finally, there has been a call for understanding transnationalism from below as well as from above. As Guarnizo and Smith (1998) have emphasized, there are a range of ways to examine such lived flows and everyday contradictions, and it is critical that we examine such experiences and practices ethnographically and systematically:

> [I]t is crucial to systematically study the translocal micro-reproduction of transnational ties. Specifically, it is crucial to determine how trans-national networks work, and in that sense, how principles of trust and solidarity are constructed across national territories. ... What discourses and practices hold these principles in place? How do trans-national relations interact with local power structures, including class, gender and racial hierarchies? More generally, how does trans-locality affect the sociocultural basis supporting transnational relations and ties? (p. 26)

representative work on transnational literacies

Applying the tools and approaches of sociology, Schein (1998) has described the role of social practice in forging transnational identities (e.g. among Hmong refugees living in Southeast Asia), while Goldring (1998) focuses on the contested nature of the transnational social space, especially when movement across borders involves movement between different hierarchies of distinction. With a focus on transnational migration processes and experiences of Dominicans moving between the Dominican Republic and the United States, Sorensen (1998) has examined the transnational space as a contested space where shared participation does not always translate into shared experiences and where meanings are produced through social practice:

> If we understand space as being culturally constructed, and already hierarchically ordered by a set of *difference producing relations*, that is, understand 'difference' as the end-product of analysis, rather than the starting point, then we may become able to see the attachment and fixation of people to places, as well as the construction of transnational communities and identities, as something worthy of explanation. (p. 245)

In raising questions about the assumed relationship between geographic space and social identification, Sorensen draws attention to some of the central tensions in the study of transnationalism while also demonstrating how to begin investigating them. Smith (1998) too examines the contested nature of the transnational social space. He argues that 'it is not necessary to either abandon the concept of community altogether, nor accept it as an unproblematic given' (p. 202) and recommends directing attention 'towards the creation of shared meanings and shared practices' as well as on 'the bewildering tensions that can result from the differing class positions, cultural orientations, and role expectations that often form within transnational migrant circuits' (p. 204).

Blommaert and his colleagues (e.g. Blommaert et al. 2005a,b; Collins & Slembrouck 2005) have examined the consequences of globalization with a specific focus on the role of multilingual language practices and with the 'neighborhood' as the primary unit of analysis. This work shows that multilingualism is both 'a matter of conditioned resources as well as interactionally "framed" practices' (Blommaert et al. 2005b: 197) and that 'densely layered patterns of multilingualism allow us to analyze the production of locality in the globalized era in which old and new forms of transnational movement and intra-national response intermingle' (Blommaert et al. 2005a: 205). This represents one example of looking closely at language practices to understand global processes and flows and to illuminate the ways in which diasporas are in fact social processes that are reconfigured both structurally and discursively over time.

With an interest in expanding definitions and understandings of two key constructs (the 'local' and the 'interactional'), Rampton's recent works (2005, 2006) examine how classroom interaction intersects with global and transnational processes. Dismantling binary distinctions within discussions of transnationalism and globlization, Rampton argues that global cities provide unique contexts for studying processes of linguistic innovation or improvisation, cultural 'mixing', and ultimately transnational identity formation:

> As a point where a plurality of different transnational and diaspora flows intersect, this is an environment that generates high levels of local meta-cultural learning and awareness (cf. Hannerz 1996: 135–7; Portes 1997), and although there will be different combinations and processes in different locations, this produces a post-colonial experience 'defined, not by essence or purity, but by the recognition of a necessary heterogeneity and diversity; by a conception of 'identity' which lives with and through, not despite, difference; by hybridity' (Hall 1990: 235–6). (Rampton 2006: 8)

Like Rampton, Wortham (2006) complicates representations of the influence of global events and processes on 'local' (and interactional) phenomena by invoking notions of intersecting timescales (Lemke 2000) and 'nested spaces' to describe the relationship between situated cognition, social identification, and academic learning in multilingual, multinational, and multiethnic classroom contexts. Similarly, Blommaert (2003) Blommaert et al. (2005a,b; see also Collins & Slembrouch 2005) have demonstrated the value of applying the theories and tools of linguistic ethnography and linguistic anthropology to the study of spatializing practices and diasporic processes. They have illuminated the need for an explicitly spatial analysis of the factors that influence whether, and in what contexts, one might be considered 'competent' (Blommaert et al. 2005b) as well as the ways in which 'regimes of interactional practice' might influence the 'production of locality in the globalized era in which old and new forms of transnational movement and intra-national response intermingle' (Blommaert et al. 2005a).

In addition to the ethnographic work described above, there have been a number of important contributions in recent years to the systematic investigation of transnational processes such as immigration and refugee resettlement through the lens of literacy as a social practice. In the U.K. context, for instance, Gregory (2000) has examined the literacy practices used at home and in the community by Bangladeshi-British women and children living in Britain, with a particular focus on the relationship between reading, writing, work, and class. Also located in the U.K. context, Pahl's (2004) linguistic ethnography explored the multiple literacies, subject positions, and identities experienced by transmigrants living in a multilingual area of London. Focusing on autobiographical accounts of mobility, immigration, and exclusion, Pahl (2004) analyzes 'home-produced narratives' as literacy practices that illuminate complicated aspects of their transnational experiences and identities. Pahl and Rowsell (2005) have also edited a collection that investigates the role of literacy as a social practice in constituting 'the interface between the local and the global' (p. 5) as well as 'the ways in which multimodality [is] tied to global or local identities and practices' (p. 8). Recently, Prinsloo and Baynham's edited volume *Literacies, Global and Local* (2008) has provided a set of chapters that collectively examine the material, interactional, institutional, ideological, and semiotic dimensions of literacy as a social practice, with a particular emphasis on the ways that literacy illuminate power relations, global-local intersections, and the role of time and space in our theorizing.

With respect to research conducted in the Canadian context, Duff (2005) and Auerbach (2005) invoke but complicate the global-local distinction in their discussions of multilingualism, new literacies, and social change. With a focus on the influence of globalization, migration, and mobility on the language learning, literacy, and work experiences of adult immigrants, Duff examines 'the pressures of globalization' (p. 342) on adult learners of English trying to participate in English-dominant work environments and communities. Reflecting similar concerns, Auerbach urges language educators to examine the forces of globalization on the language learning and literacy practices of adult learners of English and calls attention to the 'false contradiction between the global and the local' in a lot of educational research.

Focusing on the U.S. context, contributors to a special issue of *Linguistics and Education* on 'Transnational Literacies: Immigration, Language Learning, and Identity,' combine theoretical insights from the study of transnationalism with the investigation of specific literacy practices that have transnational influences and implications. Bartlett (2007) focuses on how specific literacy practices create or break down boundaries (literal and figurative) between chains of communicative events and moments in time. She not only interrogates what it means to perform 'the good student identity', but she also complicates notions of how access to those cultural models might be provided to students. Sánchez (2007) explores how the sustained transnational movement between the United States and Mexico provides particular linguistic and cultural resources for U.S. immigrant children. In this article, Sánchez describes how second-generation Latina youth used a variety of different language and literacy practices to represent themselves and author a meta-narrative about Mexican immigrant families and children who make annual pilgrimages to their country of origin. Richardson Bruna (2007) and McGinnis et al. (2007) investigate the creative and performative use of multimodal literacy practices by immigrant youth living in local contexts but influenced by global processes.[1] Richardson Bruna's piece explores the situated learning and identity construction involved when Mexican newcomer youth use available semiotic resources as 'literacies of display' to enact and perform their transnational identities. She claims that the use of informal literacy practices in the classroom does not always represent defiant behavior but rather might indicate structures of feeling that students use to construe particular transnational identities in the classroom context. McGinnis et al (2007) too explore how transnational youth display their contested situated identities through hybrid textual practices of online communication sites. Warriner's (2007b) analysis of the material and ideological effects of particular assessment practices demonstrates that the 'ideological consequences of literacy' are realized locally but with transnational implications. The work in this volume is noteworthy for the ways in which each author documents and analyzes 'how these local practices and identities are profoundly rooted in processes of globalization, and how they constantly shift and develop across time and space' (Hornberger 2007: 325). The collection also demonstrates 'a commitment to researching pedagogical sites and research relevant to pedagogical sites from a transnational perspective, part of what one might call a re-engagement with pedagogy of the New Literacy Studies' (Baynham 2007: 335).

Similar to Bartlett's (2007) investigation of the transnational literacy practices utilized by a young Dominican woman to navigate the academic demands of her new school, Rubinstein-Avíla (2007) has examined the literacy practices of Dominican immigrant youth to question 'what counts as literacy and whose literacies count in an era of globalization.' By showing how the transnational space might be considered both a physical (literal) space and a symbolic one, Rubinstein-Avíla explores not only how immigration and literacy are social processes but also how 'living in a transnational space both shapes and is shaped by a young Dominican woman's expanding literacy practices' (p. 571).

Interested in the intersections between transcultural flows, global Englishes, performativity, and social identification, Pennycook (2007) has worked to 'escape from debates over globalization and localization' (p. 7) with his sociolinguistic analysis of hip-hop in non-U.S. contexts, demonstrating that cultural and linguistic flows often result in 'a reorganization of the local' (ibid.) rather than in homogenization. This work illuminates the critical role of multimodal practices in constituting meaning, dialogue, and voice while 'break[ing] down the distinction between oral and literacy modes of communication' (p. 10). In related work, Alim and Pennycook (2007) examine 'hip-hop culture(s), identities, and the politics of language education' in order to show that 'hip-hop is always both local and global' (p. 92) and that notions of nation are complicated by the global spread of English accompanied by the global flow of hip-hop culture (p. 95).

future directions and remaining questions

Lavie and Swedenburg (1996) have described how displacement might be experienced in various ways across time and space such that 'many geographies of identity' and 'historically grounded subject positions' (pp. 4–5) are constructed. In the study of transnational literacies, we focus on the 'transcontextualized and transcontextualizing potentials' (Brandt & Clinton 2002) of any given literacy practice while exploring how intimately connected and in dialogue the local, global, and transnational are. With the goal of discovering and then articulating exactly 'what is localizing and what is globalizing in what is going on' (ibid.: 347) in any particular context, the study of transnational literacies has much to contribute to our understanding of the many intersections between global flows and social practices.

Just as insights from transnational studies add a great deal to the examination of global-local connections that are of interest in Literacy Studies scholarship, the systematic examination of literacy as a social practice permits specific accounts of the potential links between cultures, peoples, identities, and specific places by describing the actual ways in which 'global' processes and transnational flows are lived, experienced, reconstituted, even transformed at the local level, and by individual actors. Of primary interest in both areas of inquiry are questions about transnational, translocal movement in relation to social practice; the role (and nature) of boundary maintenance or disruption in global, transnational, and translocal flows; and the lived experiences of individuals on the front lines of global, transnational, and translocal processes.

In moving toward a research agenda that prioritizes the study of transnational literacies, especially with regard to their educational implications, a number of important research agendas have been created. First, as the work described here demonstrates, it is clear that 'transnational flows are not limited to transmigrants' bodily geographic mobility. They also include multiple exchanges of monetary and non-monetary resources, material and symbolic objects, commodities and cultural values' (Guarnizo & Smith 1998: 21). This is evident in the renewed focus on discursive, material, and ideological intersections. It is also evident in the many recent studies of 'transnationalism from below' and 'transnational literacies' which convey how transnationality interacts with local power structures in profound and lasting ways. Finally, this research agenda has shaped contemporary thinking about relationships between global flows and social practices, embodied realizations of ideological processes, the relationship between national identity formation and processes of 'deterritorialization', and the many ways in which displacement is experienced across time and space.

At the same time, the study of transnational literacies as described here leaves unanswered key questions about theory and methodology. For instance, we are still trying to figure out how to 'look at space outside, across, and beyond the nation-state, while at the same time retaining an ethnographic perspective that situates these transnational spaces in the bodies of people with feelings and desires' (Low & Lawrence-Zuniga 2003: 30). In addition, scholarship in both areas of inquiry (transnational studies and New Literacy Studies) continues to grapple with questions regarding how we describe commonalities while still presenting theories and accounts that accurately represent the complexities of the distinct and varied experiences of immigrant, refugee, and indigenous populations. While many facets of the transnational literacies approach outlined here might be relevant to the examination of the language contact experiences and literacy practices of indigenous people moving across the borders of sovereign nations, it is not entirely clear what additional theoretical frameworks or methodological approaches are required for the systematic investigation of such practices within and between indigenous groups in the U.S. and elsewhere. Such questions represent a few of the many promising future directions in the study of transnational literacies, and I eagerly await the studies not yet undertaken as well as the rich ethnographic accounts not yet written.

note

1. Like Lam's (2004, 2006) recent work, McGinnis's (2007) piece is noteworthy for the ways that she brings discussions of multimodal communicative practices into conversations with both NLS scholarship and the anthropological study of transnationalism.

references

Alim, H. Samy and A. Pennycook (2007) Glocal Linguistic Flows: Hip-Hop Culture(s), Identities, and the Politics of Language Education. *Journal of Language, Identity, and Education*, 6(2), 89–100.

Appadurai, A. (1991) Global ethnoscapes: notes and queries for a transnational anthropology. In R. Fox (ed.) *Recapturing Anthropology*. Sante Fe: School of American Research, 191–210.

Appadurai, A. (1996) *Modernity at Large: Cultural Dimensions of Globalization*. Minneapolis: University of Minnesota Press.

Appadurai, A. (1996, 2003) Sovereignty without territoriality: notes for a postnational geography. In S. M. Low and D. Lawrence-Zuniga (eds), *The Anthropology of Space and Place: Locating Culture*. Malden, MA: Blackwell, 337–49.

Auerbach, E. (2005) Connecting the local and the global: a pedagogy of not-literacy. In J. Anderson, M. Kendrick, T. Rogers, S. Smythe (eds), *Portraits of Literacy across Families, Communities and Schools*. Mahah, NJ: Lawrence Erlbaum Associates, Publishers, 363–79.

Bartlett, L. (2003) Social Studies of Literacy and Comparative Education: Intersections (Guest Editorial Introduction). *Current Issues in Comparative Education*, 5(2), 67–76.

Bartlett, L. (2007) Bilingual Literacies, Social Identification, and Educational Trajectories. *Linguistics and Education*, 18(3&4), 215–31.

Barton, D. and M. Hamilton (2005) Literacy, reification and the dynamics of social interaction. In D. Barton and K. Tusting (eds) *Beyond Communities of Practice: Language, Power and Social Context*. Cambridge, UK and New York: Cambridge University Press, 14–35.

Basch, L., N. G. Schiller and C. Szanton Blanc (1994) *Nations Unbound: Transnational Projects, Postcolonial Predicaments and De-territorialized Nation-States*. Langhorne, PA: Gordon and Breach.

Baynham, M. (2004) Ethnographies of Literacy: An Introduction. *Language and Education*, 18(4), 285–90.

Baynham, M. (2007) Commentary: Transnational literacies: Immigration, Language Learning and Identity. *Linguistics and Education*, 18(3&4), 335–8.

Blommaert, J. (2003) Commentary: A Sociolinguistics of Globalization. *Journal of Sociolinguistics*, 7, 465–623.

Blommaert, J., J. Collins and S. Slembrouck (2005a) Polycentricity and Interactional Regimes in 'Global Neighborhoods.' *Ethnography*, 6(2), 205–35.

Blommaert, J., J. Collins and S. Slembrouck (2005b) Spaces of Multilingualism. *Language and Communication* 25, 197–216.

Bourdieu, P. (1984) *Distinction: A Social Critique of the Judgement of Taste*. Trans. by Richard Nice. Cambridge, MA: Harvard University Press.

Brandt, D. and K. Clinton (2002) Limits of the Local: Expanding Perspectives on Literacy as a Social Practice. *Journal of Literacy Research*, 34(3), 337–56.

Chamberlain, M. and S. Leydesdorff (2004) Transnational Families: Memories and Narratives. *Global Networks*, 4(3), 227–41.

Chandler, Nahum D. (1996) The figure of the X: an elaboration of the Du Boisian Autobiographical example. In S. Lavie and T. Swedenburg (eds) *Displacement, Diaspora, and Geographies of Identity*. Durham: Duke University Press, 235–72.

Collins, J. and S. Slembrouck (2005) Editorial: Multilingualism and Diasporic Populations: Spatializing Practices, Institutional Processes, and Social Hierarchies. *Language and Communication 25*, 189–95.

Duff, P. (2005) Thinking globally about English and the New Literacies: multilingual socialization at work. In J. Anderson, M. Kendrick, T. Rogers and S. Smythe (eds), *Portraits of Literacy across Families, Communities and Schools*. Mahah, NJ: Lawrence Erlbaum Associates, Publishers, 341–62.

Favell, A., M. Feldblum and M. P. Smith (2006) The human face of global mobility: a research agenda. In M. P. Smith (ed.), *The Human Face of Global Mobility: International Highly Skilled Migration in Europe, North America and the Asia-Pacific*. New Brunswick (USA): Transaction Publishers, 1–28.

Glick, S. N. (1997) The Situation of Transnational Studies, *Identities, 4*(2), 155–66.

Goldring, L. (1998) The power of status in transnational social fields. In M. P. Smith and L. Guarnizo (eds) *Transnationalism from Below*. New Brunswick: Transaction Publishers, 165–95.

Gregory, E. (2000) *City Literacies: Learning to Read across Generations and Cultures*. New York: Routledge.

Guarnizo, L. E. (1994) Los Dominicanyorks: The Making of a Binational Society. *Annals of the American Academy of Political and Social Science*, 533, 70–86.

Guarnizo, L. and M. P. Smith (1998) The locations of transnationalism. In M. P. Smith and L. Guarnizo (eds) *Transnationalism from Below*. New Brunswick: Transaction Publishers, 3–34.

Gupta, A. (2003) The song of the nonaligned world: transnational identities and the reinscription of space in late capitalism. In S. M. Low and D. Lawrence-Zuniga (eds), *The Anthropology of Space and Place: Locating Culture*. Malden, MA: Blackwell, 321–36.

Gupta, A. and J. Ferguson (1992) Beyond 'Culture': Space, Identity, and the Politics of Difference. *Cultural Anthropology* 7(1), 6–23.

Hall, S. (1990) Cultural identity and diaspora. In Jonathan Rutherford (ed.) *Identity: Community, Culture, Difference*. London: Lawrence and Wishart, 222–37.

Hannerz, U. (1996) *Transnational Connections*. London: Routledge.

Hornberger, N. H. (2007) Commentary: Biliteracy, Transnationalism, Multimodality, and Identity: Trajectories across Time and Space. *Linguistics and Education*, 18(3&4), 325–34.

Hymes, D. (ed.) (1997) *Ethnography, Linguistics, Narrative Inequality: Towards an Understanding of Voice*. London: Routledge.

Kearney, M. (1995) The Local and the Global: The Anthropology of Globalization and Transnationalism. *Annual Review of Anthropology, 24*, 547–65.

Kivisto, P. (2001) Theorizing Transnational Immigration: A Critical Review of Current Efforts. *Ethnic and Racial Studies, 24*(4), 549–77.

178 the future of literacy studies

Kothari, U. (2007) Global peddlers and local networks: 'Migrant cosmopolitanisms.' Paper presented at Living on the Margins Conference, Stellenbosch, South Africa.

Lam, W. S. E. (2004) Second Language Socialization in a Bilingual Chat Room: Global and Local Considerations. Language Learning and Technology, 8(3), 44–65.

Lam, W. S. E. (2006) Re-Envisioning Language, Literacy, and the Immigrant Subject in New Mediascapes. Pedagogies: An International Journal, 1(3), 171–95.

Lavie, S. and T. Swedenburg (1996) Introduction. In S. Lavie and T. Swedenburg (eds), Displacement, Diaspora, and Geographies of Identity. Durham, NC: Duke University Press.

Lemke, J. (2000) Across the Scales of Time. Mind, Culture, and Activity, 7, 273–90.

Low, S. M. and D. Lawrence-Zuniga (2003) Locating culture. In S. M. Low and D. Lawrence-Zuniga (eds), The Anthropology of Space and Place: Locating Culture. Malden, MA: Blackwell, 1–47.

Luke, A. (2003) Literacy and the Other: A Sociological Approach to Literacy Research and Policy in Multilingual Societies. Reading Research Quarterly, 38(1), 132–41.

Luke, A. (2004) On the Material Consequences of Literacy. Language and Education, 18(4), 331–5.

Mahler, S. (1998/2006) Theoretical and empirical contributions toward a research agenda for transnationalism. In M. P. Smith and L. E. Guarnizo (eds), Transnationalism from Below: Comparative Urban and Community Research, Volume 6. New Brunswick, NJ: Transaction Publishers, 64–100.

McGinnis, T., A. Goodstein-Stolzenberg and E. C. Saliani (2007) 'indnpride': Online spaces of transnational youth as sites of creative and sophisticated literacy and identity work. Linguistics and Education, 18(3&4), 283–304.

Ong, A. (1999) Flexible Citizenship: The Cultural Logics of Transnationality. Durham, NC: Duke University Press.

Orellana, M., B. Thorne, A. Chee and W. S. E. Lam (2001) Transnational Childhoods: The Participation of Children in Processes of Family Migration. Social Problems, 48(4), 572–91.

Orellana, M., J. Reynolds, L. Dorner and M. Meza (2003) In Other Words: Translating or 'para-phrasing' As a Family Literacy Practice in Immigrant Households. Reading Research Quarterly, 38, 12–34.

Pahl, K. (2004) Narratives, Artifacts and Cultural Identities: An Ethnographic Study of Communicative Practices in Homes. Linguistics and Education, 15, 339–58.

Pahl, K. and J. Rowsell (2005) Travel Notes from the New Literacy Studies: Instances of Practice. Clevedon: Multilingual Matters.

Pahl, K. and J. Rowsell (eds) (2006) Travel Notes from the New Literacy Studies: Instances of Practice. Clevedon: Multilingual Matters.

Papen, U. (2005) Adult Literacy as Social Practice: More Than Skills. New York: Routledge.

Pennycook, A. (2007) Global Englishes and Transcultural Flows. New York: Routledge.

Portes, A. (1997) Globalization from Below: The Rise of Transnational Communities. Oxford: ESRC Transnational Communities Working Paper WPTC-98-01. http://www.transcomm.oxford.ac.uk.

Portes, A. (2001) Introduction: The Debates and Significance of Immigrant Transnationalism. *Global Networks: A Journal of Transnational Affairs*, 1(3), 181–94.

Portes, A., L. E. Guarnizo and P. Landolt (1999) The Study of Transnationalism: Pitfalls and Promise of an Emergent Research Field. *Ethnic and Racial Studies*, 22(2), 217–37.

Pratt, M. L. (1991) Arts of the Contact Zone. *Profession*, 91, 33–40.

Pratt, M. L. (1992) *Imperial Eyes: Travel Writing and Transculturation*. London: Routledge.

Prinsloo, M. and M. Baynham (eds) (2008) *Literacies, Global and Local*. Philadelphia: John Benjamins Publishing Company.

Rampton, B. (2005) *Crossing: Language and Ethnicity among Adolescents*. London: Longman.

Rampton, B. (2006) *Language in Late Modernity: Interaction in an Urban School*. New York: Cambridge University Press.

Richardson, B. K. (2007) Traveling Tags: The Informal Literacies of Mexican Newcomers in and Out of the Classroom. *Linguistics and Education*, 18(3&4), 232–57.

Rubinstein-Avíla, E. (2007) From the Dominican Republic to Drew High: What counts as literacy for Yanira Lara? *Reading Research Quarterly*, 42(4), 568–89.

Sánchez, P. (2007) Cultural Authenticity and Transnational Latina Youth: Constructing a Meta-Narrative across Borders. *Linguistics and Education*, 18(3&4), 258–82.

Schein, L. (1998/2006) Forged transnationality and oppositional cosmopolitanism. In M. P. Smith and L. E. Guarnizo (eds), *Transnationalism from Below: Comparative Urban and Community Research, Volume 6*. New Brunswick, NJ: Transaction Publishers, 291–313.

Smith, M. P. (2003) Transnationalism, the State, and the Extraterritorial Citizen. *Politics & Society*, 31(4), 467–502.

Smith, R. (1995) Los ausentes siempre presentes: The Imagining, making, and politics of a transnational community between Ticuani, Puebla, Mexico and New York City. PhD Dissertation, Department of Sociology, Columbia University.

Smith, R. (1998/2006) Transnational localities: Community, technology and the politics of membership within the context of Mexico and U.S. migration. In M. P. Smith and L. E. Guarnizo (eds), *Transnationalism from Below: Comparative Urban and Community Research, Volume 6*. New Brunswick, NJ: Transaction Publishers, 196–238.

Sorensen, N. N. (1998/2006) Narrating identity across Dominican worlds. In M. P. Smith and L. E. Guarnizo (eds), *Transnationalism from Below: Comparative Urban and Community Research, Volume 6*. New Brunswick, NJ: Transaction Publishers, 241–69.

Street, B. (2003) What's 'New' in New Literacy Studies? Critical Approaches to Literacy in Theory and Practice. *Current Issues in Comparative Education*, 5(2), 77–91.

Street, B. (2004) Futures of the Ethnography of Literacy? *Language and Education*, 18(4), 326–30.

Waldinger, R. and D. Fitzgerald (2004) Transnationalism in Question. *American Journal of Sociology*, 109(5), 1177–95.

Warriner, D. S. (2003) 'Here without English you are Dead': Language Ideologies and the Experiences of Women Refugees Enrolled in an Adult ESL Program'. Unpublished Doctoral Dissertation.

Warriner, D. S. (2004) 'The Days Now Is Very Hard for My Family': The Negotiation and Construction of Gendered Work Identities among Newly Arrived Women Refugees. *Journal of Language, Identity, and Education,* 3(4), 279–94.

Warriner, D. S. (2007a) Introduction. Transnational Literacies: Immigration, Language Learning, and Identity. *Linguistics and Education,* 18(3&4), 201–14.

Warriner, D. S. (2007b) 'It's Just the Nature of the Beast': Re-Imagining the Literacies of Schooling. *Linguistics and Education,* 18(3&4), 305–24.

Wortham, S. (2001) Language Ideology and Educational Research. *Linguistics and Education,* 12, 253–59.

Wortham, S. (2006) *Learning Identity: The Joint Emergence of Social Identification and Academic Learning.* New York: Cambridge University Press.

9

texting the future: work, literacies, and economies

lesley farrell

work, literacies and economies

The idea of a technologically enabled Knowledge Economy assumes literate engagement on a global scale. This is not so much because people need to be literate to *produce* new knowledge, but more because global economic activity needs people to be literate to *trade* knowledge (both new and established) in a globally distributed economy. Global economic activity is conducted through textual practices, mostly through electronic texts of various kinds. It relies on literate actors to interpret, modify and enact the texts, to make the global economy happen. This is not to say that local workplaces do not rely on their own local, and sometimes idiosyncratic, literate practices to get their work done on a day-to-day basis, or to produce the new knowledge that drives innovation. On the contrary, we know that people in local workplaces develop highly specialized and productive literate practices that are embedded in their histories and geographies and in the local economic and political landscapes of which they are a part. What is distinctive about global economic activity is that it demands, and to some extent produces, a repertoire of literate practices that have the potential to join up local, geographically specific, workplaces and work-ers, simultaneously exploiting local knowledge-building potential and standardizing literate practice (and all that it entails, including the per-vasive use of English) across space and time. Although common literate practices may be necessary to create the ligatures that join up the glo-bal economy, however, they cannot completely replace the local literate practices that sustain local work practices. In local workplaces all over the world global literacies and local literacies are in constant conversation, producing new textual forms that foreground certain types of knowledge and marginalize other types, that foreground certain kinds of working identities and marginalize others. In much of the debate around the globalisation of work and the Knowledge Economy the centrality of literate practice is acknowledged as important, but conceptually unproblematic, and the debate moves on. For Literacy Studies as a field, however, the centrality of literate practice in the globalisation of work is both critically important and conceptually challenging.

First, and most obviously, the centrality of literate practice for global work makes the workplace an important site for sophisticated literacy research to occur. To date, most empirically based literacy studies have occurred in school and community settings. This is understandable; schools are recognized as places where children and young people learn the valued literate practices of their societies and community settings are the well springs of local literacies. Workplaces have only relatively recently been understood to be sites in which literacy is not only used but also learned and produced.

Second, it foregrounds the complex theoretical challenge of understanding the relationships between the local and remote sites in which literate practices are produced. Literacy Studies has offered important new insights into the ways in which literate practices are developed collaboratively in specific local settings. We are, however, only at the beginning of understanding how global practices and local practices shape, constrain and elaborate each other, and what the implications are for the social production of knowledge and identities in the contemporary workplace. The point is not that the global and local interact; it is that the global and the local constitute each other and we need to understand how literate practice is simultaneously instantiating this and enabling this to occur.

Third, it highlights the importance of continuing to bring Literacy Studies as a field and a methodological approach into conversation with other disciplines dealing with new forms of work and work practice. Literacy Studies has the potential to contribute unique understandings of the microprocesses of the globalization of work when it takes sophisticated account of the broad geopolitical contexts in which workplace literacy events occur.

Finally, the impact of technologies on textual formation has been an important dimension of Literacy Studies, especially the expansion of semiotics. In general, this research has focused on young people in their relation to school (either in it or outside of it) or in relation to popular culture, not on young people as participants in workplaces. A focus on textual formation in workplaces encourages an analysis, not only of what technology permits but also on the social construction of the technologies themselves and the ways in which software can be understood to be a kind of 'master text' which simultaneously produces and is produced by the social relationships that constitute local and globally distributed workplaces.

In the sections which follow I take up these issues and explore them in a little more detail, canvassing some of the research that has been done from a Literacy Studies perspective and suggesting some new directions.

literacy and the knowledge economy

There has been a durable, publicly acknowledged, connection between literacy, work and economic productivity in the West since the Industrial Revolution, although the straightforward equation – that a literate workforce equals a productive workforce – has certainly been contested. At first, employers were concerned that a literate workforce might well mean a less easily governable, more subversive, workforce and some actively campaigned against literacy education for working people (Donald 1991). The extent to which a literate workforce is more governable or less governable than an illiterate one remains a matter for debate, but the connection between literacy, work and productivity is now rarely questioned. Contemporary studies from both a Literacy Studies perspective (e.g. Folinsbee 2004; Geisler 2005; Gee, Hull and Lankshear 1996) and an Organizational Studies perspective (e.g. Roberts 2001) have highlighted the centrality of literate practice to work practice in any kind of globally distributed production.

The idea of the Knowledge Economy is now also generally taken for granted, at least in public rhetoric in the West. From the World Bank's perspective, a knowledge-based economy

> relies primarily on the use of ideas rather than physical abilities and on the application of technology rather than the transformation of raw materials or the exploitation of cheap labour. (World Bank, Lifelong Learning for the Global Knowledge Economy 2003: 1)

In this context 'knowing' is both an intellectual and an economic activity that relies on language, especially literate practices, rather than physical performance. This definition of global economic activity within the framework of a Knowledge Economy is, however, a conceptualization, not a neutral description (Peters and Beasley 2006; David and Foray 2003) and it is a conceptualization that is far from neutral in its effects. As Peters and Beasley argue, one effect of this kind of conceptualization is to configure education as a subset of economic policy rather than a broad social good. Another effect is to dramatically recalibrate established hierarchies of social relationships in societies with abundant raw materials and cheap labour but restricted access to communications technologies. It is, therefore, not surprising that the idea of the Knowledge Economy is not taken for granted, but rather is strongly contested, in many parts of the non-Western world. In the Arab States, for instance, Mazawi (2007) argues that the Knowledge Economy is often interpreted as a politically motivated way of viewing economic activity that allows the West to construct the Arab States as having a 'knowledge deficit' which results 'from authoritarian, non-democratic and corrupt political systems, rampant poverty and illiteracy, centralized economies and failed industrialization' (p. 254). Constructed in such a way, the Arab States (and many other non-Western nations) are identified as being in dire need of Western technologies, political systems and, underpinning all of these, (English) literacy.

Large-scale surveys like The International Survey of Adult Literacy, which provides statistical data on 14 OECD countries, conceptualize literacy as a form of human capital, and promote the view that increased literacy leads to increased economic productivity. The Australian Bureau of Statistics (ABS), for instance, frames its analysis of the 2006 ISAL with the comment that

> Technological innovation and labour force changes, as well as the application of new work practices, have led to major changes in the occupational composition of the Australian Labour force and the tasks and skills required of workers. (ABS 2008: 4)

In doing so this survey presents literacy as one of a suite of important skills required of the workforce if Australia (along with other OECD countries) is to maintain its productivity in the new economy. In treating literacy as a cognitive skill like any other the report presents a view of literacy analogous to the autonomous perspective identified by Street (1985). It appears to follow Goody (1977) in understanding literacy as the primary cause of technological (and consequently economic) advancement. It reproduces an implicit 'Great Divide' in which the world's people are divided into those who are literate – and therefore capable of abstract thought, technological advancement and economic prosperity in a Knowledge Economy – and those who are illiterate and doomed to technological stagnation and the ensuing poverty that must follow. However, as Graff (1987) has demonstrated, the relationship between literacy and productivity is not a simple one. While there was for some time an assumption of direct cause and effect, we now know that improved literacy is just as much likely to be the result of economic growth as the cause.

The powerful concept of the Knowledge Economy, however, equates literacy and work in fundamental ways – in a practical sense it becomes difficult to disaggregate work practice and literate practice. From this perspective, literacy education seems like an unproblematic good. International aid agencies promote and fund universal literacy programs on the stated basis that literacy (usually in English but sometimes in another widely used European language) is a fundamental requirement for participation in technologically enabled global economic activity (and, therefore, it assumes, all meaningful work). In Africa, for instance, Oxenham et al. found that

Livelihoods and literacy are now so closely intertwined that it is no longer realistic to speak of two [distinct] approaches [to education]. (2002)

Brock-Utne (2000) argues that it is not so much that vocational education is intertwined with literacy education as that literacy education has completely subsumed vocational education. Many aid projects in sub-Saharan Africa and elsewhere focus on the development of literacy, usually in English, to the exclusion of local, work-related, skill development that might reasonably lead to self-employment or employment in the local community (Iman 2005; Chase–Dunn 1999; Wickens and Sandlin 2007).

In some cases this seems to be more a matter of standardizing the processes of global production by ensuring that global economic activity can be sustained by a minimally English-literate workforce than bridging a Great Divide to support local entrepreneurial activity. This has a potentially coercive effect on many fragile economies by effectively determining what and how literacy is taught. Punchi argues that the World Bank and UNESCO

dictate many national policies on education and literacy through stipulations on loans that emphasise standardisation, efficiency and measures of productivity. (Punchi 2001)

From this perspective, then, literacy (understood as a generic, 'basic', work-related skill) is comprehensively and explicitly linked to the Knowledge Economy, but in routine and instrumental ways arising from a 'top down' perspective on globalization (Appadurai 2000).

Research on literate practice and the Knowledge Economy from a Literacy Studies standpoint, however, uses a different approach, adopting a 'bottom up' (or 'grassroots' – see Appardurai 2000) perspective on globalization and a close focus on the textual practices produced in local workplaces. These studies analyse the ways in which groups of workers at specific local worksites produce the textual practices that solve problems and generate new knowledge. South African studies reported in Prinsloo and Breier (1996), and later work by Schultz and Prinsloo, emphasize the collaborative nature of literate practice at work, and the way it is embedded in the social, economic and political relations of the local site. Schultz and Prinsloo's (2001) study of literacy in a hydraulic manufacturing plant shows the way that Knowledge Economy demands for English-literate workers challenges and changes the race and gender dynamics of a South African workplace.

My own work in an automotive textile manufacturing plant in Australia also demonstrates the link between literate practice, working knowledge and gender identities. In that case, too, the literacy demands of the Knowledge Economy change the power dynamic in the textile manufacturing company by changing how working knowledge is legitimated and made visible. For many years, problem-solving (an important kind of workplace knowledge making) had occurred onsite and with minimal documentation. People knew (or thought they knew) who had certain kinds of knowledge and skill and they would form into informal working parties to address problems as they arose. However, as the company became more securely located in the global automotive supply chain, solving problems was not enough, the solutions, and the problem-solving processes that went with them, had to be documented. To be legitimated, the knowledge used to solve the problem had to be presented in a highly explicit textual form than could be easily transported from one worksite to another around the globe. It was not enough to solve the problem in practice at the local worksite. This privileging of literate practice over other work practices recalibrated gender relations in very complex ways (Farrell 2006). The established dominance of the largely male technical workforce was challenged by female workers, who had greater control of the valued literate practices.

A significant body of research raises issues like these, identifying the ways in which the literacy demands of the Knowledge Economy contribute to the capacity of global corporations to promote certain working identities and discourage others, and to maintain surveillance and control at a distance (e.g. Hull 1997, 2000; Hull and Zacher 2007; Farrell 2000; Iedema and Scheeres 2003) while simultaneously encouraging apparently autonomous, self-realizing work groups. I'll take up this question of the part that literate practice plays in regulating the relationships between people and the organizations for which they work, both locally and remotely, again below; but first I would like to consider the role that literate practice plays in joining up people and practices in global economic webs.

literacy and locality

A defining feature of New Literacy Studies has been its focus on local literate practice. Starting from the position that literacy only has meaning in the particularity of its own context – in its 'location' – it has built on Street's 'ideological model' (1995) of literacy in which literacy is understood to be produced by the immediate social, cultural and political contexts in which it is rooted.

Often, in practice, 'local' has meant a specific physical location – a school, a neighborhood, a worksite. The particular power of this analysis has been its capacity to get at complexity, and at the embedded-ness of literate practice. We are invited to view literate practice as social – embedded in the unique economic, political, cultural and other social practices of place. In workplace Literacy Studies this approach has provided a welcome challenge to the dominant view of literacy as a generic, transferable, cognitive skill which accrues to the individual worker, is the responsibility of the individual worker to maintain and update, and which can be transferred from one workplace, or industry, context to another with almost no effort. It has demonstrated that, far from merely 'using' literacy skills, people work collaboratively to produce new literate practices to get specific jobs done in the unique contexts in which they find themselves. They solve workplace problems, and make new knowledge for the Knowledge Economy, through innovative literate practice. The politics of the local is not ignored in these analyses; in fact it is foregrounded. These studies have demonstrated that literate practices produce and entrench power hierarchies at local sites, as much as they challenge and transform them.

What is less visible in these analyses, however, is the power of remote sites, and remote literate practices, and the ways in which these shape and constrain local literate practices and the work, working identities and working relationships of specific local sites. International standards frameworks, like ISO9000 for instance, demand standardized documentary evidence that local workplaces meet 'universal' standards.

If producers of any kind (cotton growers, automotive textile manufacturers, food producers) wish to trade on a global market (and that could include selling to the farm next door, if it is owned, as it is increasingly likely to be, by a global agribusiness) then they must keep exhaustive records of their products, and their production processes, in a standardized format and be prepared for regular audits. If any company wishes to be a preferred supplier of one of the major global corporations then they must comply with more extensive Quality Assurance demands. Quality Manuals from major global corporations can dictate not just the specifications of the goods produced by their suppliers but also the problem-solving processes involved in production (Farrell 2006; Jackson 1995, 2004). These remotely determined literate practices do not generally replace local practices; they are brought into conversation with them and used and interpreted in specific local ways (Kleifgen 2005; Hunter 2007).

While the aim is to standardize production across the whole globally distributed supply chain, documents like Quality Manuals are taken up and used in very different ways in different places, according to the social, political and historical contexts of the local site, and the pragmatic conditions under which they operate.

Texts like these do, theoretically and practically, have global reach. They not only move across contexts, they constitute contexts, especially when the members of the community are geographically and temporally remote from each other. They challenge us to reconsider what we mean by the term 'local' and to consider extending our methodologies in ways which take account of new forms of locality that are not primarily geographically bounded. Within the global automotive supply chain, for instance, workers in the United States, South Africa, Germany, Australia and Korea may be joined together by a single Quality Manual and a system of documentation that shapes local practice in standardized ways, but they may be simultaneously joined by technological platforms (an intranet is a simple example) which permit individual workers in one part of the world to communicate with other individual workers in another part of the world to produce a single product (a car, say, or a bottle of fruit juice) in ways that may be more, or less, constrained.

It is not surprising that the concept of the 'local' is up for debate from many disciplinary perspectives, including Literacy Studies (e.g. Brandt and Clinton 2002; Reder and Davilia 2005). With regard to research on literacy and work, the expansion of our understanding of local/remote, and local/global binaries, and the re-theorizing of the relationships between these concepts as mutually constitutive, offers potential for powerful new research. In fact it is unlikely that we can get much further in addressing the pressing research questions around literacy, identity, power and knowledge in workplaces, without confronting these issues conceptually and methodologically. To address some of these issues, which have become pressing in my own research, I am developing the concept of work*space* (Farrell 2006; Farrell and Holkner 2004) to try to capture the spatial and temporal dimensions of globally distributed work activity which is defined and bounded by traditional and technologically enabled literate practice:

> Physical work*places* [form] local nodes of a complex network of people, technologies and practices that constitute a potentially globally distributed work*space*. [Work*spaces* are] dynamic, fluid, often transient, working units defined and bounded by regular, routine information and communications technology routes. (p. 17)

The question of how we might understand the 'local' in a context where a network of familiar, routine communications join up distinctive physical locations, both spatially and temporally, might be usefully addressed by calling on economic geographers (e.g. Peck 2002). These issues have also been taken up through Actor Network Theory (e.g. Edwards and Nicoll 2007). Critical engagement with new forms of ethnography which take account of new ways of understanding space and time, like global ethnography (e.g. Burraway et al. 2000) and ethnographies of circulations (e.g. Appadurai 2000; Farrell 2006a) could suggest productive new ways forward. A more complex understanding of 'locality' may also help us to understand the part that literacy plays in the regulation of work practices and working identities at local sites.

literacy and workforce regulation

Texts in the global economy can be understood to have global reach, even though the ways they are taken up and used rely heavily on local conditions. In the same way, the workforce can usefully be understood to be a global workforce, not because workers are interchangeable, or even especially mobile, but because, almost wherever they are in the world, even if they never leave their home town, they are joined to each other, and to the institutions that regulate their work practice, by the robust textual ligatures of the global economy. This relationship between people, and between people and organizations, and the ways in which the relationship is textually enabled and realized, is a critical one in studies of work-related literacy.

One aspect of the textual regulation of the global workforce is surveillance and control. The increasing role of documentation and textual accountability in contributing to surveillance and control in workplaces is a recurring theme in much critical management literature, although the processes by which this occurs (or, indeed, the processes by which it can be disrupted) are not generally closely examined. In the most concrete sense, the micro-surveillance involved in various forms of electronic monitoring exploits the textual character of work by recording every key stroke contemporary workers make on their computers. Similarly, the coercive effect of call centre operators being required to read their screen, and follow their script without deviating, even where this involves assuming a different cultural identity (either implicitly or explicitly) is now well documented (e.g. Mirchandani 2004; Farrell and Pittard 2006). However, while these forms of regulation are obvious, they are not necessarily the most powerful form of regulation occurring in global/local workplaces.

All literate practices involve the social and ideological production of identities and relationships, and this is no less true of work than of any other activity. One of the effects of the increasing textualization of work, however, is the potential it offers to regulate working identity and working relationships in unobtrusive ways, rather than the direct coercion that the call centre operators referred to above experience. This is essentially a matter of monitoring and controlling the relationships between individual workers and between workers and the organizations with which, directly or indirectly, they are engaged. Dorothy Smith sets texts at the heart of institutional relations:

> Ruling relations form a complex file of co-ordinated activities, based on print and increasingly on communications technologies. They are activities in and in relation to texts, and texts co-ordinate them as relations. Text-mediated relations are the forms in which power is generated and held in contemporary societies. (1999: 79)

This conceptualization of the regulatory power of texts in joining the local and the remote, and the effects this has on the regulation of people and practices at local sites has been taken up by a number of scholars in the field of Literacy Studies from a conceptual point of view (Barton and Hamilton 2005; Farrell 2006b) and as the basis for empirical work (Reimer). A limitation of her work at present, however, is the conceptualization of the text itself as both relatively static and more or less print-based. By that I mean that, although Smith acknowledges the electronic transmission of texts, and all that this entails as far as texts being ligatures that make communities and produce and maintain power relations, she does not address the question of technologically mediated texts as extending and shifting the concept of text itself (Farrell and Beavis 2007). So, while the field of Literacy Studies has much to gain by engaging with Smith and others' work on Institutional Ethnography to understand the textual practice of work, Institutional Ethnography also has much to gain by engaging with the kinds of microanalyses of institutional regulation, realized in specific literate practices and events, that Literacy Studies allows.

Similarly, Barton and Tusting's collection of essays (2005) on the possibilities and limitations of Communities of Practice demonstrates the contribution that a Literacy Studies perspective can bring to a mainstream Workplace Learning concept like Communities of Practice. The concept of a Community of Practice has its roots in Lave's work on situated cognition (Lave and Wenger 2001) but has become popularized through the work of Wenger (2003) and others (e.g. Hildreth and Kimble 2004). While Communities of Practice theories sit well with Literacy Studies in their promotion of knowledge as socially produced and occurring 'in action', they tend to take a generally uncritical view of the power relationships of communities and to take the textual character of the community itself for granted. This is the case even where the focus is on spatially and temporally distributed communities which clearly rely on electronic texts to produce and maintain communities across space and time. Barton and Tusting's collection foregrounds the textual character of communities of practice and in doing so highlights the way power is produced and used in communities of practice in workplaces. In calling for a greater awareness of the extent to which the 'practice' on which communities of practice rely is literate practice; this collection proposes a potentially productive focus on the regulatory power of communities of practice in global networks of production.

An emerging issue in research on literacy and workforce regulation is the question of the role of what Fairclough calls the 'discourse technologist' (1996). Fairclough has argued that the global economy demands people who intervene in the textual practices of local sites (like a local office or factory) to shift local literate practices to the standardized global literate practices that global economic activity demands. Institutional regulation is not, then, achieved merely by imposing standardized literate practice from afar; the process needs to be far more active than that. What global organizations require is someone who animates global discourses at local sites, teaching people how to take up global discourses and insert them into their local settings. Very often, as I have argued (e.g. Farrell 2001) discourse technologists in workplaces are workplace educators, commonly but by no means always, Workplace English Language and Literacy educators. Brandt's (2005) concept of the Literacy Sponsor fills something of the same position but is somewhat more benignly constructed. Discourse technologists clearly occupy an ambiguous position in the workplace, teaching and promoting the literate practices that allow people and organizations to take part in global economic activity but, in doing so, introducing views, values and orientations to work and identity that may be regarded by local workers as alien or hostile.

literacy and multimodality at work

It has become commonplace to remark that work practice has become literate practice. What often goes less remarked is that the kinds of texts that constitute the literate practices of work practice are changing all the time. The workspace is, like everywhere else, or, perhaps, even more than everywhere else, multimodal. Multiple generations of technologies coexist at many worksites– print, fax, pagers, telephone landlines, voice recorders, mobile phones (for voice and text messaging), email, shared virtual 'workspaces' and more elaborate business to business (B2B) exchanges. Sophisticated computer software allows multifunctional teams to form and collaboratively design new products and processes (a car, a bridge, an investment strategy, a corporate restructure), or solve problems, across many countries, time zones, companies, industry sectors and professions. We inhabit those workspaces and animate those technologies routinely, as part of our everyday working lives.

Workspaces also include less familiar textual formations – wikis, blogs, social networking sites like Facebook and multiplayer online games like World of Warcraft– some (but by no means all) imported into the workspace by workers and not associated with the workplace in a formal way. The blurring of work and personal life (and, therefore, working and other identities) through these literate technologies is evident. Technologies like these have the potential to disrupt accepted understandings of what counts as working knowledge, and the ways in which new knowledge might be made and used in globally distributed workspaces. For instance, all forms of social networking provide a company with potentially valuable new networks and professional contacts – networks and contacts that might be crucial to the development of an innovative new product or to the development of a new market in a new location. Workers with skill and experience in engaging in these new textual formations can be valuable. They can be offered a high degree of apparent autonomy and encouraged to develop their social networking as a means of enhancing the resources available to them and their employer. Similarly, multiplayer online games can be viewed as a means of enhancing a worker's capacity to communicate, form relationships and solve problems in online environments (Gee et al. 1996; Farrell and Beavis 2007). One famous example is the US military's use of the World of Warcraft to train military personnel. In other work environments, of course, logging on to a social networking site or a videogame could be viewed grounds for dismissal.

The pervasiveness of these kinds of technologies (which seem, on the face of it, to provide the opportunity to obscure national, gender and class differences) has been one of the reasons why commentators present the world as 'borderless' and argue, as Michael Hammer (1996) does, that difference has become obsolete:

> Connections, background, ethnicity, race religion and gender no longer count. The process organization is a true meritocracy, the original American ideal and the realisation of Dr Martin Luther King's dream that men and women may be judged only by the content of their character. (p. 264)

Global economies in general, and global corporations in particular, rely heavily on technologically enabled communication to communicate and get work done across spatially and temporally distributed supply chains and networks. What has become evident, however, is that while technologies are notionally context free and available all over the world they are neither neutral nor equally available. While a business to business exchange, a company intranet site or an interactive diagnostic program may seem to be a neutral (context-free) text, this neutrality is illusory. These software programs, the programming language of which can be understood as a technological text, and the literate practices that they provoke, are as socially embedded as any other. Any business to business exchange, for instance, will have embedded in it the hierarchical relationships between the participating businesses (either existing or desired) and assumptions about what kind of access to technology is available and who at the worksite has access to it (Farrell 2006b).

Software programs need to be understood as both socially embedded and ideological if we are to understand the literate practices and literacy events that develop around them and the different local sites where they are taken up and used. So, for instance, a multinational corporation might make a new interactive, continuously updating, Operations Manual available to all suppliers simultaneously, whether they be in Aceh in Indonesia or Sydney Australia. In Sydney the document might be downloaded in a couple of minutes to the personal computer of anyone who needs it without interrupting any other activities. In Aceh, where far less bandwidth is available, and it is relatively much more expensive, it may take several hours to download to one of the few computers available and mean that no bandwidth is available for other members of the community (like the school, other businesses etc.). The scarcity of bandwith in Aceh may well promote innovative uses of other technologies, especially print and fax, and the development of new, local, literate practices that accommodate the demands of global corporations in the context of local conditions. But the scarcity of bandwidth in Aceh is also likely to promote innovative literate practices (possibly involving fax and print) in Sydney. Workers in Sydney cannot assume that co-workers in Aceh are working from the same document, making the same assumptions about what that document means, or developing the same literate practices around it. The point here is that, far from erasing difference, technologically enabled texts are produced by difference and produce difference. Technologically enabled texts are as socially produced as any other form of literate engagement. While they are generated from remote sites they are bound to the geographic, economic, social and political relations of where they are taken up.

This makes a difference to the way we conceptualize literacy education in a technologized workspace. The challenge stops being fundamentally concerned with mastering successive generations of digital literacies and becomes more concerned with learning to navigate, with sensitivity and political acuity, the technologically and culturally hybrid textual context of work.

texting the future at work

Workplace literate practices are shaping our future, and they are doing it in unpredictable ways. Local workplaces are the sites where the global movement of people, capital and ideas play out in urgent ways, generating new literate practices from the local and remote resources available to them, and the new identities, relationships and institutions that attend these new practices. While they may start at the workplace, however, they will not end there. As we have seen, when identities, relationships and institutions are challenged in the workplace the ramifications extend well beyond the workplace, reconfiguring social relationships and social institutions in the rest of people's lives. The challenge to Literacy Studies as a field is to accept the complexity of the global workspace and to find new ways to understand it.

references

Appadurai, A. (2000) Grassroots globalisation and the research imagination. *Globalisation*. Durham and London, Duke University Press, 1–21.

Australian Bureau of Statistics (ABS) (2008) Adult Literacy and Life Skills Survey http://www.abs.gov.au/AUSSTATS/abs@.nsf/DOSSbytitle/2D7F8204FEA1D124 CA2572E9008079F1?OpenDocument. Accessed on 13 August 2009.

Barton, D. and K. Tusting (eds) (2005) *Beyond Communities of Practice: Language, Power and Social Context*. Cambridge, UK: Cambridge University Press.

Barton, D. and M. Hamilton (2005) Literacy, reification and the dynamics of social interaction. In D. Barton and K. Tusting (eds) *Beyond Communities of Practice: Language, Power and Social Context*. Cambridge, UK: Cambridge University Press.

Brandt, D. (2005) Writing for a Living Literacy and the Knowledge Economy. *Written Communication*, 22(2), 166–97.

Brandt, D. and K. Clinton (2002) Limits of the local: expanding perspectives on literacy as social practice. *Journal of Literacy Research*, 34(3), 337–56.

Brocke-Utne, B. (2000) *Whose Education for All? The Colonization of the African Mind*. New York, NY: Falmer Press.

Burawoy, M. (2000) Grounding globalisation. In M. Burawoy, Joseph A. Blum, S. George and Z. Gille (eds), *Global Ethnography: Forces, Connections and Imaginations in a Postmodern World*. Berkeley: University of California Press, 337–50.

Chase-Dunn, C. (1999) Globalization: A World-Systems Perspective, *Journal of World-Systems Research*, 2, 187–215.

David, P. A. and D. Foray (2003) Economic Fundamentals of the Knowledge Society. *Policy Futures in Education*, 1(1), 20–49.

Donald, J. (1991) How illiteracy became a problem and literacy stopped being one. In C. Mitchell and K. Weiler (eds), *Rewriting Literacy: Culture and the Discourse of the Other*. New York: Bergin and Garvey.

Edwards, R. and K. Nicoll (2007) The ghost in the network Globalisation and workplace learning. In L. Farrell and T. Fenwick (eds) *Educating the Global Workforce: Knowledge, Knowledge Work and Knowledge Workers*. World Year Book of Education 2007. London: Routledge, 300–10.

Fairclough, N. (1996) Technologisation of discourse. In C. Caldas-Coulthard and M. Coulthard (eds) *Texts and Practices*. London: Routledge, 71–83.

Farrell, L. (2000) Ways of Doing, Ways of Being: Language, Education and 'Working' Identities. *Language and Education*, 14(1), 18–36.

Farrell, L. (2001) Negotiating Knowledge in the Knowledge Economy: Workplace Educators and the Politics of Codification. *Studies in Continuing Education* 23(2), 201–14.

Farrell, L. (2006) *Making Knowledge Common: Literacy and Knowledge at Work*. New York: Peter Lang & Co.

Farrell, L. and B. Holkner (2004) Points of Vulnerability and Presence: Knowing and Learning in Globally Networked Communities. *Discourse*, 25(2), 133–44.

Farrell, L. and C. Beavis (2007) Institutional Ethnography and the challenge of multi-modal, globally distributed, 'cyber texts' in Contexts, Organizations and Texts: Institutional Ethnographers in Transnational Dialogue Conference, Management Centre, Deakin University, November 20–1.

Farrell, L. and M. Pittard (2006) Regulating/educating global workers: the role of work-related education in global workspaces. SCUTREA 2006 Inter-cultural perspectives on research into adult learning: a global dialogue, Leeds, UK, Lifelong Learning Institute, University of Leeds and SCUTREA.

Folinsbee, S. (2004) Paperwork as the lifeblood of quality. In M. E. Bellfiore, T. A. Defoe, S. Folinsbee, J. Hunter and N. S. Jackson (eds), *Reading Work. Literacies in the New Workplace*. Mahwah, New Jersey: Lawrence Erlbaum Associates.

Gee, J. P. (2005) *What Video Games Have to Teach Us about Learning and Literacy*. New York: Palgrave Macmillan.

Gee, J. P. and G. Hull, and C. Lankshear (1996) *The New Work Order: Behind the Language of the New Capitalism*. St Leonards, NSW: Allen and Unwin.

Geisler, C. (2005) Textual Objects: Accounting for the Role of Texts in the Everyday Life of Organizations. *Written Communication*, 18(3), 296–325.

Goody, J. (1977) *The Domestication of the Savage Mind*. Cambridge (UK): Cambridge University Press.

Graff, H. (1987) *The Labyrinths of Literacy: Reflections on Literacy Past and Present*. New York: Falmer Press.

Hammer, M. (1996) *Beyond Reengineering: How the Process-Centred Organization Is Changing Our Work and Our Lives*. New York: Harper Collins.

Hildreth, P. and C. Kimble (eds) (2004) *Knowledge Networks: Innovation through Communities of Practice*. Hershey, PA: Idea Group Publishing.

Hull, G. (ed.) (1997) *Changing Work, Changing Workers Critical Perspectives on Language, Literacy and Skills*. New York: SUNY.

Hull, G. (2000) Critical Literacy at Work. *Journal of Adolescent and Adult Literacy*, 43(7), 648–52.

Hull, G. and J. Zacher (2007) Identity formation and literacy development within vocational education and work. In L. Farrell and T. Fenwick (eds) *Educating the global workforce: Knowledge, Knowledge Work and Knowledge Workers*. World Year Book of Education 2007. London: Routledge.

Hunter, J. (2007) Language, Literacy and Performance: Working Identities in the Back of the House. *Discourse: Studies in the Cultural Policies of Education*, 28(2), 243–57.

Iedema, R. and H. Scheeres (2003) From Doing Work to Talking Work: Renegotiating Knowing, Doing and Identity. *Applied Linguistics*, 24(3), 316–37.

Jackson, N. (1995) 'These things just happen': *Talk, Text and Curriculum Reform*. In M. Campbell and A. Manicom (eds), *Knowledge, Experience and Ruling Relations. Studies in the Social Organisation of Knowledge*. Toronto: Toronto University Press, 164–80.

Jackson, N. (2004) Introduction. In M. E. Belfiore, T. A. Defoe, S. Folinsbee, J. Hunter and N. S. Jackson (eds), Reading Work *Literacies in the New Workplaces*. Mahwah New Jersey: Lawrence Earlbaum Associates, 1–15.

Kleifgen, J. (2005) ISO 9002 as Literacy Practice: Coping with Quality-Control Documents in a High-Tech Company. *Reading Research Quarterly*, 40(4), 450–68.

Lankshear, C. (1998) Language and the New Capitalism. *Journal of Inclusive Education*, 1(4), 309–21.

Lave, J. and E. Wenger (1991) *Situated Learning: Legitimate Peripheral Participation*. New York: Cambridge University Press.

Mazawi, A. (2007) 'Knowledge Society' or work as 'spectacle'? Education for work and the prospects of social transformation in Arab societies. In L. Farrell and T. Fenwick (eds) *Educating the Global Workforce: Knowledge, Knowledge Work and Knowledge Workers*. London: Routledge.

Mirchandani, K. (2004) Practices of Global Capital: Gaps, Cracks and Ironies in Transnational Call Centres in India. *Global Networks*, 4(4), October, 355–74.

Oxenham, J., A. Daillo, A. Katahoire, A. Petkova-Mwangi and O. Sall (2002) *Skills and Literacy Training for Better Livelihoods: A Review of Approaches and Experiences*. Bonn, Germany: World Bank.

Peck, J. (2002) Political Economies of Scale: Fast Policy, Interscalar Relations, and Neoliberal Workfare. *Economic Geography*, 78(3), 331–60.

Peters, M. and A. C. Besley (2006) *Building Knowledge Cultures: Education and Development in the Age of Capitalism*. Lanham, MD: Rowman and Littlefield.

Prinsloo, M. and M. Breier (Eds) (1996) – *The Social Uses of Literacy* Amsterdam: Benjamins.

Punchi, L. (2001) Resistance towards the Language of Globalization – The Case of Sri Lanka. *International Review of Education*, 47(3–4), 361–78.

Reder, S. and E. Davila (2005) Context and Literate practices. *Annual Review of Applied Linguistics*, 25, 170–87.

Reimer, M. (1995) Downgrading clerical work in a textually mediated labour process. In M. Campbell and A. Manicom (eds), *Knowledge, Experience and Ruling Relations*. Toronto: Toronto University Press, 193–208.

Roberts, J. (2001) The Drive to Codify: Implications for the Knowledge-based Economy. *Prometheus*, 19(2), 99–116.

Scholtz, S. and M. Prinsloo (2001) New Work Places, New Literacies, New Identities. *Journal of Adolescent and Adult Literacy*, May, 710–13.

Street, B. (1985) *Literacy and Theory and Practice*. Cambridge: Cambridge University Press.

Wenger, E. (2003) *Communities of practice and social learning systems.* In D. Nicolini, S. Gherardi, D. Yanow (eds) Knowing in Organisations: A Practice-Based Approach. New York: Armonk, 76–99.

Wickens, C. and J. Sandlin (2007) Literacy for What? Literacy for Whom? The Politics of Literacy Education and Neo-colonialism in UNESCO and World Bank Sponsored literacy programs. *Adult Education Quarterly*, 54(4), 275–92.

World Bank (2003) *Lifelong Learning for the Global Knowledge Economy: Challenges for Developing Countries.* Washington DC: World Bank.

10
literacy, media, and morality: making the case for an aesthetic turn

glynda a. hull and
mark evan nelson

introduction: of blacksmiths and representation

Media scholar Roger Silverstone (2007) opens his provocative meditation on the role of media in a global world by recounting a story that we find powerfully emblematic. It is emblematic of his book, which theorizes the potential of media to constitute a moral public space, and of our chapter, which proposes aesthetics, or one's sense of what is beautiful or right,[1] as an organizing principle for future Literacy Studies. Silverstone recounts a brief interview that was broadcast on BBC Radio in the midst of the US war in Afghanistan not long after 9/11 and the World Trade Center attack. This interview featured an Afghani blacksmith, who had his own take on why so many bombs were falling on his village. It was because, his translated voice proposed, 'Al Qaeda had killed many Americans and their donkeys and had destroyed some of their castles' (p. 1). What interested Silverstone about the blacksmith's account was that, for a brief moment, it reversed the 'customary polarities of interpretation' (p. 4) 'in which we in the West do the defining, and in which you are, and I am not, the other' (p. 3). Silverstone believes that the quintessential characteristic of media in our global and digital world is its potential to link strangers to each other, across geographic, social, and historical space. Indeed, he argued that the images of strangers, mediated by television, computers, cell phones, radio, and the like, largely constitute our understanding of the world. The insistent question, of course, is what are we to make of these mediated images, how are we to respond in our turn. In Silverstone's words: 'So here is the blacksmith speaking, and he is speaking, albeit briefly, about us. Here he is talking about us in his terms, through his view of the world. Are we going to listen? What are we going to hear' (p. 2)?

This chapter is our response to these questions as we consider the future of Literacy Studies. That is, if we want to position ourselves and our students to be able to listen, hear, and respond to Silverstone's blacksmith—if we see this as a paradigmatic instantiation of a critical function that literacies need to serve in the twenty-first century, which we do—how might we conceptualize Literacy Studies and literacy education now?

As will be explored in what follows, we believe that being prepared, in both senses of being able and willing, to communicate and understand across differences in language and other modes and media for communication, in ideology, in culture, and in geography is at the heart of what it means to be literate now. Indeed, such capacities and desire stand at the center of other proposed dispositions for identity, thought, and action, such as civic engagement, cosmopolitanism, and 'productive diversity' (Cope & Kalantzis 1997; Kalantzis & Cope 2000; New London Group 1996) which are considered by some to be crucial, and crucially needed at present, as habits of mind and activity in a global world. Further, as we consider the need to communicate and understand across differences, we, as do a growing number of our colleagues (e.g. see Barton 2007; Gee 2003, 2004; Harris 2001; Hull 2003; Hull & Nelson 2005; Kress 2003, 2005; Kress & van Leeuwen 1996; Lankshear & Knobel 2003; Lemke 1997, 1998; New London Group 1996; Wysocki et al. 2004), take as a given that we now need to define literacy as a multimodal enterprise, one that recognizes and tries to account for necessary interrelationships among language, written and oral, sound, image, gesture, movement, and even silence (Stein 2007). No longer is it practical or theoretically defensible, we believe, to separate the teaching and conceptualization of written language from other semiotic systems. Partly this stance is driven empirically by the shift that many have observed from the dominance of print to digitally enabled multimodality (e.g. Kress 2003; Lemke 1997); but partly, too, it is a theoretical predilection, informed by a vision of meaning-making and symbolization as a human activity that of necessity relies on many senses and modes of knowing (Finnegan 2002). Last, drawing on the multimodal impulse in digital communication today, and combining that with the crucial need to communicate respectfully and intelligently and compassionately across differences—in Silverstone's terms, to exhibit 'hospitality' when we engage images and words of the 'other'—we offer the beginnings of an artistic, aesthetic grounding for Literacy Studies.[2]

In the sections that follow, we draw upon empirical studies that we and others have carried out principally over the past five years and that feature explorations of new literacies along the lines discussed above; that is, literacies that are multimodal, aesthetically alert, and morally attuned. Our own work has centered on digital storytelling,[3] and more recently social networking as well, and it has taken place usually, although not always, in extra-school or out-of-school contexts, and often the targeted participants have been children, youth, and adults who generally have not always flourished within usual educational environments such as school or who otherwise are considered 'at risk' in their communities or society at large. In this work we have analyzed the social functions that the creation of digital stories and digital music has served for youth and young adults (Hull & Katz 2006; Hull & James 2007). We have also examined the social and pedagogical settings in which such work seems to flourish (Hull & Schultz 2001; Hull & Greeno 2006; Hull et al. 2006) as well as the pedagogical, ethical (Nelson & Hull 2008), and evaluative (Stornaiuolo, Hull & Nelson 2009) challenges that it offers. And finally, we have attempted to conceptualize and carry out analyses of multimodal digital products, creating a framework for analyzing digital stories that begins to account for their semiotic and aesthetic power (Hull & Nelson 2005; Nelson 2006, 2008; Nelson & Hull 2008). Our primary approach has been to construct comparative case studies (cf. Bogdan & Biklen 1992; Dyson & Genishi 2005) that reveal patterns of identity formation and literate development conceived to include emerging expertise in multimodal communication. We have focused on individuals or groups of youth linked through their participation at sites or by age and gender. Our current work, and this chapter, examines multimodal meaning-making not only on a personal and local level but also on its global reach through social networking, explained and illustrated below.

We would offer a few caveats before proceeding. Along with some others who are interested in youth and young adults, media, and multimodality, we have located a significant portion of our work in out-of-school contexts to circumvent the constraints that so many schools and teachers face in this accountability obsessed era (Meier & Wood 2004). Such extra-school contexts are the best means that we personally have had, at a particular historical moment, to attempt to impact positively and directly at least a modest number of participants, and we hope a larger number indirectly through the sharing of materials, approaches, research, and theorizing (cf. Hill 2007). This positioning does not mean that we aren't aware of the limitations of working outside of the powerful institution of schooling, or that we don't see a need to bridge in-school and out-of-school literacies, as well as to interrogate all implied by the connection metaphor. Nor does it mean, of course, that we would discourage anyone from centering their intellectual projects and activist efforts on schools. Far from it, engaging with out-of-school contexts has also meant, for us, helping to create tools, programs, participant structures, and collaboratives to cross institutional contexts that more typically, to paraphrase W. H. Auden (Autumn Song 1936), sit with separate hands on separate knees: university; public, charter, and private schools; and community-based and faith-oriented organizations. In point of fact, two of three empirical examples discussed to follow are drawn from somewhat hybridized contexts: these settings, while ostensibly school- (South Africa) and university-based (Japan), happily afforded a flexibility and features more typically characteristic of after-school programs, clubs, and other out-of-school settings. This crossing and blurring of institutional boundaries will, we believe, increasingly need to be a core concern of Literacy Studies, not least because hybridity and synthesis are defining features of new and emerging literacy practices themselves.

Akin to the location of our work outside schooling as formally and traditionally construed is the privileging of new and still untraditional genres and forms of communication. As already stated, this includes a focus on multimodal texts made possible largely through the spread of various kinds of digital media, and the exploration of what seems distinctive about particular kinds of digital texts as new forms of meaning-making. Even a cursory look suggests that such texts provide a distinctive contrast with the school-based essay, including the formulaic five-paragraph piece and essay types much valued in current high-stakes assessment, such as the literary interpretive essay. Our brief but necessary point here is that we don't, through our own focus, mean to imply a devaluation of such school-based literacy types. On the contrary, we recognize that they are important for the construction of particular kinds of knowledge (including the chapters in this edited volume), and that they currently serve not-to-be-ignored gate-keeping functions, such as certification of graduation from high school and entrance to college and graduate school. We maintain, however, that we are on the cusp at the current moment of a broadening of communicative means and opportunities that begs a reevaluation of what counts as a valued text. It is to the exploration of the implications of this broadening that we hope to contribute.

Thus, ours has not been solely a research enterprise, as traditionally defined, but something more akin to the design-based approaches that captured the imagination of cognitive scientists in the recent past (Brown 1992; Collins 1992; di Sessa 2000), or to the recent involvement by anthropologists such as Appadurai (1996, 2000) to provide intellectual tools and economic opportunity to participants along with theoretical categories and analyses for the field. We hope that many helpful varieties of deep, sustained, and durable participation on the part of university-based researchers both within (Heath 1983; Scribner & Cole 1981; Street 1984) and across local and global communities will be a mainstay of literacy scholarship in the future. Combining in-depth investigation of local sites with attention to the interrelations between them is in our view a critical focus.

looking anew at the new literacy studies

Our postmodern world is one of shifting boundaries and alignments, and, as Appadurai (1996) explains, this is largely due to the easy transportability of people and media around the globe. Media theorist Henry Jenkins discusses this phenomenon in terms of 'convergence culture,' defined by the ready flow of content across media platforms, populations, and borders. A profound consequence of this convergence is a fundamental alteration in 'the relationship between existing technologies, industries, markets, genres, and audiences' (Jenkins 2006: 15–16; cf. Jenkins et al. 2006). Accordingly, since the primary role of literacy education is to prepare present and future generations to achieve fulfillment in life and work, in recent years, literacy scholars have perceived and addressed the urgent need to understand the interrelations and pedagogic implications of these social, semiotic, and economic shifts.

A landmark move toward such an understanding was made by the New London Group (1996), who asserted that 'classroom teaching and curriculum have to engage with students' own experiences and discourses, which are increasingly defined by cultural and sub-cultural diversity and the different language backgrounds and practices that come with this diversity' (p. 36). The pedagogy they proposed therefore privileges the 'designing of meaning' over the dissemination of information and related notions have been conceptually elaborated by other scholars since, particularly those interested in the incorporation of popular media and digital technologies within education (cf. Buckingham 2003; diSessa 2000; Dyson 1997, 2003; Gee 2003, 2004; Jocson 2006; Morrell 2004; Resnick et al. 1998; Sefton-Green 1999; Vasudevan 2006). For example, in a constructionist (cf. Papert 1980, 1993) vein, Resnick and colleagues (1998) assert that engagement in personally relevant computer-enabled design activities allows users to 'make' understandings about technology, themselves and the world around them. As well, Gee (2003, 2004) has argued that generally schooling neither values nor capitalizes on the complex-thinking, problem-solving, and collaborative interaction that engagement with popular media, like video games, can stimulate. Another influential, consonant perspective is diSessa's (2000) notion of 'two-way literacies,' which describes the transformative effect on knowledge of associated creative processes of consumption and production with virtual environments.

Clearly, the current prevailing attitude among those concerned with literacy education is that literacy as a construct needs reformulation, evidenced in part by the formation in 2004 of the Partnership for 21st Century Skills,[4] a US-based coalition of experts from academia, government, and industry convened to solve the problem of how to equip young people with the 'skills' necessary to successfully navigate the global, digital landscape of today and tomorrow. And while the issues of accommodating cultural and semiotic diversity have thus far been widely examined, we feel that the existing scholarship on new literacies has yet to adequately account for the almost limitless quality of connectivity—across personal, linguistic, cultural, and national boundaries—that many forms of new media communication are coming to exhibit. In particular, social networking represents one of the most powerful new forms of Internet-enabled interaction.

The Pew Internet and American Life Project (Lenhart & Madden 2007) reports that of nearly one thousand American teens sampled in 2006, over 50 percent belonged to at least one online social networking community. Of those who belonged, more than half accessed these communities once per day or more. The recent trend toward building social networking capability into 'standard' display-type websites (e.g. media-sharing sites like Flickr and YouTube) can only serve to intensify this trend. According to industry leaders, as recently reported in the *New York Times*, social networking sites are set to become 'as ubiquitous as regular Web sites' ('Social Networking's Next Phase,' 2007). Perhaps unsurprisingly, too, there is emerging, compelling evidence of concomitant, complex patterns of power distribution, virtual population shifts, and ideological clashes, which may convey consequential impacts. Boyd (2007), for instance, identified a growing demographic gulf between members of MySpace and Facebook respectively; She found that MySpace users were increasingly characterized by lower socio-economic status, while the opposite was true in the case of *Facebook*. As well, Barnes (2006) has examined privacy issues and the exchange of personal information within social networking communities, describing the false sense of security that may come of revealing personal information to those one never really sees. Notwithstanding the work of these and other pioneer researchers (e.g. Diaz 2003, Dwyer 2007; Heer & Boyd 2005; Lam 2000, 2006; Liu et al. 2006; Perkel 2008), more rigorous scholarly scrutiny must be put to trends like this, to understand the complex interweavings of textual, personal, interpersonal, and cultural aspects of meaning within social networking worlds.

Digitally supported social networks are powerful facilitators of the 'cultural flows' (Appadurai 1996: 35) that veritably define this historical moment and these flows are especially important and apparent in global youth culture. So, it follows that new media literacy in a global world not only requires a facility with coordinating relationships of meaning among pictures, language(s), and others modes, but it also demands a sensitivity toward the ideologies, mores, and dispositions that structure the multimodal meanings differentially made and understood by people whose life-worlds may be very unlike one's own: people whose own principles of relevance, beauty, reality, and even fundamental truth may differ radically from ours. As a simple example, consider that an image of a crescent moon would likely evoke different kinds of associations for a Norwegian-American girl in Minnesota as for a Pashto-speaking boy in Pakistan. As such, the aesthetic parameters for integrating or interpreting such an image within a multimedia composition would likely be different as well. Thinking broadly about literacy, then, we see that noticing textual manifestations of difference and imagining points of connection and synthesis beyond these differences are requisite skills for success in the twenty-first century, skills that arts-oriented literacy practices cultivate (cf. Messaris 1994: 182).

With this understanding in mind, we have begun to formulate a new theoretical direction for the New Literacy Studies (Gee 1996; Street 1993), an orientation that we believe promises to reconcile the two aforementioned central constructs of *designing meaning*, and *connectivity*. This orientation centers not just on the integration of multiple semiotic systems (language, imagery, etc.), a need helpfully identified by the New London Group and others; it takes into account also a holistic view of aesthetic practices and their relation to personal and cultural contexts of production. Admittedly, this is a marked departure from skills-based and functional approaches that have long informed normative notions of literacy and schooling. However, with the confluence of digital technologies, the creation of evermore hybrid and multimodal texts, and the confirmed presence of intertexuality (Kristeva 1980) as an interpretive habit of the late-modern mind, we have strongly concluded that arts practices and aesthetic principles should be at the base of a newly invigorated Literacy Studies. Below we briefly sketch our current thinking about aesthetics as an organizing theory for the intersection of learning and digital media.

While for most of the twentieth century, one-size-fits-all approaches and methods for literacy education predominated, these programs and methods have recently been besieged by a radical plurality with regard to the purposes, media, and material of textual meaning-making. Simply put, literacy practices at present might be described as a moment-to-moment engagement in communicative *bricolage*. Kress (2005) makes a similar claim:

> Instead of competence in relation to stable social frames and stable resources for representation, we need the notion of design, which says: In this social and cultural environment, with these demands for communication of these materials, for that audience, with these resources, and given these interests of mine, what is the design that best meets these requirements? (p. 20)

If it ever could, literacy can no longer be understood as a simple process of encoding and decoding messages according to a set of notational conventions. Again, literacy is now a necessarily multimodal, multimedial, dynamically changeable enterprise. Accordingly, the primary object of literacy education should not be to equip learners with a finite set of competencies, but rather to engender the adaptive, generative capacity to design coherent, elegant, impactful meanings out of the multiplex, shifting array of memories, emotions, ideas, and artifacts that are the stuff of everyday life. This, of course, is a capacity that has always been associated with arts practices and arts education.

Nearly a century ago, in his 'Psychology of Art,' L. S. Vygotsky (1971) professed that 'art is the supreme center of biological and social individual processes in society...it is a method for finding an equilibrium between man and his world, in the most critical and important stages of his life.' In explanation of this statement, Vygotsky adds, 'art is the organization of our future behavior. It ... forces us to strive beyond our life toward all that lies beyond it.' (p. 253) Complementarily, Dewey (1934/2005) saw artworks not merely as aesthetic objects, but rather as focal points of processes of sense-making and 'worldmaking', to adapt Nelson Goodman's (1978) phrase—art as (receptive and productive) experience in itself as well as meeting ground at which multiple life experiences may be better understood and reconciled. And even today, these ideas persist in philosophies of arts education. For instance, arts education scholar Eliot Eisner (2002) asserts that two necessary functions the arts serve are to 'help us to notice the world' and 'provide permission to engage the imagination as a means for exploring new possibilities' (p. 10). We believe that these arts functions of awareness and imagination have much to offer literacy education, not only in recognizing and motivating connections of meaning within a multimedia text, of course, but also in understanding the co-texts with which and contexts within which these texts are deployed.

The importance for young people of art as a means through which to interpret and transform individual and social lives is readily apparent in recent literature onto youth culture and global youth studies (Hull et al. in press). Accounts of youth's participation in popular cultural forms, especially music and media-related consumption and production, are frequent in this literature, marking a shift from the older tradition of documenting and theorizing the class-based resistance of young people (cf. Bucholtz 2002; Nayak 2003). It is surely important to consider why it is that many youth who would be considered at risk in every category, and many of whom are disenchanted with school, reveal themselves to be remarkably devoted to and adept at the sophisticated and skillful interpretation and creation of popular cultural forms (cf. Hull & Nelson 2005; Hull & Schultz 2002; Kirkland 2007; Muñoz & Marín 2006). We interpret the aesthetic turn among youth and young adults not only as a venue on the part of some for engaging in collective politically alert activity but as also the expression of a quintessentially human need to make meaning by engaging in what Willis (1990) termed 'symbolic creativity.' Through language, visual arts, dance, music, or a multimodal combination of these (cf. Finnegan 2002), youth express themselves through performance, the production of artifacts, and the stylization of their bodies. The aesthetic activities of youth, we and others submit (cf. Muñoz & Marín 2006), join palpably the pleasures of making meaning with the pleasures of constructing and enacting a self. This is quite a potent combination. In their study of music in Columbian youth cultures, Muñoz and Marín assert that participation in an artistic process, such as music-making, 'leads young people towards self-creation, to the production of new subjectivities—to the search for, and generation of, *something else* in the domains of ethics, politics, art and forms of knowledge converted into praxis' (p. 132). They describe what they term the 'motor forces of creation,' (p. 132) that drive or liberate creativity in youth cultures. One example is the ethos of DIY or 'do it yourself,' which encourages young people to believe that 'anyone can,' including them. Another example is the importance of searching for one's own style and making one's own mark within a culture, which is a hip-hop mantra.

Moreover, new media seem to amplify the creative and cooperative potential of youth, and all individuals for that matter. Yet, the present condition of the world seems to demonstrate as well that potentials of new media communication will not be likely to automatically obtain. This is a gap that a new literacy pedagogy must fill, though the fluidity and sheer complexity of present-day life and communication practices present significant challenges to learners and teachers alike. Crucially, we maintain that there will be a prominent role for ethically, morally, and aesthetically alert educators and multimodal artists to play in filling this gap. Next we turn to three brief examples—the cases of 'Gorou', Randy, and 'Layla'[5]—which illustrate the challenges and opportunities for multimodal, textual self-expression in a digitally mediated and interconnected global world.

the challenge and the promise: designing multimodal meanings

Perhaps the most distinctive characteristic of communication via multimodal electronic media is that the Self that one presents to the online community is most often both 'narrated' and 'displayed,' to use Gunther Kress's (2003) terms, which is to say that language and photographs are co-deployed in the service of self-expression, along with graphics, illustrations, voice, and music, among other typically represented semiotic modes and devices. For example, the wildly multimodal MySpace pages of many new media authors, youth and adults alike, confront one at once with myriad channels of often chaotically arranged information that takes minutes even to take in. Of course, multimodal coherence may not be the point in these so-called mash-ups; multiplicity or even cacophony (metaphorically speaking) may in fact be the point.

However, it may be, too, that a coherent, cohesive multimodal statement is the desired, but elusive result.

gorou[6]

By way of example, consider the case of 'Gorou', a Japanese university student engaged in the multimodal practice of digital storytelling in English whose process was followed and documented over four months during 2005–2006. Gorou's multimedia narrative is titled 'Aomori: The Place That Shaped Me,' and the thematic thread that runs through his piece is his connection to and appreciation of his birthplace, a rural precinct of Aomori Prefecture, the northernmost prefecture in the northerly Tohoku region of Japan. More particularly, Gorou's intent was to express how the natural and cultural features of Aomori influenced the person he had become and to suggest ways in which his home prefecture might in its turn benefit from the cultural influences he had accrued while living in the Tokyo area.

Gorou's multimedia design strategy was to divide his piece into four thematic sections, each presenting one defining feature of his life that was rooted in some way in his Aomori experience. We categorically describe these sections as *Aomori Landscape, Alcohol, Nature and Fishing,* and *Festivals and Music.* In each of these thematic segments, each roughly two minutes in duration, Gorou's plan was to orchestrate a progressive change in the quality of relation between sequentially deployed images and the theme of the section, from what he explained as 'low impact' to 'high impact.' Impact, to Gorou's way of thinking, was a function of the degree to which the images disambiguated, that is, gave away, the theme. For example, consider the series of images represented below. This sequence of eight photos is taken from the second of the four thematic sections (Alcohol[7]) and includes (1) a traditional Japanese storefront, (2) vats in a sake distillery, (3) a factory beside a river, (4) distillation tanks, (5) a person smelling a whiskey sample, (6) an assortment of Japanese spirits, (7) Gorou's own collection of Western-style spirits, and (8) Gorou's own collection of Japanese *shochu* liquor (see Figure 10.1).

In a Peircian sense, we might say that Gorou intended a more-or-less measured progression from a vaguely *indexical sign*, that is, a storefront image to *index* or point to the concept of his relationship to alcohol, to a more directly *iconic sign*, an image of his bottles of alcohol to represent the concept of his relationship to alcohol (Peirce 1940/1955). Gorou expected that paring away layers of ambiguity by degrees in each of his four sections would be an effective means of engaging his audience.

Figure 10.1   Gorou's alcohol sequence (left to right, top to bottom)

Midway through the composing process, Gorou explained his plan in a written journal entry:

> For example, about Aomori, I don't want to use only the pictures which symbol Aomori prefecture directly like a map of there. However, probably I'm going to use such pictures, but I want to treasure the order of them. In conclusion, I will use such a direct picture as final one in one theme. Before that, I want to choose pictures about Aomori in order with intensity of association ... My effect can catch an attention of visual and listening too. Because my effect can't work without speaking part. I want to let audience guess 'How can this picture be connected with this story' when each parts start, and then they will surely want to listen to that story carefully. (November 18, 2005)

In sum, Gorou felt that purposefully, steadily increasing the 'intensity of association' in the visual mode in each section would stimulate the curiosity, and engagement, of his audience.

When asked later if he felt his expressive intentions had been realized in the end product, Gorou responded:

Gorou:	The shochu bottle here these pictures are, were the big impact for me, but it's not enough I felt. My planning was more, how can I say?
Interviewer:	You can say it in Japanese if you want.
Gorou:	*Haba no aru.*
Interviewer:	More wide?
Gorou:	Wide. More wide between low to high. So they can't receive the, they already know that.

Gorou is displeased with what he believes was an unsuccessful attempt at creating suspense in each of the thematic sections: although the organization of the images achieves the desired progression from low impact to high impact, the linguistic channel—what he is saying in the piece as the images are deployed—quickly nullifies this effect. In the case of the alcohol section again, the first two of the eight images above, the storefront and the vats, appear on screen for two and six seconds respectively. Simultaneously, Gorou says, 'We people from the Tohoku District often are asked "Are you a heavy drinker?"' So, eight seconds into the two-minute section, the cat is already out of the bag, as it were. As carefully considered as Gorou's plan for the visual component of his story may have been, he was not able to fully anticipate the semiotic effect that integrating language into a multimodal design would have. He explains in the journal excerpt above that his effect 'can't work without [the] speaking part,' but it seems that he has achieved a synthesis that actually flies in the face of his overall expressive purpose. Image and language 'mutually contextualize one another,' (Lemke 2002: 322; cf. Mitchell's (1995) notion of 'imagetext') and as such the lack of specificity that the image in isolation affords, that his visual organization was predicated upon, is 'filled in,' to adapt Kress's (2003) terminology, by the labeling function of language.

A critical component of multimedia literacy in any incarnation is to understand not only the affordances for meaning-making of individual modal components, like language or imagery but also the semiotic affordances and constraints and aesthetic properties that these entail in combination. Clearly, the whole can mean very differently from the sum of its parts. Understanding and leveraging these semiotic and aesthetic parameters is, we believe, at the heart of literacies newly conceived for a new media age.

randy

For a second illustration we reintroduce a young man from whose artistry as a digital storyteller and musician we have already learned a great deal. We first met him eight years ago at a community technology center where courses were provided for children and adults on digital storytelling, and his demonstrated ability to orchestrate or braid different modes of communication (images, music, spoken language) allowed him to create, we have argued elsewhere (Hull & Nelson 2005), a distinctive kind of multimodal meaning. In contrast to Gorou, Randy was able to layer modal channels to advantage, such that a complete and powerful whole was perceived to emerge from his collection of digital elements.

Figure 10.2   The first nine frames of 'Absolute' (left to right, top to bottom)

Over the years Randy has continued to create digital stories as well as digital music. His most recent digital story, 'Absolute,' is yet another masterful multimodal piece, one that braids modes in ways that magnify potential meaning.[8] 'Absolute' refers to 'absolute truth', the truth that he is ready to tell but that he believes people aren't ready to hear. It is thus about speaking truth to power. He started with the idea that he wanted 'to do something political' and composed a basic driving beat, which he meant to sound ominous and simultaneously began searching for images on the Internet. In his words, 'I had the beat in the works, but I started pulling the images that supported the theme.' He searched for images associated with genocide, Darfur, Rwanda, and war, and he noted that, were others to search using those words, some of the same images that he used in his story would be called up, which for him amplified the truth he was telling through his digital story; 'Hence the moniker, "Absolute,"' as he put it.

After an opening image that establishes Randy's affiliation with the hip-hop movement (see Figure 10.2), the linguistic script for the story begins to unfold: 'Get ready! Here it comes! You think you want it? You don't want none! I'm gonna take you on a trip, but this isn't a vacation.'

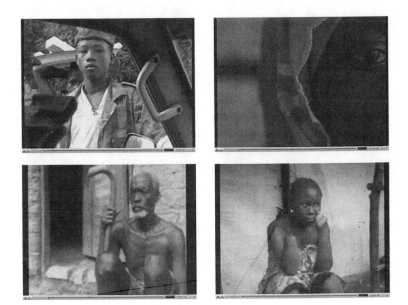

Figure 10.3   Brother, auntie, granddaddy, sister (left to right, top to bottom)

Simultaneously, images of war and conflagration appear on the screen, followed by images of mutilated women, people who've died and whose bodies are abandoned in the dust, children who've lost limbs or have been pressed into military service—all the horrors that we perhaps have become deadened to, so frequently do we see them on the news. Randy's story re-contextualizes those images by gradually juxtaposing them to horrific images from the history of slavery in the United States and current events. As it builds, the story develops a powerful coherence on multiple levels. For instance, on the level of individual image-language pairings, Randy deftly manipulates the 'narrative' and 'display' functions of language and image respectively. The four images in Figure 10.3 correspond in the story to the following lines:

Top-Left: *Convinced my brother to sell my brother.*
Top-Right: *Say goodbye to my auntie, goodbye to grandmother.*
Bottom-Left: *Goodbye, granddaddy. And even though you're gone, I know you're still smilin' at me.*
Bottom-Right: *This pain is full-grown. My sister's so strong. She done been through enough but she's still holdin' on.*

In each of these image-language pairings, Randy capitalizes on the narrative ambiguity in the images and the accordant possibility of effectively naming or labeling them, afforded by language. In this way, a child-soldier becomes *his* brother, a wounded and disfigured girl *his* sister, and so on, effecting a potent fusion of Randy's world and, as we participate as viewers, our world, with the tragic circumstances of the depicted victims of war.[9] Especially expertly, in the top-right image he exploits the obscurity of a covered head, a naked cheek, and a single open eye as minimum common visual criteria for iconic representation of both an auntie and a grandmother; by side-stepping overt indications of age in his image choice, Randy is able to accomplish both semiotic objectives in a single photo.

The absolute truth that Randy speaks lies in parallels like these, drawn in words, images, and beats, and reflecting parallel situations of suffering and lack of compassion, historical and current, within the United States and across the world. 'The pain has become mundane,' he told us in an interview; 'it's what ties everything together.' And thus Randy's story takes us through Darfur and Iraq and the United States and back again. When Randy finished 'Absolute,' he drove to a park in Oakland, California that attracts a lot of youth at night and set his computer on top of his car and played the movie again and again for passersby. He noted that the first time that people watched the story, they were driven by emotions, by anger. It 'fuels the fire.' But gradually, he believes they came to understand his message. This story, and all of Randy's art, is his attempt to make a difference in the world: 'Damn, I have something to say! I want to be part of the solution.' And significantly, in 'Absolute', he ventured to the other side of the world for images of violence to help young people in his own neighborhood 'be more thoughtful,' and 'not be so quick to destroy.'

layla

Our final illustration derives from the recent digital storytelling and social networking activities of 'Layla', a thirteen-year-old girl in South Africa. About two years ago, Layla moved from urban Cape Town to the tiny agricultural village of 'Kaap', tucked between the Cape Winelands and the Klein Karoo. She went to live with her grandmother and attend school at the behest of her parents. As did all the other 'Kaap Primêre Skool' students in grade eight, between May and October of 2008 Layla created a digital story, a short, autobiographical piece that was meant to serve as a self-introduction to an online social network for youth, which our research group had developed and offered for use. Layla was a member of South Africa's 'colored' community and spoke Afrikaans as her home language. However, she was also quite proficient in English, proudly, as a result of having attended an English-medium school in Cape Town, and chose English as the language of her story:

> My name is [Layla], and I am a proudly SA girl that's thirteen years of age and loves taking long luxurious bubble baths. As a teenage girl, I also loves taking walks and playing in our street. My hobbies are modeling and singing. We also have ten chickens and two dogs that love chasing them. I actually lives in Cape Town, but did move to [Kaap] to finish the primary school. I love to model just like Tyra Banks and to sing just like Mariah Carey. Ciara aren't too bad either. My role model is my mum. I really love her. My dad is also my role model, but my second one. One day I want to be a nurse and a part-time model for a magazine. I have plan my whole future, but it's all in the Lord's hands. Thank you.

In this, Layla's first digital story, she describes herself in terms of a number of qualities; for example, her hobbies and interests, her history, her future aspirations, her religious faith. On the surface it is a seemingly simple and straightforward sequence of still images and corresponding spoken language, which is at times difficult to hear given the poor sound quality of the recording. There is no music in the piece until the credits begin; the only evident flourishes are video effects (e.g. oscillations in image color, an aged film effect) and transition effects (e.g. fades, spins), selected from among those available within *Windows Movie Maker*, the video editing software she employed.

But this deceptively simple piece also, we believe, evidences potentially powerful habits of mind in relation to new media literacies. For instance, in the opening frame the title of the piece, in white Times New Roman script on a black background, enlarges and approaches the viewer: 'Entering Layla's world...' The visual transition between this title and the first image in the piece (an image of Layla posing beside a bright blue wall on the grounds of her school) is an expanding keyhole. With this choice, Layla intends that her audience will in a vivid sense pass through a portal, the entryway to her world, thus metaphorically signaling the beginning of her story. She explains, 'it's like when you start to press play, you put in a key and open.' Further, the second photographic image in the story is also imbued with semiotic and aesthetic intent. It is of Layla herself, wearing a shiny tracksuit and smiling broadly. Over the five-second period that this image appears on screen, in correspondence with '... proud SA girl that's thirteen years of age and loves ... ', its color continuously changes, phasing from a monochrome blue tone, to green, then yellow, then orange, then red. As with the keyhole, this prismatic color transformation is not a random aesthetic choice: it is designful and encodes a deeper significance. When asked about this decision, Layla said, 'I wanted to show them [her audience[10]], the color actually is like the flag almost, not really, but the colors of the flag shows I am proud to be South African. I don't even know where I got it from. I go in and choose something.' While this color-change effect may not be an ideal vehicle for Layla's potential meaning, as she expresses, it does suggest something of the most salient visual characteristic of 'flagness' (i.e. multiple fields of color) which is intended to index her pride in being South African, an 'SA girl.' Through the practice and processes of multimedia composition, Layla develops, we suggest, a keener, fuller, more sophisticated sense of multimodal design; her work begins to exhibit the characteristics of more experienced and expert digital artists, like Randy. Still, we would point to one other illustrative vignette from Layla's case, one that perhaps demonstrates how a purposeful design decision, such as those already discussed, can be misconstrued in what we might regard, in a Bourdieuian sense, as the 'global semiotic marketplace' (Bourdieu 1991).

When interviewed about the various design decisions comprising her digital storytelling process, including those detailed above, Layla returned several times in her explanation to a particular core theme: her sincere desire to simultaneously undertake occupations as a nurse and a part-time fashion model. She related her frustrating experience of being told by a teacher in Cape Town that she should focus on just one future aspiration and expressed her resultant determination to realize both dreams. In her own words, 'I want to be a nurse and a part-time model, and I think I can do both at the same time. And I will show the world that there are times for everything.' One way that she intended to stake a public claim to this bipartite career was through her digital story, for which she engineered a rather ingenious semiotic device for visually integrating the quality of being a nurse with that of being a fashion model. In the process of making and collecting imagery to include in her piece, Layla happened upon an advertisement for Skechers shoes, featuring pop diva Christina Aguilera in two different costumes and poses in the same picture plane, as if she were two different people interacting with one another. The ad is photographic, but highly stylized, perhaps evoking an airbrushed comic book scene or a 1950s pin-up poster image. A standing Christina is depicted on the left, wearing a white nurse's cap adorned with a red cross; a white mini-dress with a low-cut décolleté neckline; white stockings with exposed garters and white high-heeled boots. She casts an exaggeratedly suggestive look at the viewer, striking a *contrapposto* pose and holding up a comically large hypodermic needle. The other Christina sits to the left on a hospital bed, looking at the 'nurse'. This second Christina wears a pink, cropped sweatshirt, a white t-shirt, running shorts, and Skechers shoes, of course. She holds an icepack to her head, suggesting she is being treated. The Skechers name and logo appear prominently in the foreground with the name 'Christina Aguilera' included in print beneath. Layla could not remember the search term that retrieved this image, but she recalled having noticed in it a serendipitous suitability for expressing her particular meaning:

Interviewer:	And the picture that you chose to show the idea of being a nurse, why did you pick that one instead of some other nurse picture?
Layla:	The person that's on the picture is Christina, I think, but she famous, famous and kind of like a model also, so the modeling thing comes together ... When I put the picture of Christina Aguilera, it's the meaning of two, but it's one picture. She's famous and she's like a nurse. And I want to be famous and a nurse, that's why I put the pictures together ... the clothes that she is wearing is like a nurse but she is like modeling the clothes and advertising the things that she has on. It's two, but it's one person and that's why the modeling and the nurse can be one.

Again, in a very real sense, we might recognize that Layla exhibits a quality of 'semiotic awareness' (Nelson 2006) that may be critical to the kind of 'symbolic creativity' that Willis (1990) discusses. More specifically, drawing further on the work of Kress (2000, 2003), we might also say that Layla's process reveals an intuitive sense of the meaning-making affordances and aesthetic properties of the mode of the visual image, that is, its capacity to simultaneously incorporate and encode multiple meanings ('nurse-ness', 'model-ness', duality) in a way that spoken language, which typically must present single sequenced elements that unfold in time, is not so well disposed to do. Like Randy, she showed an ability to semiotically exploit the image to its best advantage in support of a larger multimodal design. Moreover, she seemed pleased and proud at having noticed the semiotic potential of this image in particular and at harnessing this potential in the service of her story.

When the social network, which we have called 'Space2Cre8', was launched in California and South Africa in early November, the first thing that each youthful participant did upon joining was to add an image to her or his individual profile page. In South Africa these ranged from photographs of self, to images of South African rugby heroes and reggae musicians. Participants were given free rein to represent themselves as they liked. Perhaps unsurprisingly, Layla chose the nurse image as her profile picture, along with the username 'Miss SA Teen'. Interestingly, when research team members in California noticed that this image was used as the 'photo' for a participant's profile, they were taken aback. They immediately worried that teachers and youth at the American school (hereafter called 'Bay Academy', a pseudonym), which had especially strict rules about language, sexuality, and behavior, would find the image inappropriate. In fact, there had been much discussion in this after-school program about what might constitute appropriate images and language within the international network. This sense of alarm is suggested in field notes written by a team member following a discussion during a research meeting. These are excerpted below:

> We were pointed ... to two of the SA students photo/user name combinations, [including] 'Miss SA Teen' with the Sketchers ad with a nurse, and 'Sexy Girl' ... These were, to our tired brains, quite alarming. Particularly when 'read' so to speak, against the backdrop of our understanding of the [school] culture ... They are combating media images that are aligned with illegal and illicit behavior on the part of men and women. In particular with women they argue for conservative dress. This came up earlier in the year when it was very warm and one of the undergraduates came to [Bay Academy] in a tank top and short shorts. (November 6, 2008)

The original intent behind the nurse image was rendered opaque within the network, at least temporarily, and this image that was imbued for Layla with so much personal meaning was most readily seen and interpreted, naturally enough, through the lens of local circumstances and concerns, as problematic. Namely, the visual likeness of the 'sexy nurse' was juxtaposed to and complicated by another risqué profile image, that of a woman posing in a 'fashion police' costume, featuring a short skirt, policeman's cap and exposing deep cleavage—that was posted at the same time by a different participant who called herself 'sexy girl.' In the light of recent events at the site, the shorts and tank top incident, and the possible concerns of parents for their children, and researchers' desire to respect these, the American team began to discuss the possibility of enabling participants to flag potentially offensive postings.

Ultimately, these and other controversial images were leveraged for purposes of constructive discussion in the program at Bay Academy, and Layla's intention was explained and understood. But this could only have eventuated because the American researchers and participants were made privy to a life-world, Layla's, in which the choice of the nurse image could hardly have seemed *more appropriate*, or more apt to uniquely fulfill a particular and personal expressive purpose, much less inappropriate. This case urges us to seriously consider what we may miss, what other powerful designs of meaning and emergent new literacy capacities may remain undisclosed to or misconstrued by us, when our imaginations (and research methodologies) are insufficiently expansive, flexible, and agile as to allow us to perceive them.

literacy, media, morality, and imagination

Though the preceding examples represent only three tiny windows onto the twenty-first-century literacy picture, we believe they serve to illustrate and underscore some of the core issues to be addressed in the broader view. In brief, Gorou, Randy, and Layla's experiences of multimedia composing seem to cogently suggest that new media meaning-making may depend not so much on what is said, shown, and the like but on what lies in-between, in the semiotic relationships and aesthetic judgments that cross-cut a great diversity of individual, social and cultural codes, and preferences. Yes, constructing coherence in new media, as we understand it, entails consciously semantically reconciling the often disparate elements of potential meaning simultaneously encoded in what M. A. K. Halliday (1978) calls the *textual, interpersonal,* and *ideational* aspects of various texts. These respectively relate, for example, to (1) knowledge of the semiotic affordances and constraints of modality and materiality; (2) the multiple 'voices' (Bakhtin 1981) or meanings that reside in texts as a product of their past and incarnations and uses; and (3) the content of one's own expressive intentions. Being literate, to this way of thinking, is tantamount to controlling *textual ecologies* rather than texts themselves. At the core of the development of this kind of capacity, we suspect, is artistic creative practice, which promotes an understanding of textual meaning-making as a fluid, context-dependent, intertextual, and fundamentally designful process.

In addition to a capacity to control textual ecologies, our work on multimodal composing and social networking, the examples of composers such as Gorou, Randy, Layla and others, as well as our observations about the potential now of their stories and other creative products to circulate locally and globally, push us to consider larger issues at stake when we consider Literacy Studies in the future, including nothing less than what constitutes ethical citizenship in a global world. Silverstone (2007) theorized the potential of media to be a moral public space, a 'mediapolis' where we see and are seen, where our worlds are represented, and where we have both a right to 'hospitality,' and thereby to be welcomed and to speak, and an obligation to be hospitable, to listen and to hear. He asserts that media must be ethically constituted:

> Insofar as they provide the symbolic connection and disconnection that we have to the other, the other who is the distant other, distant geographically, historically, sociologically, then the media are becoming the crucial environments in which a morality appropriate to the increasingly interrelated but still horrendously divided and conflictual world might be found, and indeed expected. (p. 8)

Like political philosophers Appiah (2005, 2006) and Benhabib (2002), Silverstone wrestles with seemingly divisive global and local diversity and plurality, as they are juxtaposed with the necessity of interdependence. 'Does difference,' he asks, 'condemn humanity either to indifference or to a fundamental refusal of its value' (p. 13)? Or can we adopt 'cosmopolitanism' as an ethic, whereby we 'recognize not just the stranger as other, but the other in oneself' (p. 14)?

We think of Randy's meditation on Darfur. We are encouraged by such individual examples of the appropriation of multimodal textual forms to participate, undaunted, in local and global conversations that are respectfully alert to differences. We think of Layla's self-representation and imaginings of future selves, and we wonder both how to become hospitable readers of distant texts, as well as how to teach ourselves and our students to convey desired meanings. In our view, a fundamental challenge for Literacy Studies in the future will be to determine how such conversations and such habits of mind, heart, and hand can be fostered. As a preliminary step toward meeting this challenge, we propose that the recognition of imagination—understood here as the (multi)semiotic, communicative extension of a capacity to envisage other realities and, even more, the realities of others—as a key factor in the emergence and sustenance of hospitality. Neither understanding nor empathy can exist without first exercising the conciliatory power of imagination. And this is just as true on the semiotic plane as on the social. Of the relationship between juxtaposed semiotic elements (e.g. images) that are seemingly unrelated or opposed, psychologist Rudolph Arnheim (1969) writes 'confrontation...presses for relation' (p. 62). By this Arnheim means that what a picture shows, what a color is, or what a word means is discerned in the moment by recognizing defining interrelationships with other pictures, colors, words, and so on, through a process of imaginative extension. Connections and commonalities are not preexistent; they are psychologically motivated and designed and only then materially and socially constructed, and always continuously revised and renewed. Arnheim continues

> [t]he privilege of observing everything in relation raises understanding to higher levels of complexity and validity, but it exposes the observer at the same time to the infinity of possible connections. It charges him with the task of distinguishing the pertinent relations from the impertinent ones and of warily watching the effects things have upon each other. (p. 62)

This is the kind of imaginative vigilance that Randy and Layla exhibit in the cases described above. It is an approach to meaning-making that leverages the connective power of the imagination to create coherence and cohesiveness out of apparent disjuncture and dissimilitude. Of course, it seems a significantly more difficult task to reconcile difference in the social world than in the semiotic, but it is our hope that the latter may support the former, through rendering imaginable, sensible, scrutible, and reconfigurable the multimodal textual architectures of individual life-worlds and social communities.

notes

We thank the Spencer Foundation, the UC Links Project of the University of California, and a generous private donor for their support, which allowed us to develop the perspectives reported in this chapter and in our ongoing work. We also acknowledge the following collaborators and colleagues with whom we have been fortunate to explore new media, social networking, and digital contexts for learning: Patricia Baker, Michael Carter, Emily Gleason, Adrienne Herd, Nora Kenney, Knut Lundby, David Malinowski, Stacy Marple, Ayodele Nzinga, Dan Perkel, Urvashi Sahni, Amy Stornaiuolo, Xolani Tembu, Rian

Whittle, and Duncan Winter. Special thanks to Gorou, Randy, and Layla, whose creative work provides continuing inspiration for our explorations of new literacies.

We note that order of authorship on this piece, jointly conceptualized and written, is alphabetical.

1. We recognize the vital distinction between the ethical interpretations as to what is 'right' and aesthetic interpretations; nonetheless, we also see that principles, and accordant judgments, of what constitutes accuracy, morality, and beauty are inextricably interlaced.

2. We acknowledge here the pioneering and durable scholarship of Louise Rosenblatt (1938, 1978), who helpfully explored the distinction between 'aesthetic' and 'efferent' readings of texts—respectively, the continuum of readerly attention to the personal and affective associations of words as contrasted with the public and factual. While Rosenblatt was primarily interested in the meaning-making or 'transactions' possible through the reading of literature, we hope to explore more generally the aesthetic dimensions of literacy that accrue through multimodality.

3. 'Digital storytelling' refers to a popular digital technology-supported form of creative narrative practice that may integrate still and video imagery, text, sound, music, and recorded voice (e g see Lambert 2002).

4. http://www.21stcenturyskills.org

5. The names 'Gorou' and 'Layla' are pseudonyms, as is 'Kaap', the name of Layla's village. 'Randy' is this participant's actual name, used here according to his own preference. Randy's professional name, under which he creates music and digital stories, is Relixstylz.

6. This example also appears in Nelson (2008).

7. Gorou was keenly interested in the subject of spirits and aspired to a career in some aspect of this industry.

8. Randy's latest digital story can be viewed on You Tube at http://www.youtube.com/watch?v= HeTHFHTd_xA

9. This notion of representing local, personal experience in global, universal terms is a recurrent theme in Randy's work. See Hull and Nelson (2005).

10. The audience for 'Entering Layla's World', as reported in a post-production interview, is intended by the author/artist to include her friends and 'people overseas,' viz. the youth in other countries with whom she expected to communicate via the social network.

references

Appadurai, A. (1996) *Modernity at Large*. Minneapolis: University of Minnesota Press.

Appadurai, A. (2000) Grassroots Globalization and the Research Imagination. *Public Culture*, 12(1), 1–19.

Appiah, K. A. (2005) *The Ethics of Identity*. Princeton, NJ: Princeton University Press.

Appiah, K. A. (2006) *Cosmopolitanism: Ethics in a World of Strangers*. New York: W.W. Norton.

Arnheim, R. (1969) *Visual Thinking*. Berkeley and Los Angeles: University of California Press.

Bakhtin, M. (1981) *The Dialogic Imagination*. Austin: University of Texas Press.

Barnes, S. (2006) *A Privacy Paradox: Social Networking in the United States*. First *Monday*, 11(9). Retrieved May 1, 2007 from http://firstmonday.org/issues/ issue11_9/barnes/ index.html

Barton, D. (2007) *Literacy: An Introduction to the Ecology of Written Language*. Malden, MA: Blackwell Publishing.

Benhabib, S. (2002) *The Claims of Culture: Equality and Diversity in the Global Era*. Princeton, NJ: Princeton University Press.

Bogdan, R. C. and S. K. Biklen (1992) *Qualitative Research for Education: An Introduction to Theory and Methods*, second edition. Needham Heights, MA: Allyn and Bacon.

Bourdieu, P. (1991) *Language & Symbolic Power*. Cambridge, MA: Harvard University Press.

Boyd, D. (2007) Viewing American class divisions through Facebook and MySpace . *Apophenia Blog Essay*, June 24, http://www.danah.org/papers/essays/ Class Divisions.html. Accessed on 19 September 2008.

Brown, A. (1992) Design Experiments: Theoretical and Methodological Challenges in Creating Complex Interventions in Classrooms Settings. *Journal of the Learning Sciences*, 2(2), 141–78.

Bucholtz, M. (2002) Youth and Cultural Practice. *Annual Review of Anthropology*, 31, 525–52.

Buckingham, D. (2003) *Media Education*. Cambridge, UK: Polity.

Collins, A. (1992) Towards a design science of education. In E. Scanlon and T. O'Shea (eds), *New Directions in Educational Technology*, Berlin: Springer, 15–22.

Cope, B. and M. Kalantzis (1997) *Productive Diversity: A New Australian Approach to Work and Management*. Sydney: Pluto.

Diaz, P. (2003) The Computer Clubhouse Village: A Virtual Meeting Place for an Emerging Community of Learners. *Journal of Systemics, Cybernetics, and Informatics*, 2(2), 47–50.

diSessa, A. (2000) *Changing Minds: Computers, Learning and Literacy*. Cambridge, MA: MIT Press.

Dewey, J. (1934/2005) *Art as Experience*. New York: Perigree Books.

Dwyer, C. (2007) Digital Relationships In The 'Myspace' Generation: Results From A Qualitative Study. http://csis.pace.edu/~dwyer/research/ DwyerHICSS2007.pdf. Accessed on 1 June 2008.

Dyson, A. H. (1997) *Writing Superheroes: Contemporary Childhood, Popular Culture, and Classroom Literacy*. New York: Teacher College Press.

Dyson, A. H. (2003) *The Brothers and Sisters Learn to Write: Popular Literacies in Childhood and School Cultures*. New York: Teachers College Press.

Dyson, A. H. and C. Genishi (2005) *On the Case: Approaches to Language and Literacy Research*. New York: Teachers College Press.

Eisner, E. (2002) *The Arts and the Creation of Mind*. New Haven, CT: Yale University Press.

Finnegan, R. (2002) *Communicating: The Multiple Modes of Human Interconnection*. London: Routledge.

Gee, J. P. (1996) *Social Linguistics and Literacies: Ideology and Discourses*. Second edition. London: Routledge/Taylor and Francis.

Gee, J. P. (2003) *What Videogames Have to Teach Us about Learning and Literacy*. New York: Palgrave/Macmillan.

Gee, J. P. (2004) *Situated Language and Learning: A Critique of Traditional Schooling*. New York: Routledge.

Goodman, N. (1978) *Ways of Worldmaking*. Hassocks, Sussex: Harvester.

Halliday, M. A. K. (1978) *Language as Social Semiotic: The Social Interpretation of Language and Meaning*. London: Arnold.

Harris, R. (2001) *Rethinking Writing*. London: Continuum.

Heath, S. B. (1983) *Ways with Words: Language, Life, and Work in Communities and Classrooms*. Cambridge: Cambridge University Press.

Heer, J. and D. Boyd (2005) *Vizster: Visualizing online social network*. Paper presented at the IEEE Symposium on Information Visualization, October, Minneapolis, Minnesota.

Hill, S. (ed.) (2007) *Between School and Fun: Perspectives on Out-of-School Time*. Thousand Oaks, CA: Corwin.

Hull, G. (2003) Youth Culture and Digital Media: New Literacies for New Times. *Research in the Teaching of English*, 38(2), 229–33.

Hull, G. and J. Greeno (2006) Identity and agency in non-school and school worlds. In Z. Bekerman, N. Burbules and D. Silberman Keller (eds), *Learning in Places: The Informal Education Reader*. New York: Peter Lang, 77–97.

Hull, G., J. Zacher and L. Hibbert (2009) Youth, Risk, and Equity in a Global World. *Review of Research in Education*, 33, 117–59.

Hull, G. and K. Schultz (2001) Literacy and Learning Out of School: A Review of Theory and Research. *Review of Educational Research*, 71(4), 575–611.

Hull, G. and M. Katz (2006) Crafting an Agentive Self: Case Studies on Digital Storytelling. *Research in the Teaching of English*, 41(1), 43–81.

Hull, G. and M. E. Nelson (2005) Locating the Semiotic Power of Multimodality. *Written Communication*, 22(2), 224–62.

Hull, G., N. Kenney, S. Marple and A. Forsman-Schneider (2006) *Many Versions of Masculine: Explorations of Boys' Identity Formation through Multimodal Composing in an after-School Program*. The Robert F. Bowne Foundation's Occasional Papers Series. New York: Robert F. Bowne Foundation.

Jenkins, H. (2006) *Convergence Culture: Where Old and New Media Collide*. New York: New York University Press.

Jenkins, H., K. Clinton, R. Purushotma, A. Robinson and M. Weigel (2006) *Confronting the Challenges of Participatory Culture: Media Education for the 21st Century*. Occasional Papers on Digital media and learning. John T. and Catherine D. Macarthur Foundation.

Jocson, K. (2006) 'Bob Dylan and Hip Hop': Intersecting Literacy Practices in Youth Poetry Communities. *Written Communication*, 23(3), 231–59.

Kalantzis, M. and J. Cope (2000) Changing the role of schools. In B. Cope and M. Kalantzis (eds), *Multiliteracies: Literacy Learning and the Design of Social Futures*. London: Routledge, 121–48.

Kirkland, D. (2007) The power of their text: teaching hip hop in the secondary English classroom. In K. Keaton and P. R. Schmidt (eds), *Closing the Gap: English Educators Address the Tensions between Teacher Preparation and Teaching*

Writing in Secondary Schools. Charlotte, NC: Information Age Publishing, 129–45.

Kress, G. (2000) Multimodality. In B. Cope and M. Kalantzis (eds), *Multiliteracies: Literacy Learning and the Design of Social Futures*. London: Routledge, 182–202.

Kress, G. (2003) *Literacy in the New Media Age*. London: Routledge.

Kress, G. (2005) Gains and Losses: New Forms of Text, Knowledge and Learning. *Computers and Composition*, 22, 5–22.

Kress, G. and T. van Leeuwen (1996) *Reading Images: The Grammar of Visual Design*. London: Routledge.

Kristeva, J. (1980) *Desire in Language: A Semiotic Approach to Literature and Art*. New York: Columbia University Press.

Lam, W. S. E. (2000) L2 Literacy and the Design of Self: A Case Study of a Teenager Writing on the Internet. *Tesol Quarterly*, 34(3), 457–82.

Lam, W. S. E. (2006) Re-Envisioning Language, Literacy, and the Immigrant Subject in New Mediascapes. *Pedagogies: An International Journal*, 1(3), 171–95.

Lambert, J. (2002) *Digital Storytelling: Capturing Lives, Creating Community*. Berkeley, CA: Digital Diner.

Lankshear, C. and M. Knobel (2003) *New Literacies: Changing Knowledge and Classroom Learning*. Berkshire, UK: Open University Press.

Lemke, J. (1997) Multiplying meaning: visual and verbal semiotics in scientific text. In J. Martin and R. Veel (eds), *Reading science*. London: Routledge, 87–113.

Lemke, J. (1998) Metamedia literacy: transforming meanings and media. In D. Reinking, M. McKenna, L. Labbo and R. Kieffer (eds), *Handbook of Literacy and Technology: Transformations in a Post-Typographic World*. Hillsdale, NJ: Lawrence Erlbaum, 283–302.

Lemke, J. (2002) Travels in Hypermodality. *Visual Communication*, 1(3), 299–325.

Lenhart, A. and M. Madden (2007) Teens, privacy and online social networks: How teens manage their online identities and personal information in the age of MySpace. *Pew Internet and Family Life Project*. Retrieved 10 June 2007 from http://www.pewinternet. org/pdfs/PIP_Teens_Privacy _SNS_Report_ Final.pdf

Liu, H., P. Maes and G. Davenport (2006) Unraveling the Taste Fabric of Social Networks. *International Journal on Semantic Web and Information Systems*, 2(1), 42–71.

Meier, D. and G. Wood (eds) (2004) *Many Children Left behind: How the No Child Left behind Act Is Damaging Our Children and Our Schools*. Boston: Beacon Press.

Messaris, P. (1994) *Visual Literacy: Image, Mind & Reality*. Boulder, CO: Westview Press.

Mitchell, W. J. T. (1995) *Picture Theory*. Chicago: University of Chicago Press.

Morrell, E. (2004) *Linking Literacy and Popular Culture: Finding Connections for Lifelong Learning*. Norwood, MA: Christopher-Gordon Publishers.

Muñoz, G. and M. Marín (2006) Music is the connection: youth cultures in Colombia. In P. Nilan and C. Feixa (eds), *Global Youth? Hybrid Identities, Plural Worlds* London: Routledge, 130–48.

Nayak, A. (2003) *Race, Place and Globalization: Youth Cultures in a Changing World.* Oxford and New York: Berg Publishers.

Nelson, M. E. (2006) Mode, Meaning, and Synaesthesia in Multimedia L2 Writing. *Language Learning and Technology,* 10(2), 56–76.

Nelson, M. E. (2008) Multimodal Synthesis and the 'Voice' of the Multimedia Author in a Japanese Efl Context. *Innovation in Language Learning and Teaching,* 2(1), 65–82.

Nelson, M. E. and G. Hull (2008) Self-presentation through multimedia: a Bakhtinian perspective on digital storytelling. In Knut Lundy (ed.), *Digital Storytelling, Mediatized Stories: Self-Representations in New Media.* Digital Formations Series. New York: Peter Lang Publishing.

Nelson, M. E., G. Hull and J. Roche-Smith (2008) Challenges of Multimedia Self-Presentation: Taking, and Mistaking, the Show on the Road. *Written Communication,* 25(4), 415–40.

New London Group (1996) A Pedagogy of Multiliteracies: Designing Social Futures. *Harvard Educational Review,* 66, 60–92.

Papert, S. (1980) *Mindstorms.* New York: Basic Books.

Papert, S. (1993) *The Children's Machine.* New York: Basic Books.

Peirce, C. S. (1940/1955) *Philosophical Writings of Peirce.* New York: Dover Publications.

Perkel, D. (2008) Copy and paste literacy? Literacy practices in the production of a MySpace profile. In K. Drotner, H. S. Jensen and Schroeder (eds), *Informal Learning and Digital Media: Constructions, Contexts, Consequences.* Newcastle, UK: Cambridge Scholars Press.

Resnick, M., N. Rusk and S. Cooke (1998) The computer clubhouse: technological fluency in the inner city. In D. Schon, B. Sanyal and W. Mitchell (eds), *High Technology and Low-Income Communities.* Cambridge, MA: MIT Press.

Rosenblatt, L. (1938) *Literature as Exploration.* New York: Appleton-Century.

Rosenblatt, L. (1978) *The Reader, the Text, the Poem: The Transactional Theory of the Literary Work.* Carbondale: Southern Illinois Press.

Scribner, S. and M. Cole (1981) *The Psychology of Literacy.* Cambridge, MA: Harvard University Press.

Sefton-Green, J. (ed.) (1999) *Young People and New Technologies: The Challenge of Digital Arts.* London: Routledge.

Silverstone, R. (2007) *Media and Morality: On the Rise of the Mediapolis.* Cambridge, UK: Polity Press.

Social networking's next phase (2007, March 3) *New York Times.* Retrieved March 10, 2007 from http://www.nytimes.com/2007/03/03/technology/03social.html

Stein, P. (2007) *Multimodal Pedagogies in Diverse Classrooms: Representation, Rights, and Resources.* London: Routledge.

Stornaiuolo, A., G. Hull and M. Nelson (2009) Mobile Texts and Migrant Audiences: Rethinking Literacy and Assessment in a New Media Age. *Language Arts* 86(5), 382–92.

Street, B. (1984) *Literacy in Theory and Practice.* Cambridge, UK: Cambridge University Press.

Street, B. (1993) *Cross-Cultural Approaches to Literacy.* Cambridge, UK: Cambridge University Press.

Vasudevan, L. (2006) Making Known Differently: Engaging New Modalities as Spaces to Author New Selves. *E-Learning*, 3(2), 207–16.

Vygotsky, L. (1971) *The Psychology of Art*. Cambridge, MA: MIT Press.

Willis, P. (1990) *Common Culture: Symbolic Work at Play in the Everyday Cultures of the Young*. Boulder, CO: Westview Press.

Wysocki, A., J. Johnson-Eiola, C. Selfe and G. Sirc (2004) *Writing New Media: Theory and Applications for Expanding the Teaching of Composition*. Logan: Utah State University Press.

index